SONS OF ANARCHY

EST 1967

REDWOOD ORIGINAL

VOLUME TWO

WITHDRAWN

SONS OF ANARCHY Volume Two, January 2015. Published by BOOM!
Studios, a division of Boom Entertainment, Inc. Sons of Anarchy ™ & © 2015
Twentieth Century Fox Film Corporation and Bluebush Productions, LLC. Originally
published in single magazine form as SONS OF ANARCHY No. 7-10. ™ & © 2014
Twentieth Century Fox Film Corporation and Bluebush Productions, LLC. All Rights
Reserved. BOOM! Studios™ and the BOOM! Studios logo are trademarks of Boom
Entertainment, Inc., registered in various countries and categories. All characters,
events, and institutions depicted herein are fictional. Any similarity between any
of the names, characters, persons, events, and/or institutions in this publication
to actual names, characters, and persons, whether living or dead, events, and/or
institutions is unintended and purely coincidental. BOOM! Studios does not read
or accept unsolicited submissions of ideas, stories, or artwork.

A catalog record of this book is available from OCLC and from the BOOM! website,
www.boom-studios.com, on the Librarians Page.

BOOM! Studios, 5670 Wilshire Boulevard, Suite 450, Los Angeles, CA 90036-5679.
Printed in China. First Printing.

ISBN: 978-1-60886-478-2, eISBN: 978-1-61398-332-4

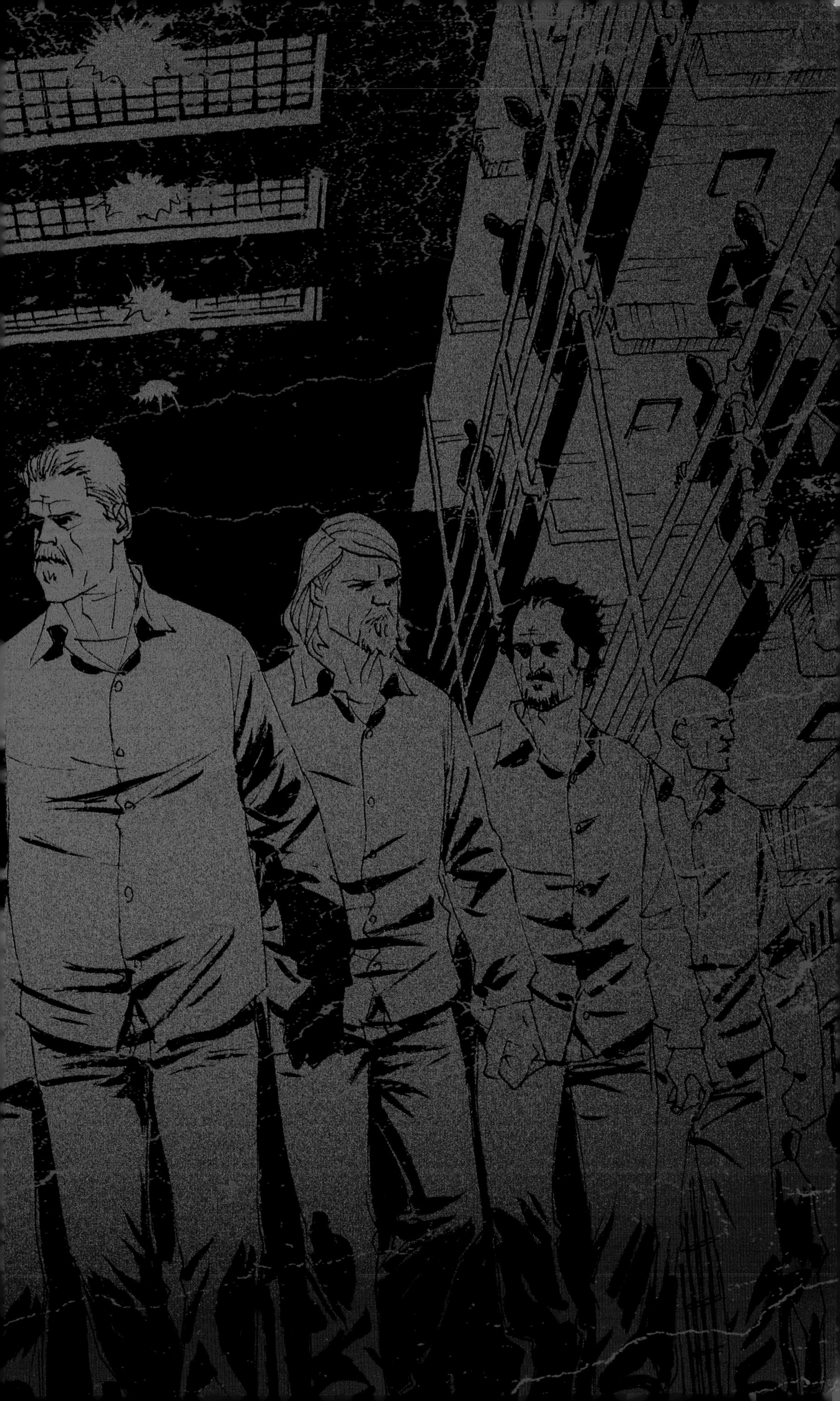

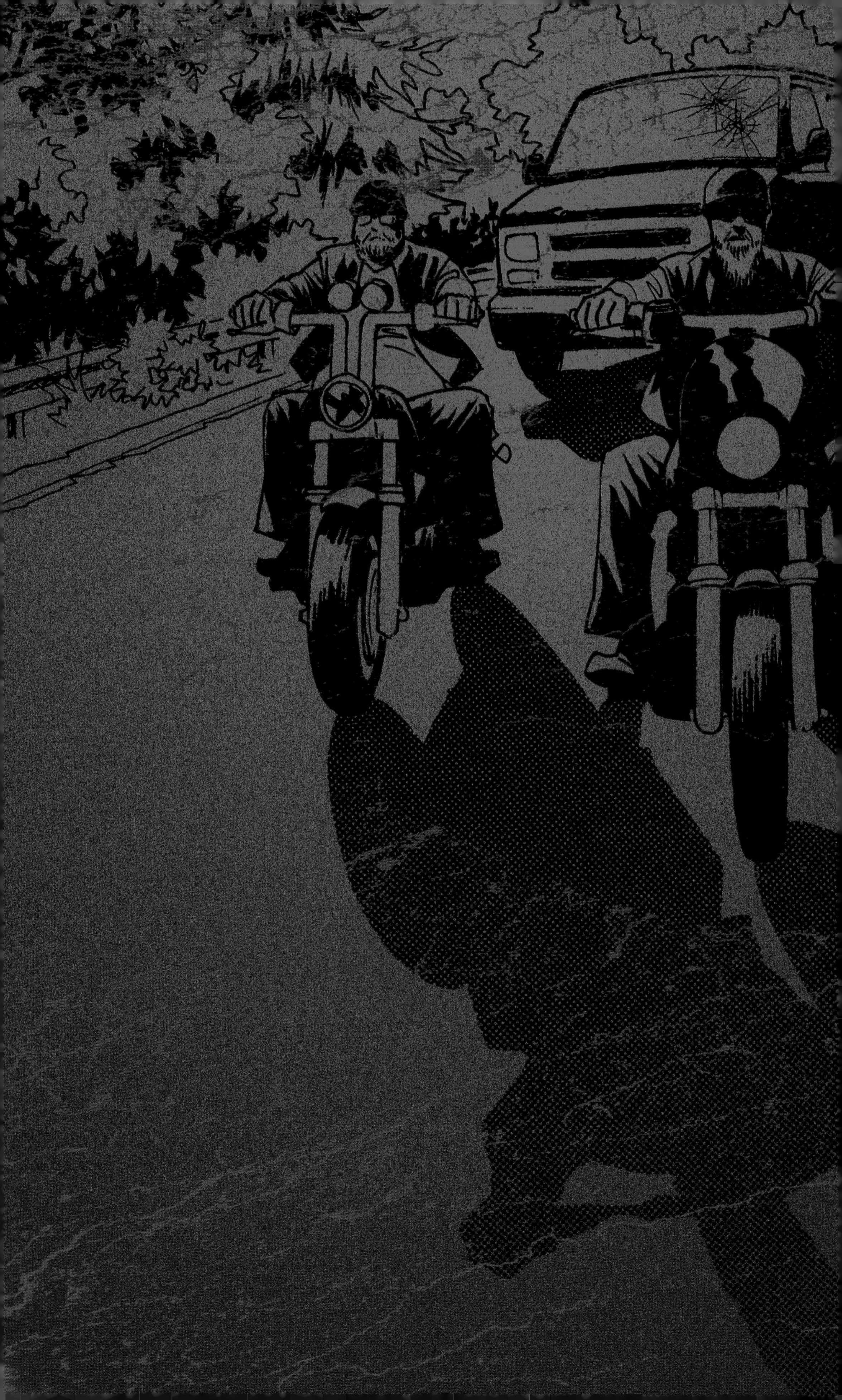

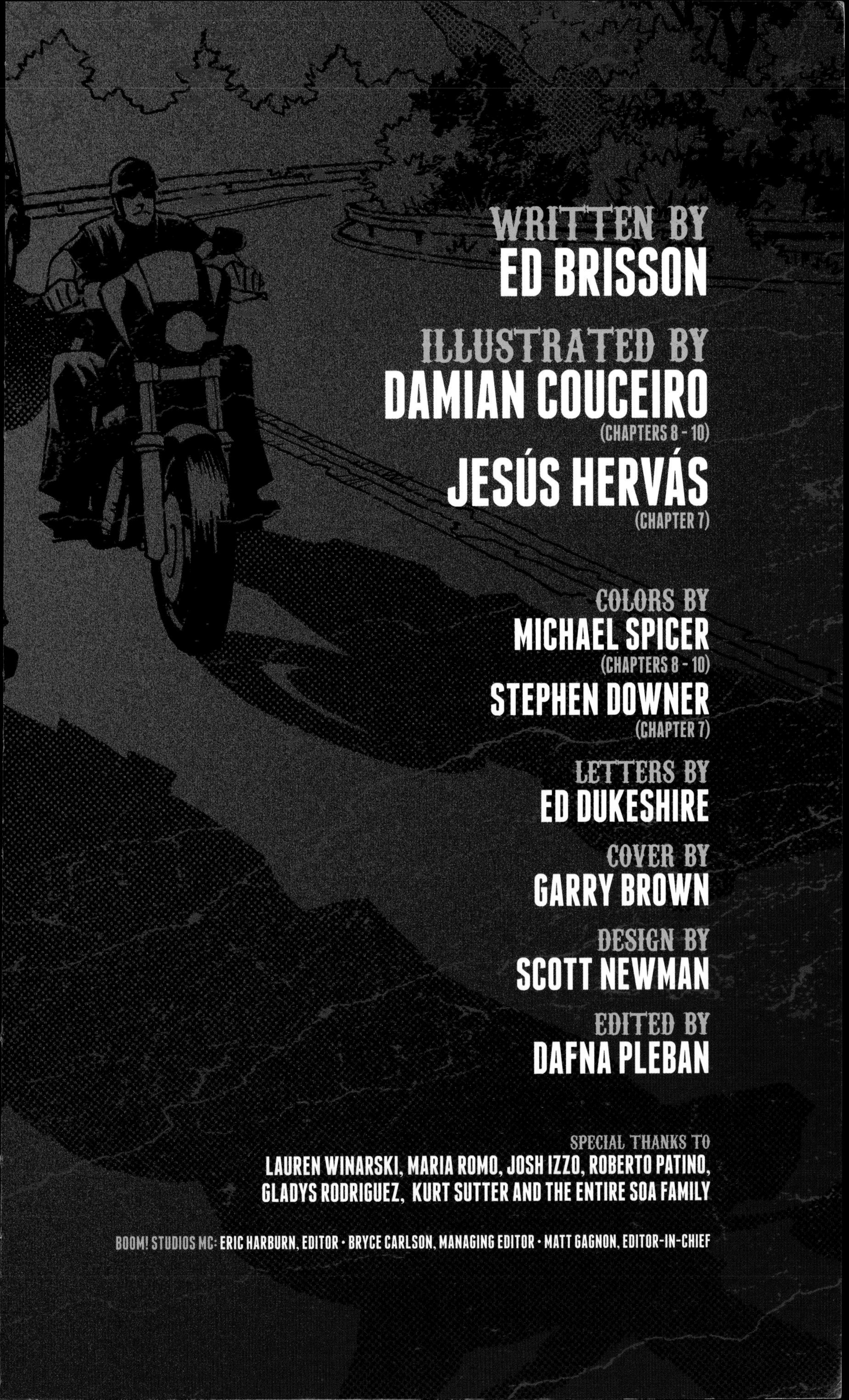

WRITTEN BY
ED BRISSON

ILLUSTRATED BY
DAMIAN COUCEIRO
(CHAPTERS 8 - 10)
JESÚS HERVÁS
(CHAPTER 7)

COLORS BY
MICHAEL SPICER
(CHAPTERS 8 - 10)
STEPHEN DOWNER
(CHAPTER 7)

LETTERS BY
ED DUKESHIRE

COVER BY
GARRY BROWN

DESIGN BY
SCOTT NEWMAN

EDITED BY
DAFNA PLEBAN

SPECIAL THANKS TO
LAUREN WINARSKI, MARIA ROMO, JOSH IZZO, ROBERTO PATINO,
GLADYS RODRIGUEZ, KURT SUTTER AND THE ENTIRE SOA FAMILY

BOOM! STUDIOS MC: ERIC HARBURN, EDITOR · BRYCE CARLSON, MANAGING EDITOR · MATT GAGNON, EDITOR-IN-CHIEF

CHAPTER 7

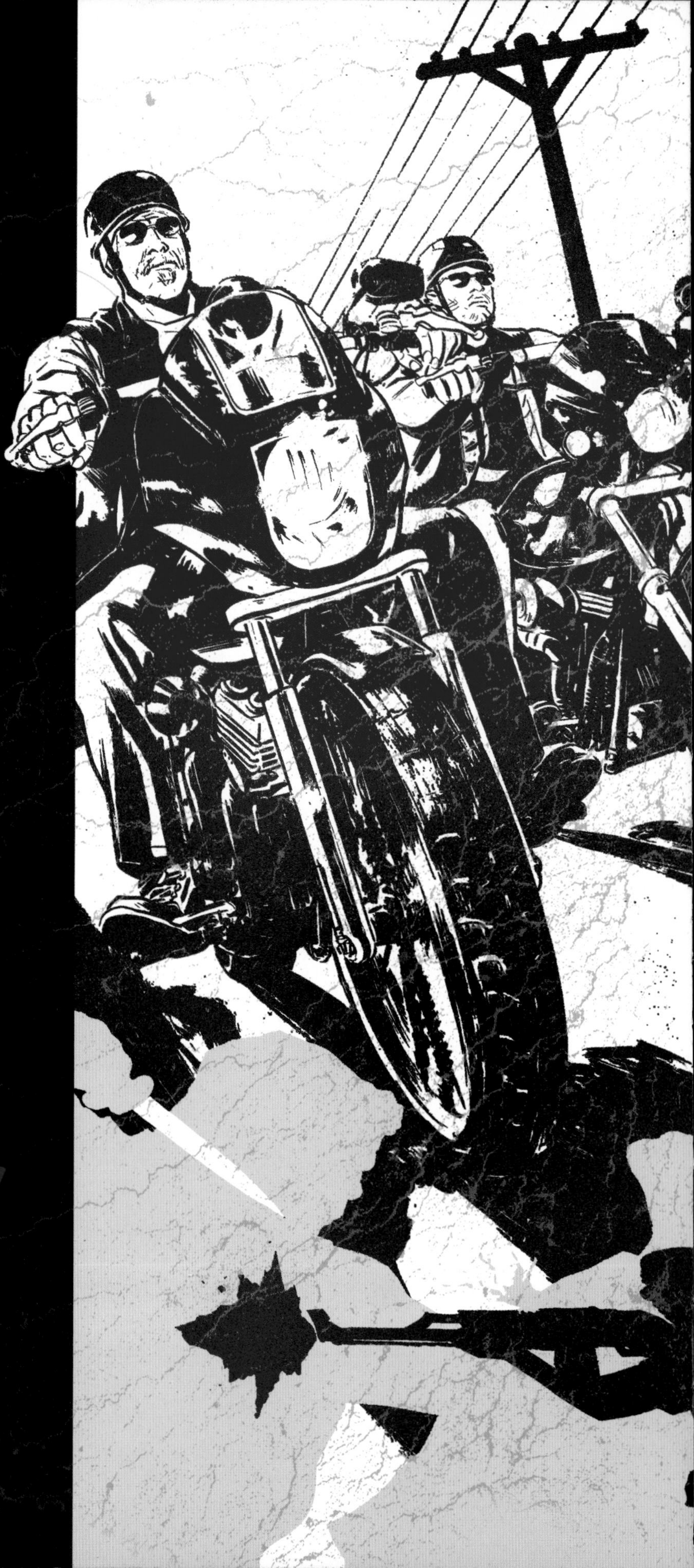

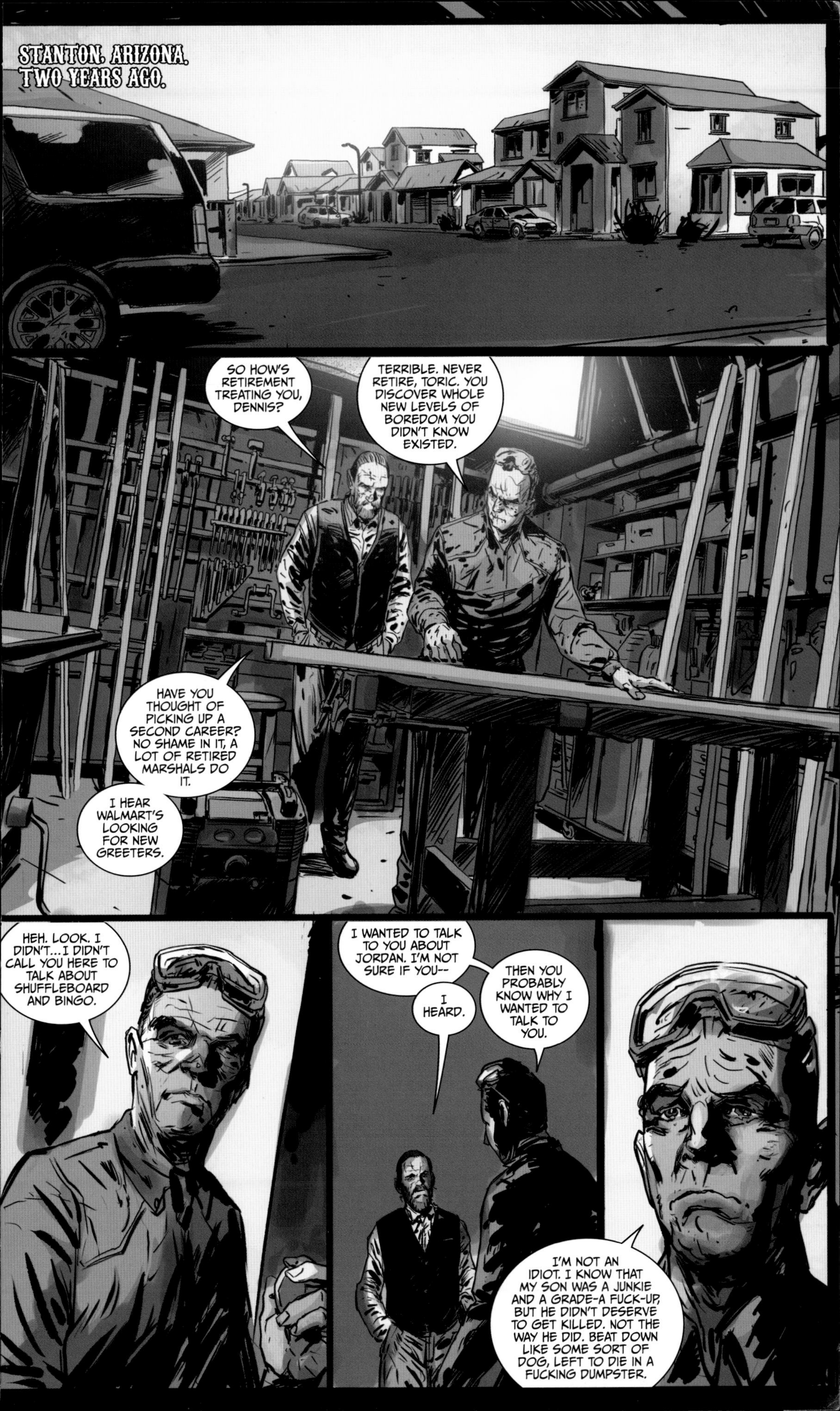
STANTON, ARIZONA. TWO YEARS AGO.
SO HOW'S RETIREMENT TREATING YOU, DENNIS?
TERRIBLE. NEVER RETIRE, TORIC. YOU DISCOVER WHOLE NEW LEVELS OF BOREDOM YOU DIDN'T KNOW EXISTED.
HAVE YOU THOUGHT OF PICKING UP A SECOND CAREER? NO SHAME IN IT, A LOT OF RETIRED MARSHALS DO IT.
I HEAR WALMART'S LOOKING FOR NEW GREETERS.
HEH. LOOK. I DIDN'T...I DIDN'T CALL YOU HERE TO TALK ABOUT SHUFFLEBOARD AND BINGO.
I WANTED TO TALK TO YOU ABOUT JORDAN. I'M NOT SURE IF YOU--
I HEARD.
THEN YOU PROBABLY KNOW WHY I WANTED TO TALK TO YOU.
I'M NOT AN IDIOT. I KNOW THAT MY SON WAS A JUNKIE AND A GRADE-A FUCK-UP, BUT HE DIDN'T DESERVE TO GET KILLED. NOT THE WAY HE DID. BEAT DOWN LIKE SOME SORT OF DOG, LEFT TO DIE IN A FUCKING DUMPSTER.

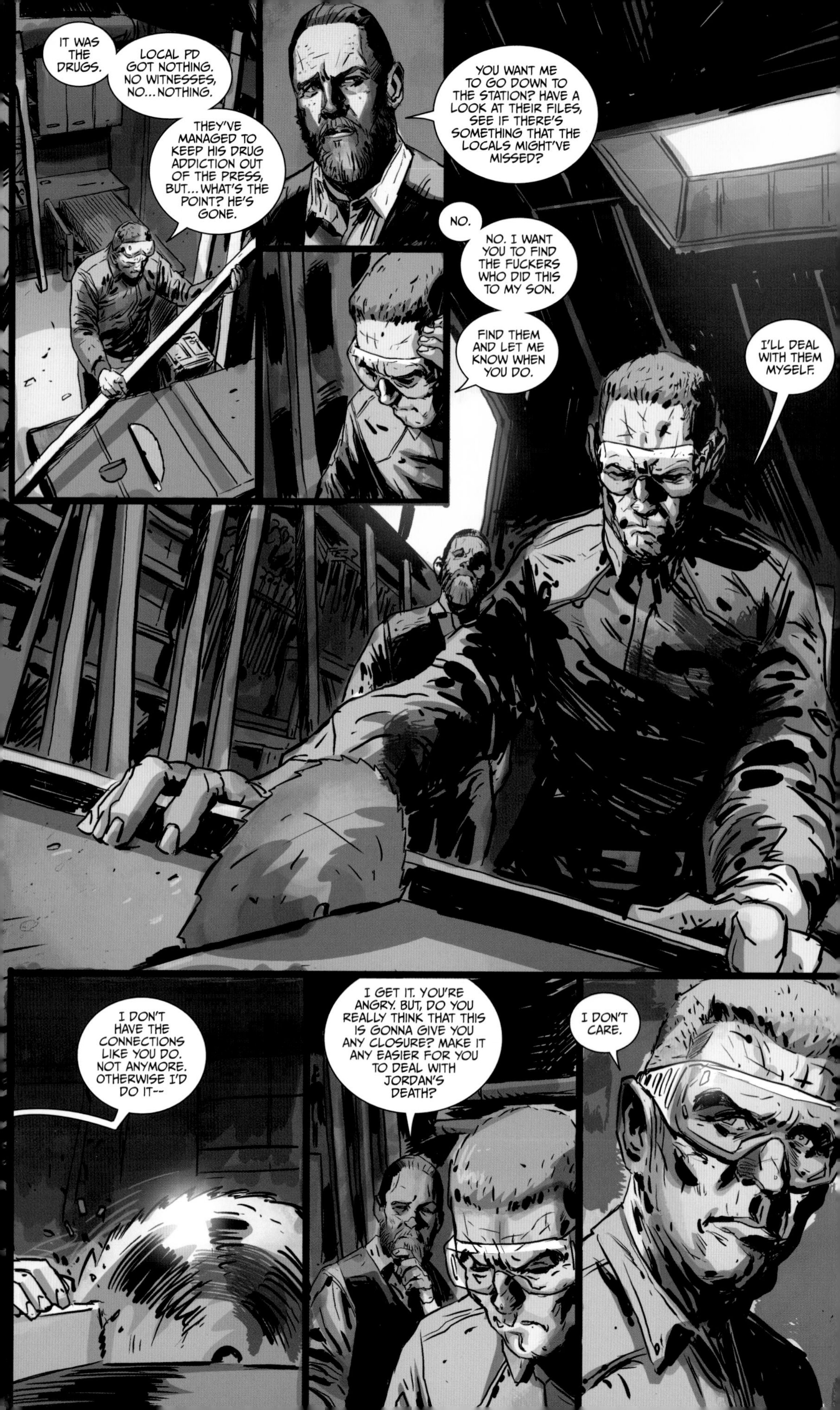
IT WAS THE DRUGS.
LOCAL PD GOT NOTHING. NO WITNESSES, NO...NOTHING.
THEY'VE MANAGED TO KEEP HIS DRUG ADDICTION OUT OF THE PRESS, BUT...WHAT'S THE POINT? HE'S GONE.
YOU WANT ME TO GO DOWN TO THE STATION? HAVE A LOOK AT THEIR FILES, SEE IF THERE'S SOMETHING THAT THE LOCALS MIGHT'VE MISSED?
NO.
NO. I WANT YOU TO FIND THE FUCKERS WHO DID THIS TO MY SON.
FIND THEM AND LET ME KNOW WHEN YOU DO.
I'LL DEAL WITH THEM MYSELF.
I DON'T HAVE THE CONNECTIONS LIKE YOU DO. NOT ANYMORE. OTHERWISE I'D DO IT--
I GET IT. YOU'RE ANGRY. BUT, DO YOU REALLY THINK THAT THIS IS GONNA GIVE YOU ANY CLOSURE? MAKE IT ANY EASIER FOR YOU TO DEAL WITH JORDAN'S DEATH?
I DON'T CARE.

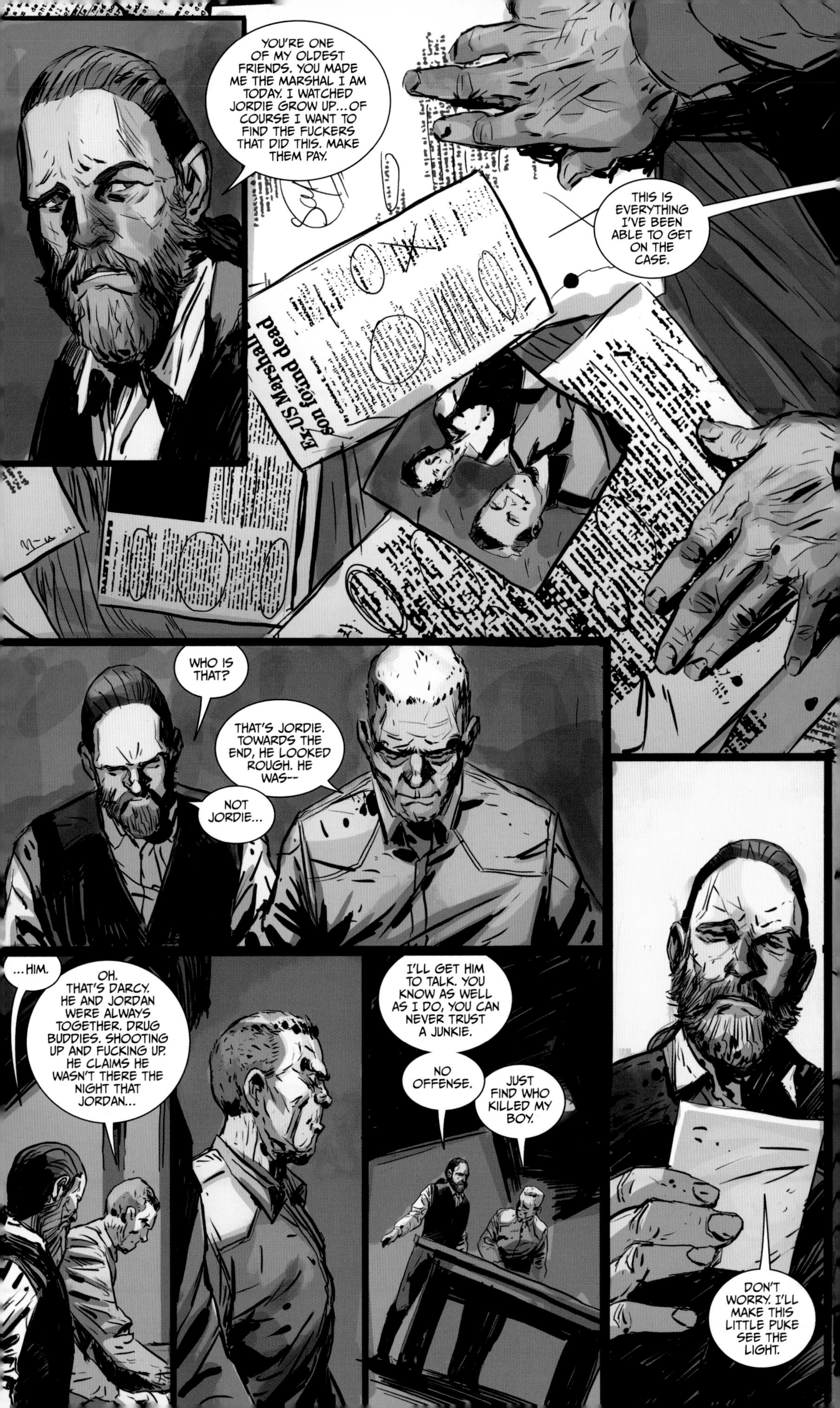
YOU'RE ONE OF MY OLDEST FRIENDS. YOU MADE ME THE MARSHAL I AM TODAY. I WATCHED JORDIE GROW UP...OF COURSE I WANT TO FIND THE FUCKERS THAT DID THIS. MAKE THEM PAY.
THIS IS EVERYTHING I'VE BEEN ABLE TO GET ON THE CASE.
Ex-US Marshall son found dead
WHO IS THAT?
THAT'S JORDIE. TOWARDS THE END, HE LOOKED ROUGH. HE WAS--
NOT JORDIE...
...HIM.
OH. THAT'S DARCY. HE AND JORDAN WERE ALWAYS TOGETHER. DRUG BUDDIES. SHOOTING UP AND FUCKING UP. HE CLAIMS HE WASN'T THERE THE NIGHT THAT JORDAN...
I'LL GET HIM TO TALK. YOU KNOW AS WELL AS I DO, YOU CAN NEVER TRUST A JUNKIE.
NO OFFENSE.
JUST FIND WHO KILLED MY BOY.
DON'T WORRY. I'LL MAKE THIS LITTLE PUKE SEE THE LIGHT.

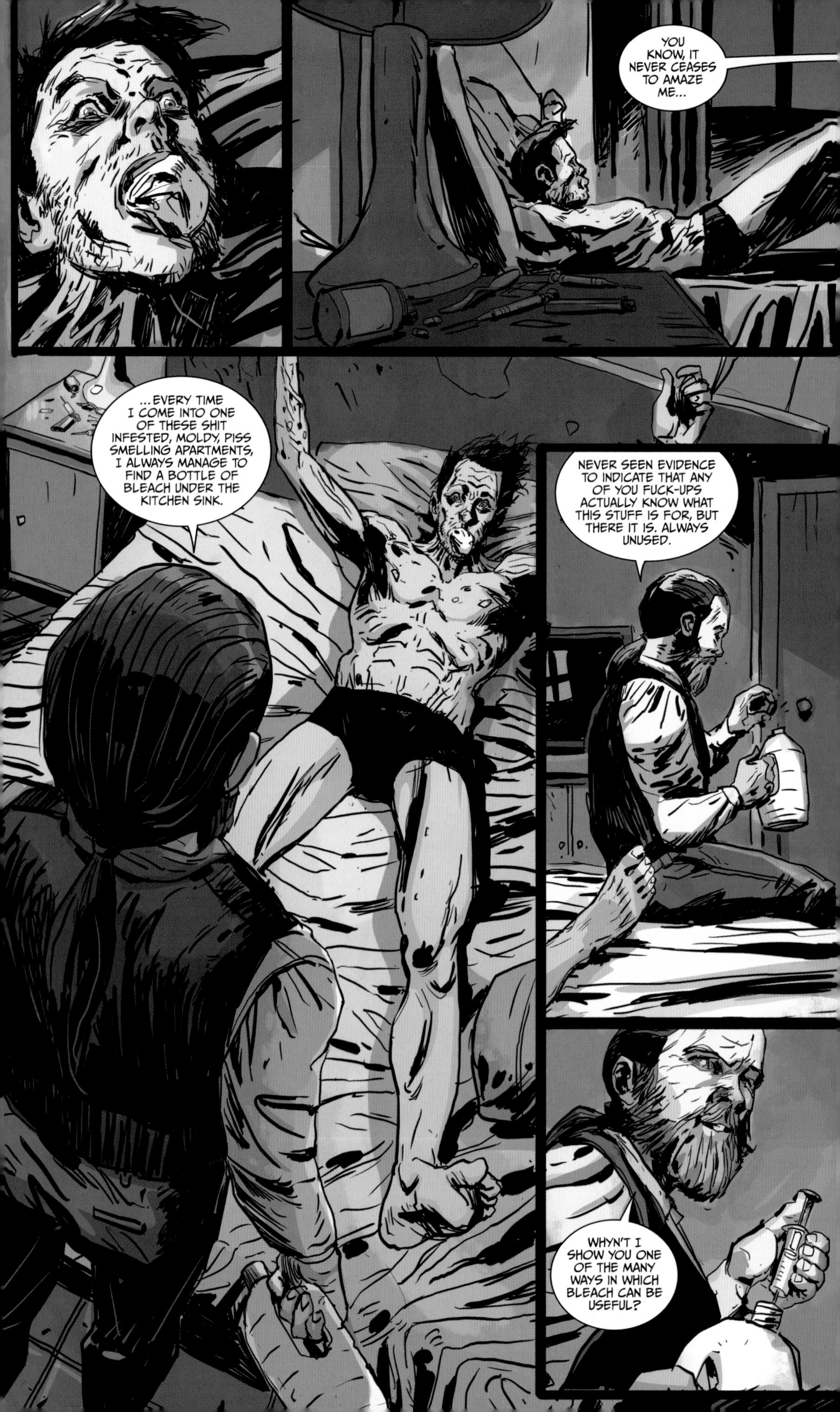
YOU KNOW, IT NEVER CEASES TO AMAZE ME...
...EVERY TIME I COME INTO ONE OF THESE SHIT INFESTED, MOLDY, PISS SMELLING APARTMENTS, I ALWAYS MANAGE TO FIND A BOTTLE OF BLEACH UNDER THE KITCHEN SINK.
NEVER SEEN EVIDENCE TO INDICATE THAT ANY OF YOU FUCK-UPS ACTUALLY KNOW WHAT THIS STUFF IS FOR, BUT THERE IT IS. ALWAYS UNUSED.
WHYN'T I SHOW YOU ONE OF THE MANY WAYS IN WHICH BLEACH CAN BE USEFUL?

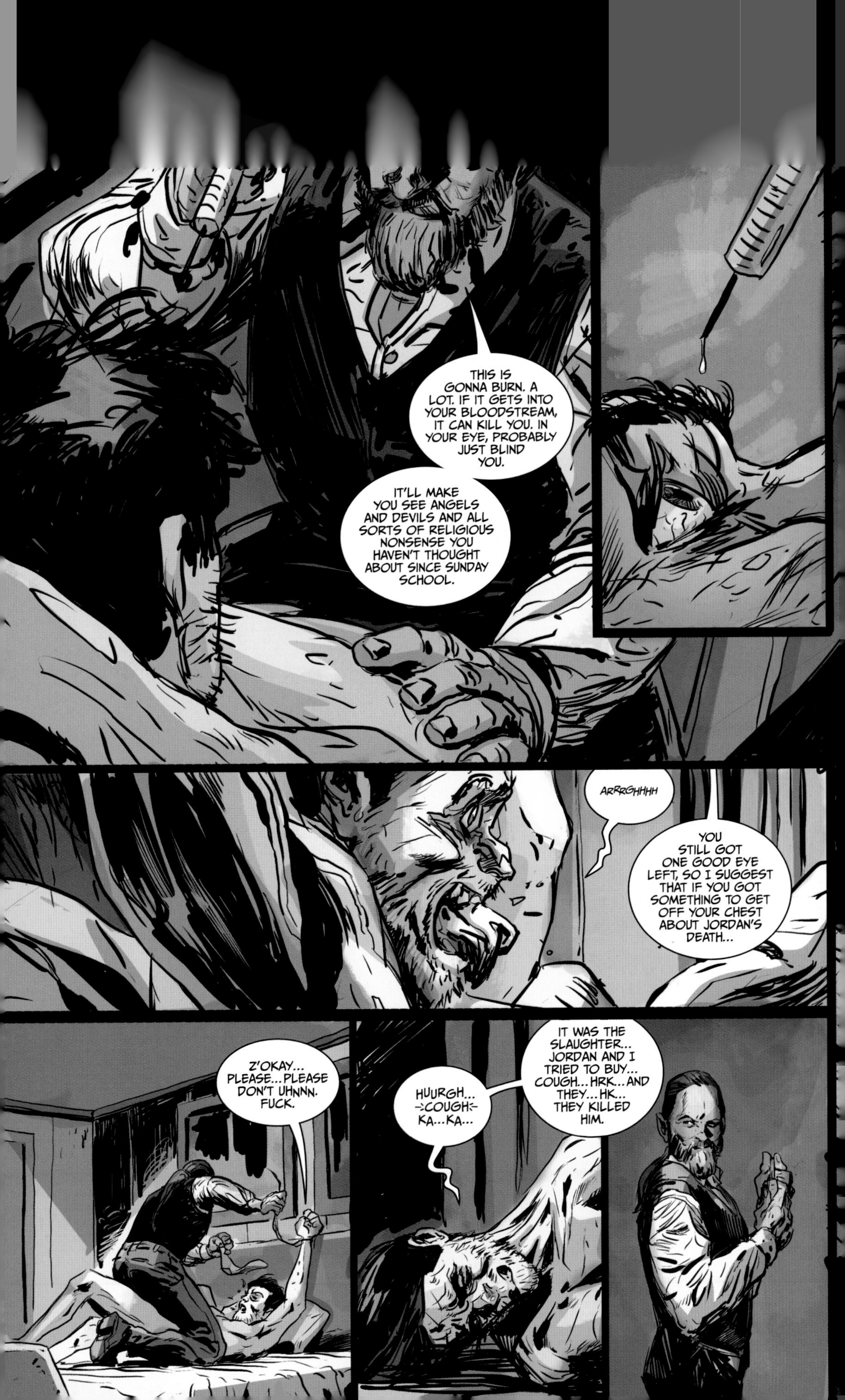
THIS IS GONNA BURN. A LOT. IF IT GETS INTO YOUR BLOODSTREAM, IT CAN KILL YOU. IN YOUR EYE, PROBABLY JUST BLIND YOU.
IT'LL MAKE YOU SEE ANGELS AND DEVILS AND ALL SORTS OF RELIGIOUS NONSENSE YOU HAVEN'T THOUGHT ABOUT SINCE SUNDAY SCHOOL.
ARRRGHHHH
YOU STILL GOT ONE GOOD EYE LEFT, SO I SUGGEST THAT IF YOU GOT SOMETHING TO GET OFF YOUR CHEST ABOUT JORDAN'S DEATH...
Z'OKAY... PLEASE...PLEASE DON'T UHNNN. FUCK.
HUURGH... COUGH KA...KA...
IT WAS THE SLAUGHTER... JORDAN AND I TRIED TO BUY... COUGH...HRK...AND THEY...HK... THEY KILLED HIM.

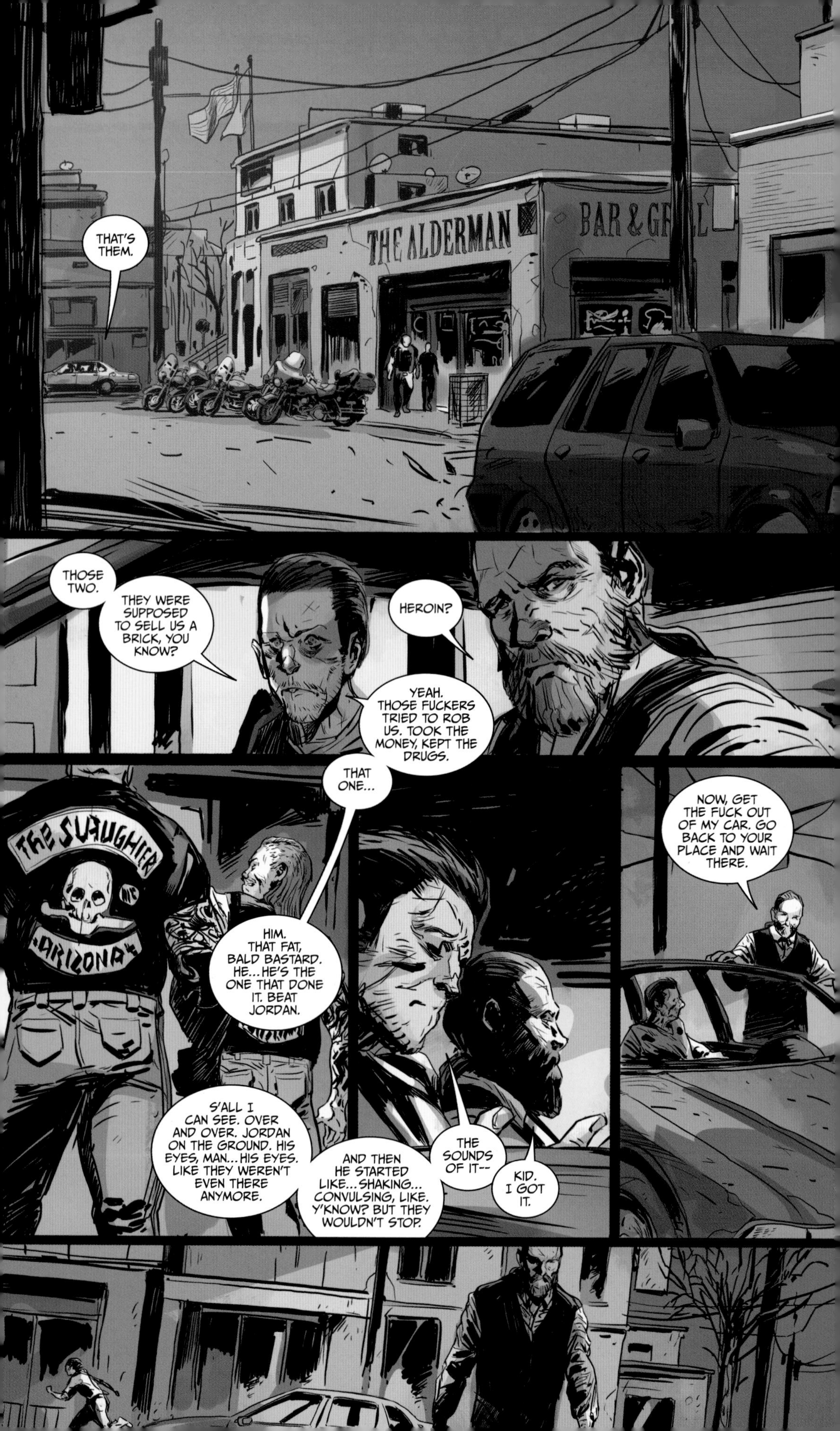
THAT'S THEM.
THE ALDERMAN
BAR & GR L
THOSE TWO.
THEY WERE SUPPOSED TO SELL US A BRICK, YOU KNOW?
HEROIN?
YEAH. THOSE FUCKERS TRIED TO ROB US. TOOK THE MONEY, KEPT THE DRUGS.
THAT ONE...
HIM. THAT FAT, BALD BASTARD. HE...HE'S THE ONE THAT DONE IT. BEAT JORDAN.
S'ALL I CAN SEE. OVER AND OVER. JORDAN ON THE GROUND. HIS EYES, MAN...HIS EYES. LIKE THEY WEREN'T EVEN THERE ANYMORE.
AND THEN HE STARTED LIKE...SHAKING... CONVULSING, LIKE. Y'KNOW? BUT THEY WOULDN'T STOP.
THE SOUNDS OF IT--
KID. I GOT IT.
NOW, GET THE FUCK OUT OF MY CAR. GO BACK TO YOUR PLACE AND WAIT THERE.

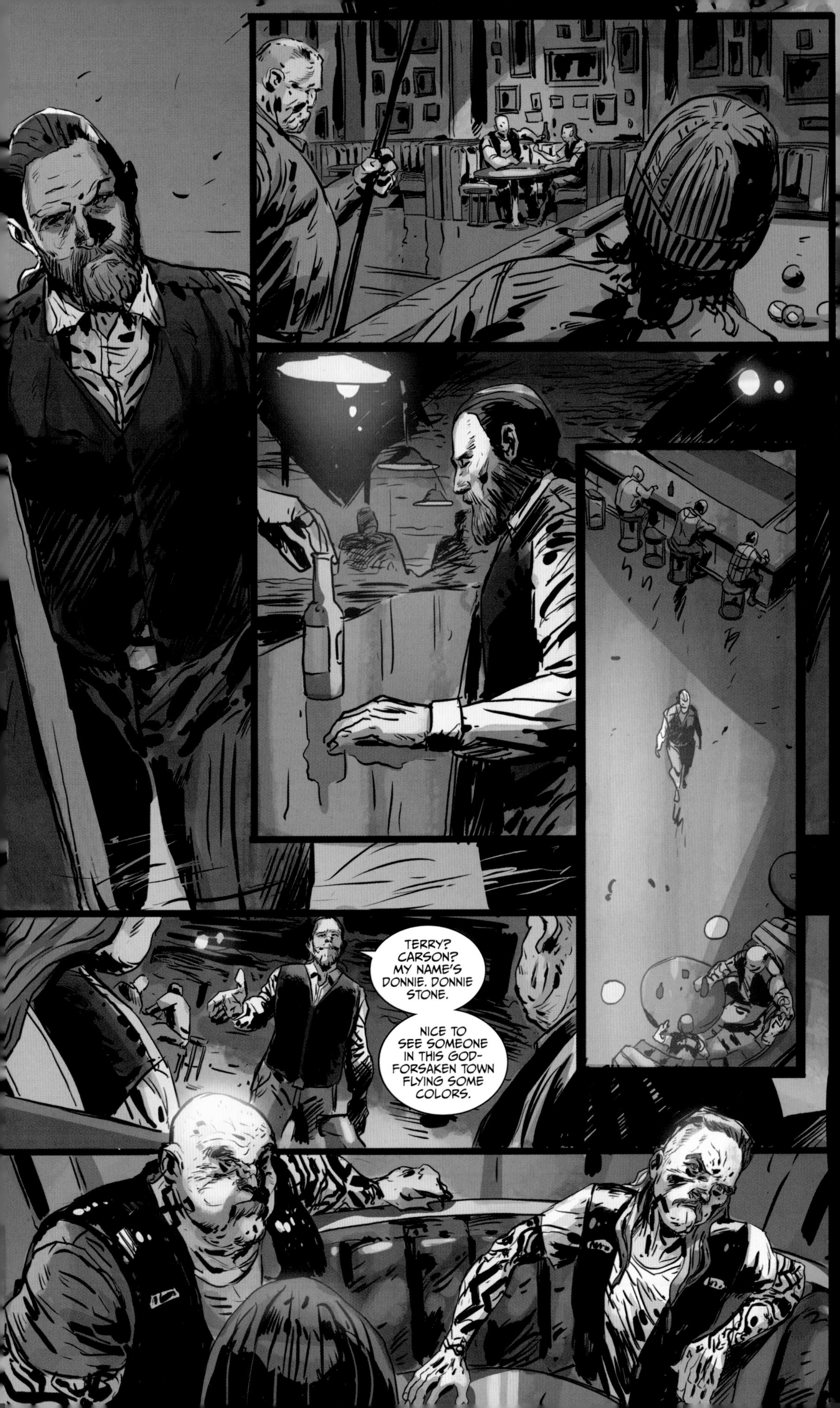
TERRY? CARSON? MY NAME'S DONNIE. DONNIE STONE.
NICE TO SEE SOMEONE IN THIS GOD-FORSAKEN TOWN FLYING SOME COLORS.

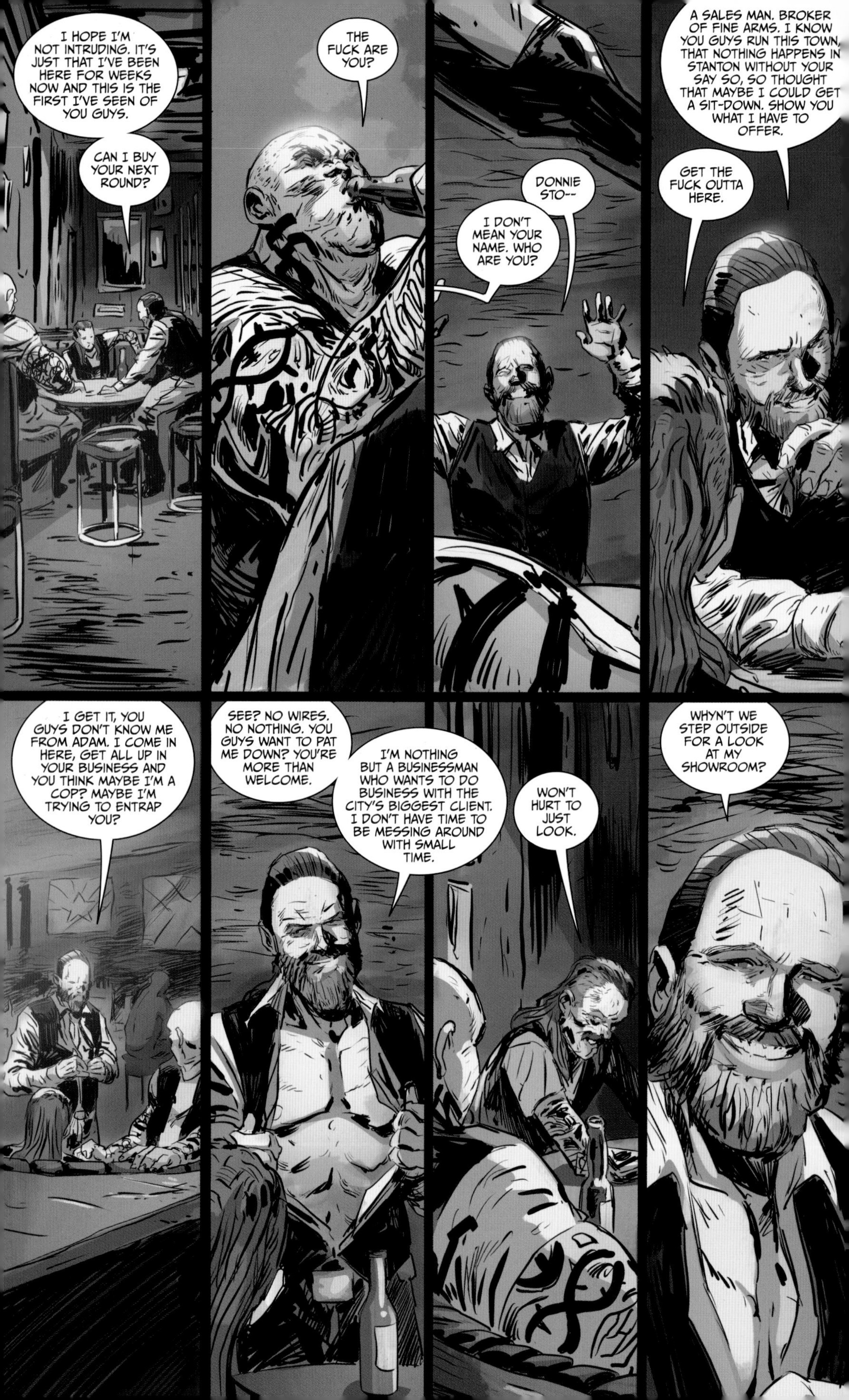
I HOPE I'M NOT INTRUDING. IT'S JUST THAT I'VE BEEN HERE FOR WEEKS NOW AND THIS IS THE FIRST I'VE SEEN OF YOU GUYS.
CAN I BUY YOUR NEXT ROUND?
THE FUCK ARE YOU?
DONNIE STO--
I DON'T MEAN YOUR NAME. WHO ARE YOU?
A SALES MAN. BROKER OF FINE ARMS. I KNOW YOU GUYS RUN THIS TOWN, THAT NOTHING HAPPENS IN STANTON WITHOUT YOUR SAY SO, SO THOUGHT THAT MAYBE I COULD GET A SIT-DOWN. SHOW YOU WHAT I HAVE TO OFFER.
GET THE FUCK OUTTA HERE.
I GET IT, YOU GUYS DON'T KNOW ME FROM ADAM. I COME IN HERE, GET ALL UP IN YOUR BUSINESS AND YOU THINK MAYBE I'M A COP? MAYBE I'M TRYING TO ENTRAP YOU?
SEE? NO WIRES. NO NOTHING. YOU GUYS WANT TO PAT ME DOWN? YOU'RE MORE THAN WELCOME.
I'M NOTHING BUT A BUSINESSMAN WHO WANTS TO DO BUSINESS WITH THE CITY'S BIGGEST CLIENT. I DON'T HAVE TIME TO BE MESSING AROUND WITH SMALL TIME.
WON'T HURT TO JUST LOOK.
WHYN'T WE STEP OUTSIDE FOR A LOOK AT MY SHOWROOM?

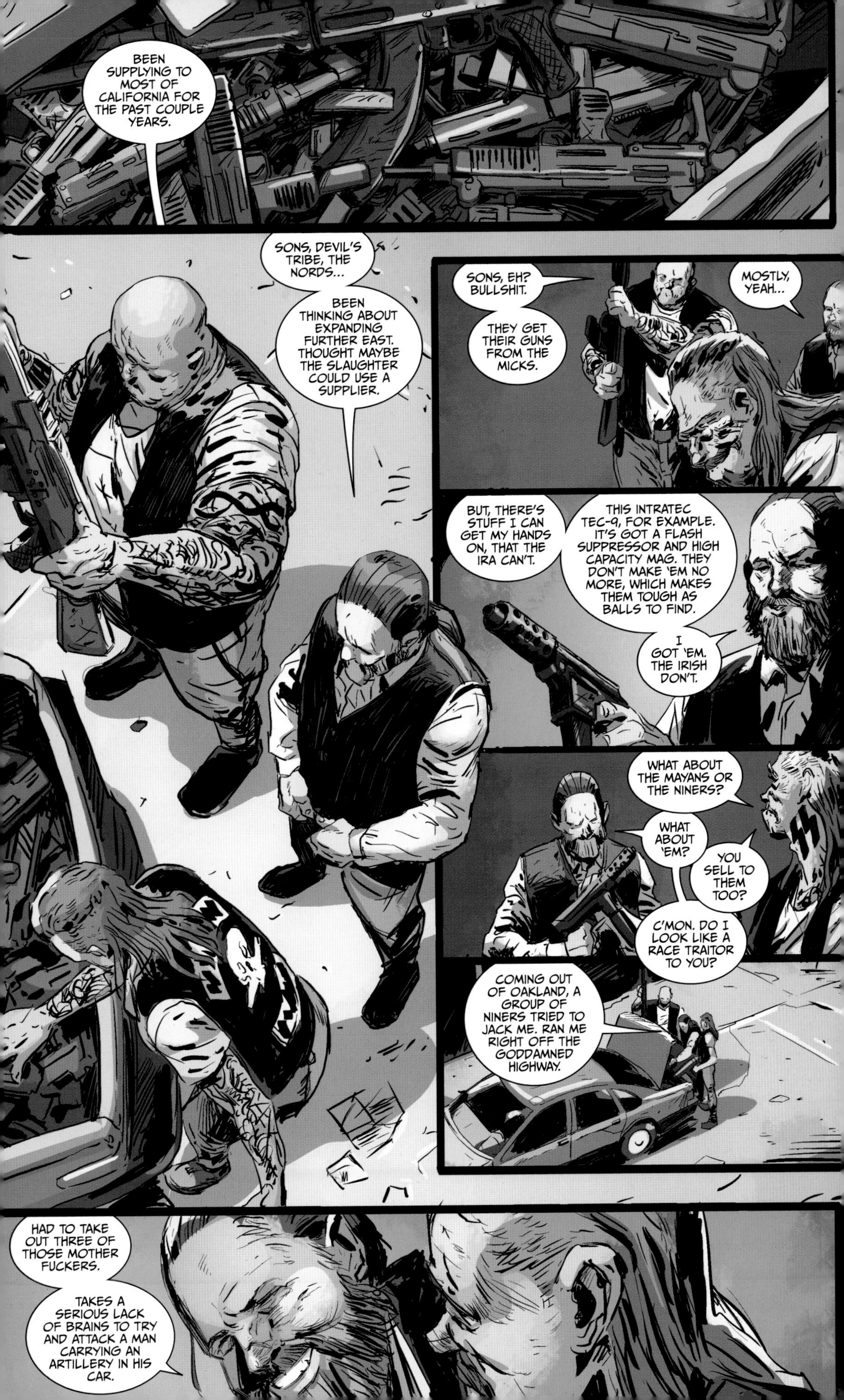
BEEN SUPPLYING TO MOST OF CALIFORNIA FOR THE PAST COUPLE YEARS.
SONS, DEVIL'S TRIBE, THE NORDS...
BEEN THINKING ABOUT EXPANDING FURTHER EAST. THOUGHT MAYBE THE SLAUGHTER COULD USE A SUPPLIER.
SONS, EH? BULLSHIT.
THEY GET THEIR GUNS FROM THE MICKS.
MOSTLY, YEAH...
BUT, THERE'S STUFF I CAN GET MY HANDS ON, THAT THE IRA CAN'T.
THIS INTRATEC TEC-9, FOR EXAMPLE. IT'S GOT A FLASH SUPPRESSOR AND HIGH CAPACITY MAG. THEY DON'T MAKE 'EM NO MORE, WHICH MAKES THEM TOUGH AS BALLS TO FIND.
I GOT 'EM. THE IRISH DON'T.
WHAT ABOUT THE MAYANS OR THE NINERS?
WHAT ABOUT 'EM?
YOU SELL TO THEM TOO?
C'MON. DO I LOOK LIKE A RACE TRAITOR TO YOU?
COMING OUT OF OAKLAND, A GROUP OF NINERS TRIED TO JACK ME. RAN ME RIGHT OFF THE GODDAMNED HIGHWAY.
HAD TO TAKE OUT THREE OF THOSE MOTHER FUCKERS.
TAKES A SERIOUS LACK OF BRAINS TO TRY AND ATTACK A MAN CARRYING AN ARTILLERY IN HIS CAR.

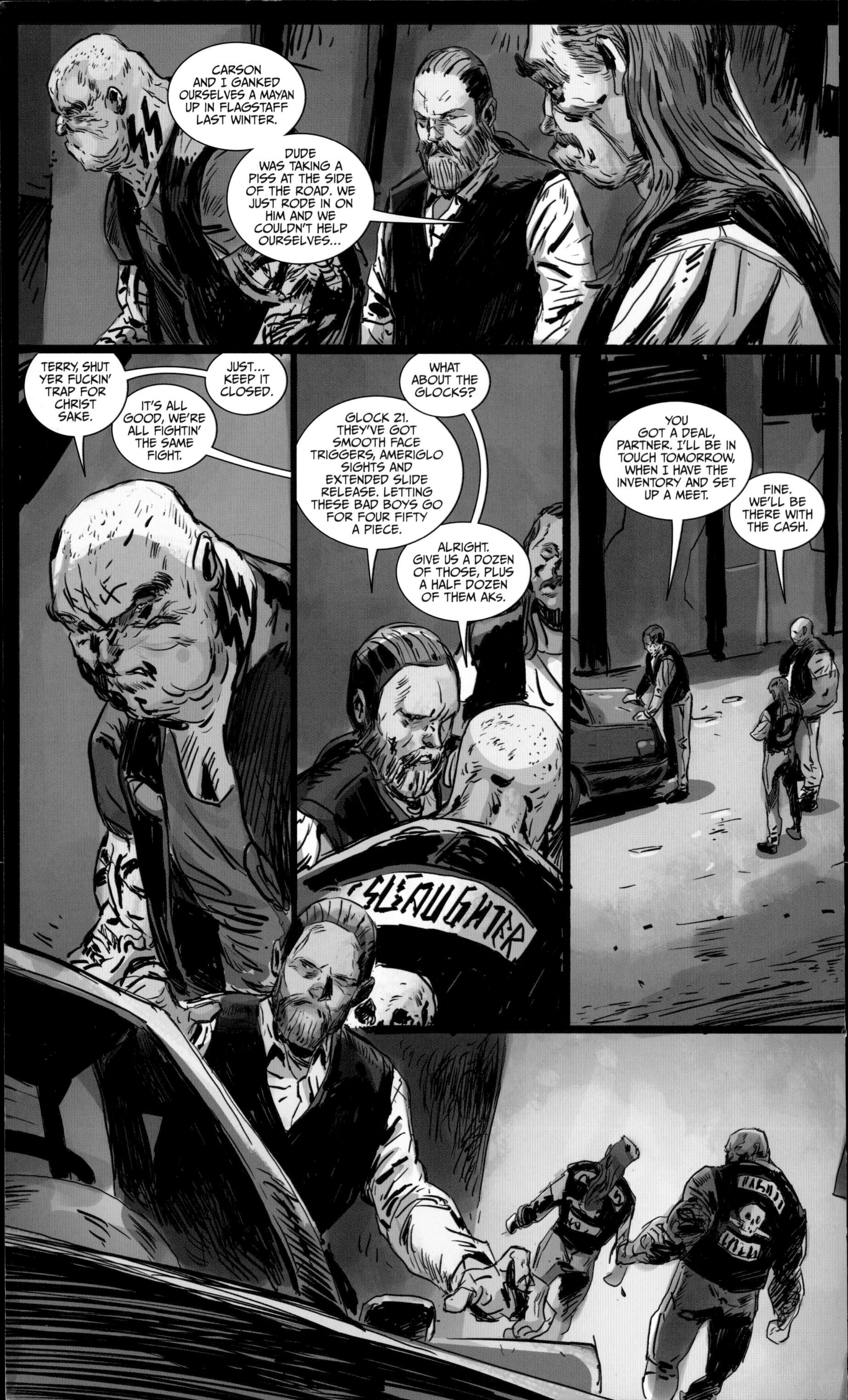
CARSON AND I GANKED OURSELVES A MAYAN UP IN FLAGSTAFF LAST WINTER.
DUDE WAS TAKING A PISS AT THE SIDE OF THE ROAD. WE JUST RODE IN ON HIM AND WE COULDN'T HELP OURSELVES...
TERRY, SHUT YER FUCKIN' TRAP FOR CHRIST SAKE.
JUST... KEEP IT CLOSED.
IT'S ALL GOOD, WE'RE ALL FIGHTIN' THE SAME FIGHT.
WHAT ABOUT THE GLOCKS?
GLOCK 21. THEY'VE GOT SMOOTH FACE TRIGGERS, AMERIGLO SIGHTS AND EXTENDED SLIDE RELEASE. LETTING THESE BAD BOYS GO FOR FOUR FIFTY A PIECE.
ALRIGHT. GIVE US A DOZEN OF THOSE, PLUS A HALF DOZEN OF THEM AKS.
SLAUGHTER
YOU GOT A DEAL, PARTNER. I'LL BE IN TOUCH TOMORROW, WHEN I HAVE THE INVENTORY AND SET UP A MEET.
FINE. WE'LL BE THERE WITH THE CASH.

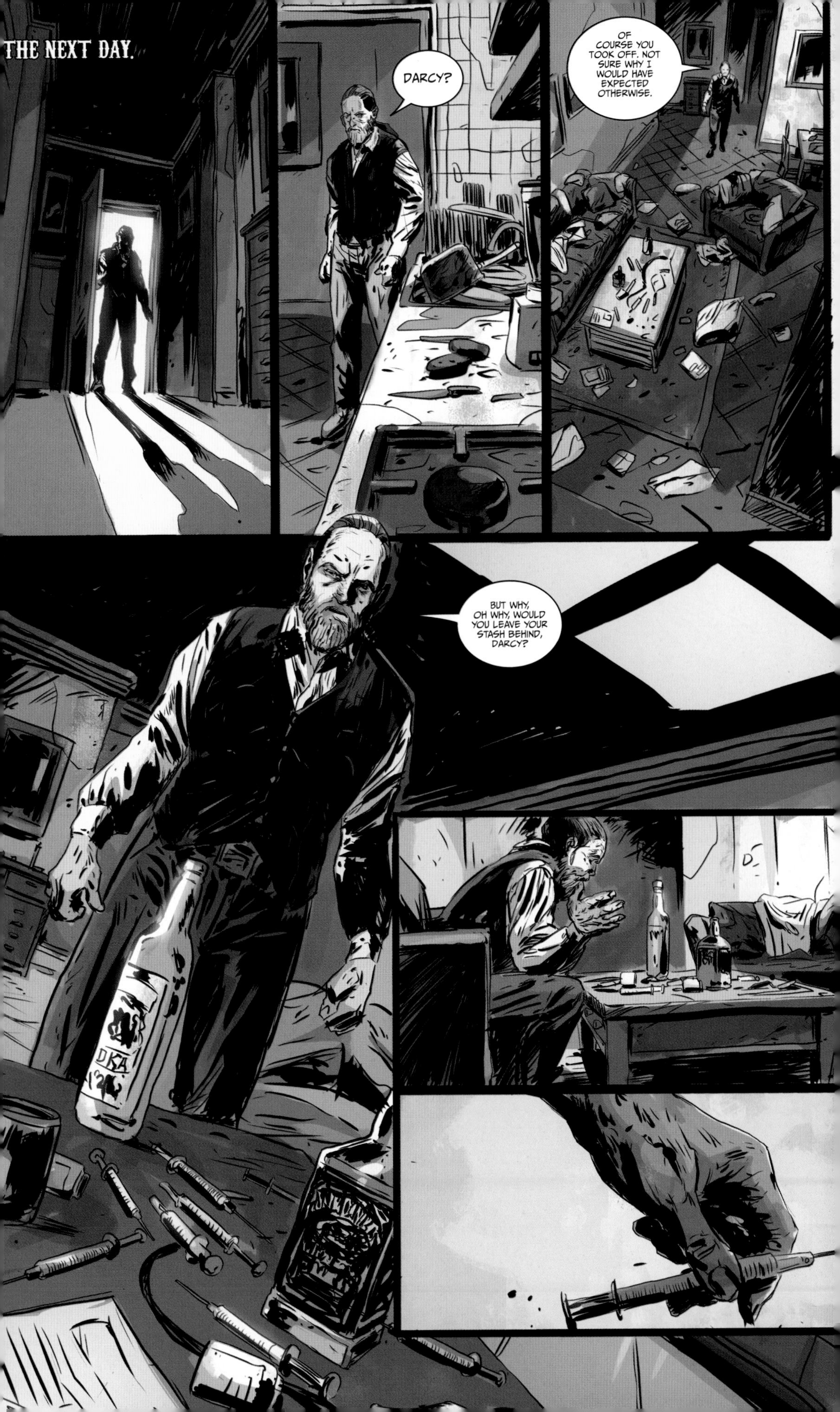
THE NEXT DAY.
DARCY?
OF COURSE YOU TOOK OFF. NOT SURE WHY I WOULD HAVE EXPECTED OTHERWISE.
BUT WHY, OH WHY, WOULD YOU LEAVE YOUR STASH BEHIND, DARCY?
DKA

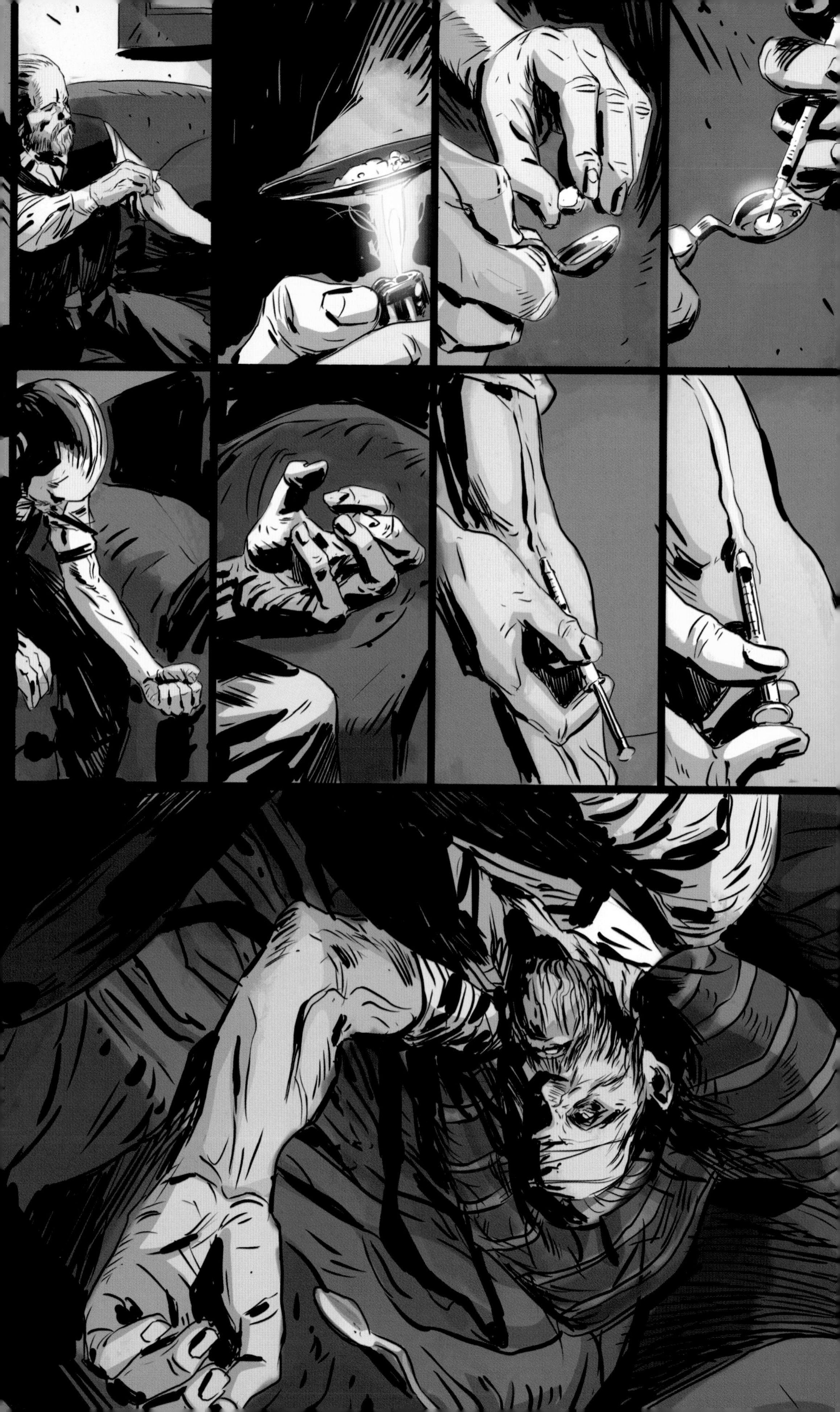

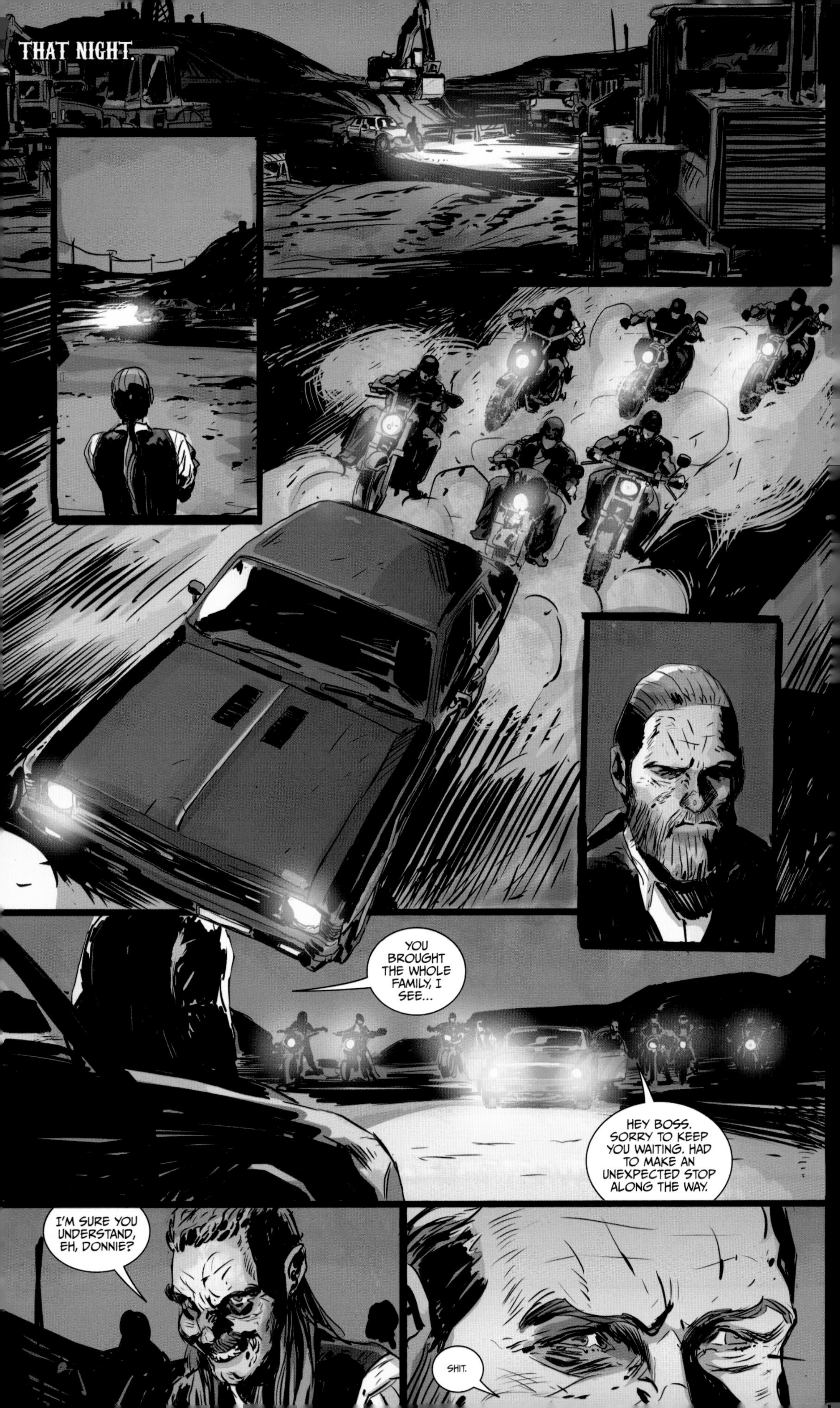
THAT NIGHT.
YOU BROUGHT THE WHOLE FAMILY, I SEE...
HEY BOSS. SORRY TO KEEP YOU WAITING. HAD TO MAKE AN UNEXPECTED STOP ALONG THE WAY.
I'M SURE YOU UNDERSTAND, EH, DONNIE?
SHIT.

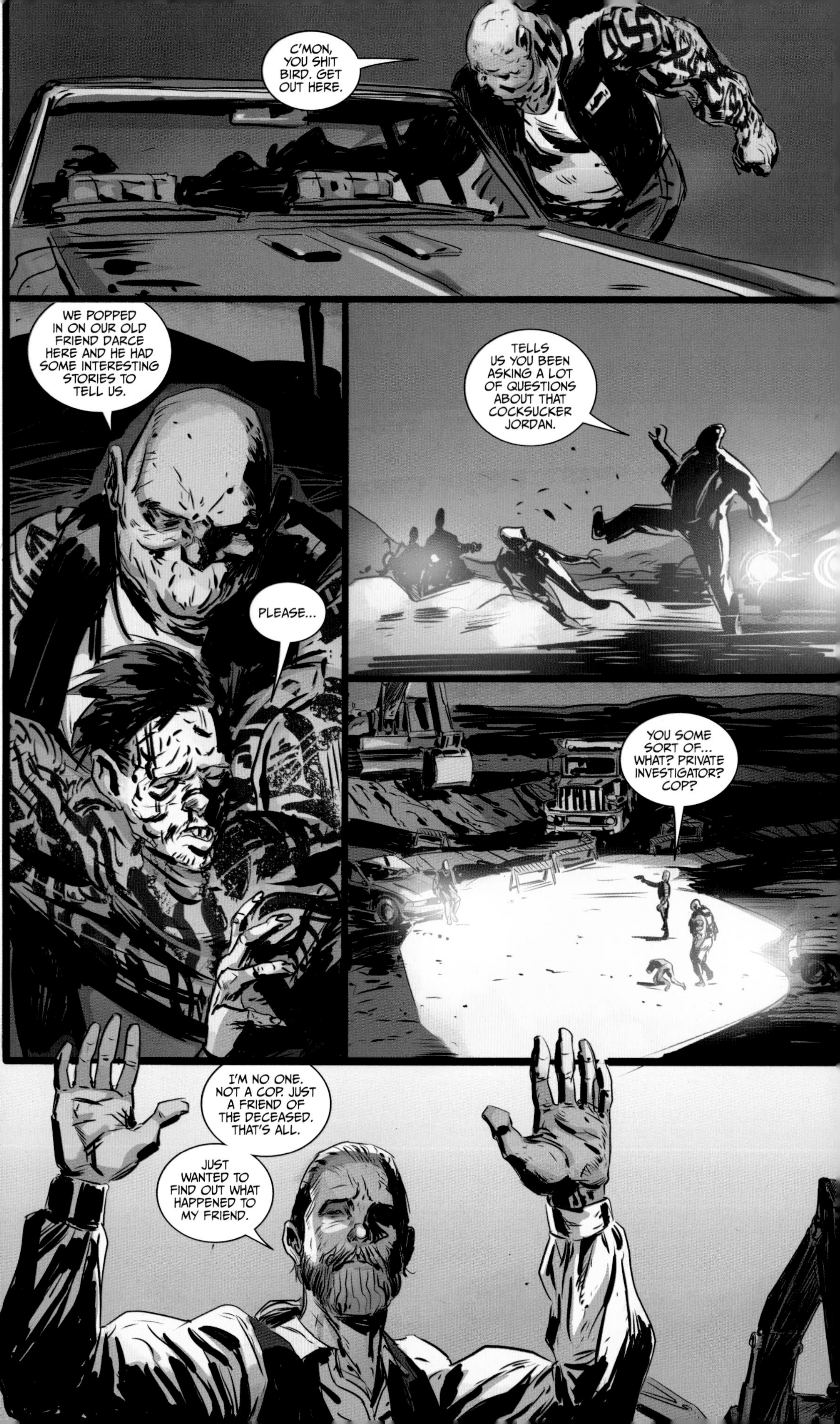
C'MON, YOU SHIT BIRD. GET OUT HERE.
WE POPPED IN ON OUR OLD FRIEND DARCE HERE AND HE HAD SOME INTERESTING STORIES TO TELL US.
PLEASE...
TELLS US YOU BEEN ASKING A LOT OF QUESTIONS ABOUT THAT COCKSUCKER JORDAN.
YOU SOME SORT OF... WHAT? PRIVATE INVESTIGATOR? COP?
I'M NO ONE. NOT A COP. JUST A FRIEND OF THE DECEASED. THAT'S ALL.
JUST WANTED TO FIND OUT WHAT HAPPENED TO MY FRIEND.

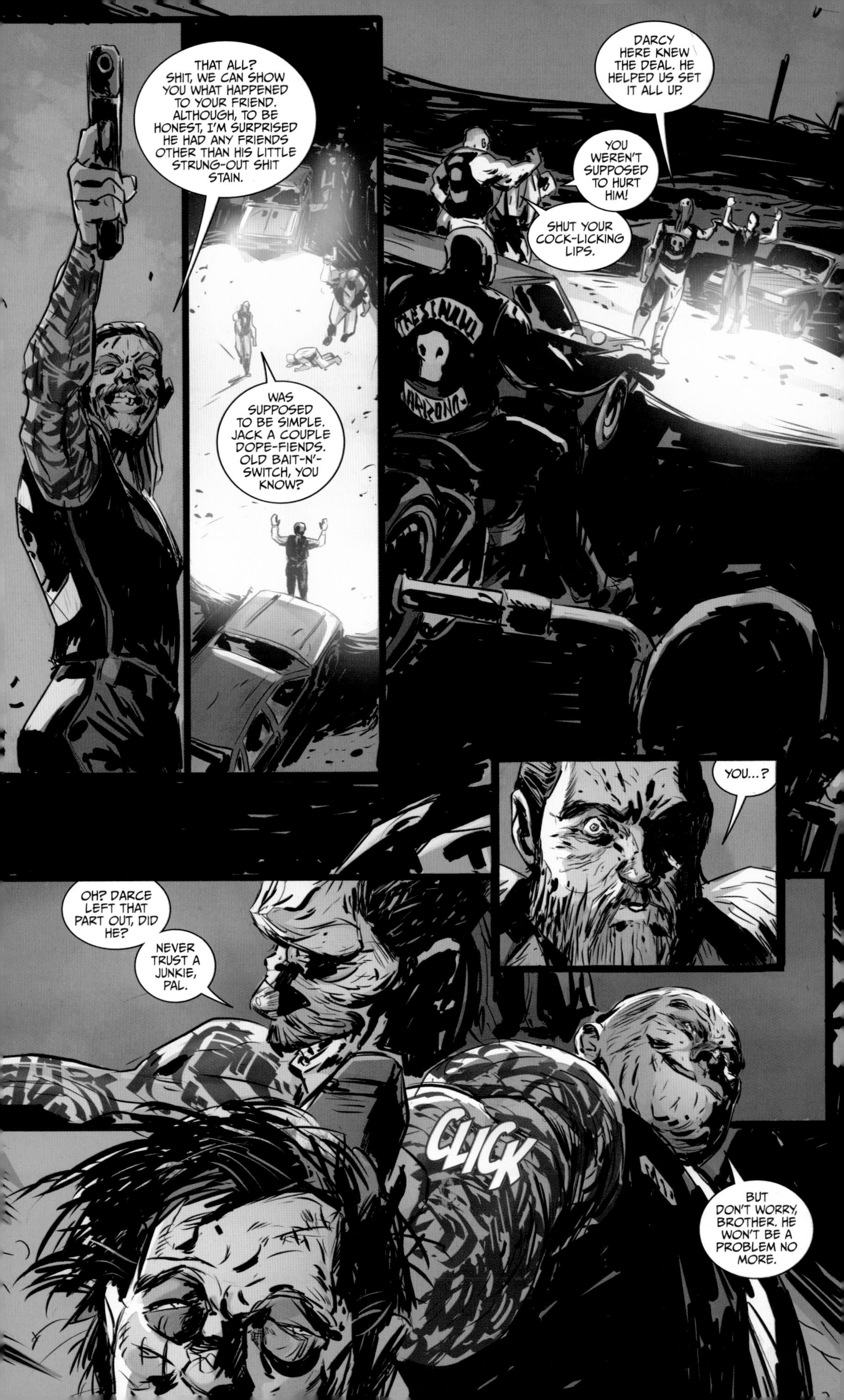
THAT ALL? SHIT, WE CAN SHOW YOU WHAT HAPPENED TO YOUR FRIEND. ALTHOUGH, TO BE HONEST, I'M SURPRISED HE HAD ANY FRIENDS OTHER THAN HIS LITTLE STRUNG-OUT SHIT STAIN.
WAS SUPPOSED TO BE SIMPLE. JACK A COUPLE DOPE-FIENDS. OLD BAIT-N'-SWITCH, YOU KNOW?
DARCY HERE KNEW THE DEAL. HE HELPED US SET IT ALL UP.
YOU WEREN'T SUPPOSED TO HURT HIM!
SHUT YOUR COCK-LICKING LIPS.
YOU...?
OH? DARCE LEFT THAT PART OUT, DID HE?
NEVER TRUST A JUNKIE, PAL.
CLICK
BUT DON'T WORRY, BROTHER. HE WON'T BE A PROBLEM NO MORE.

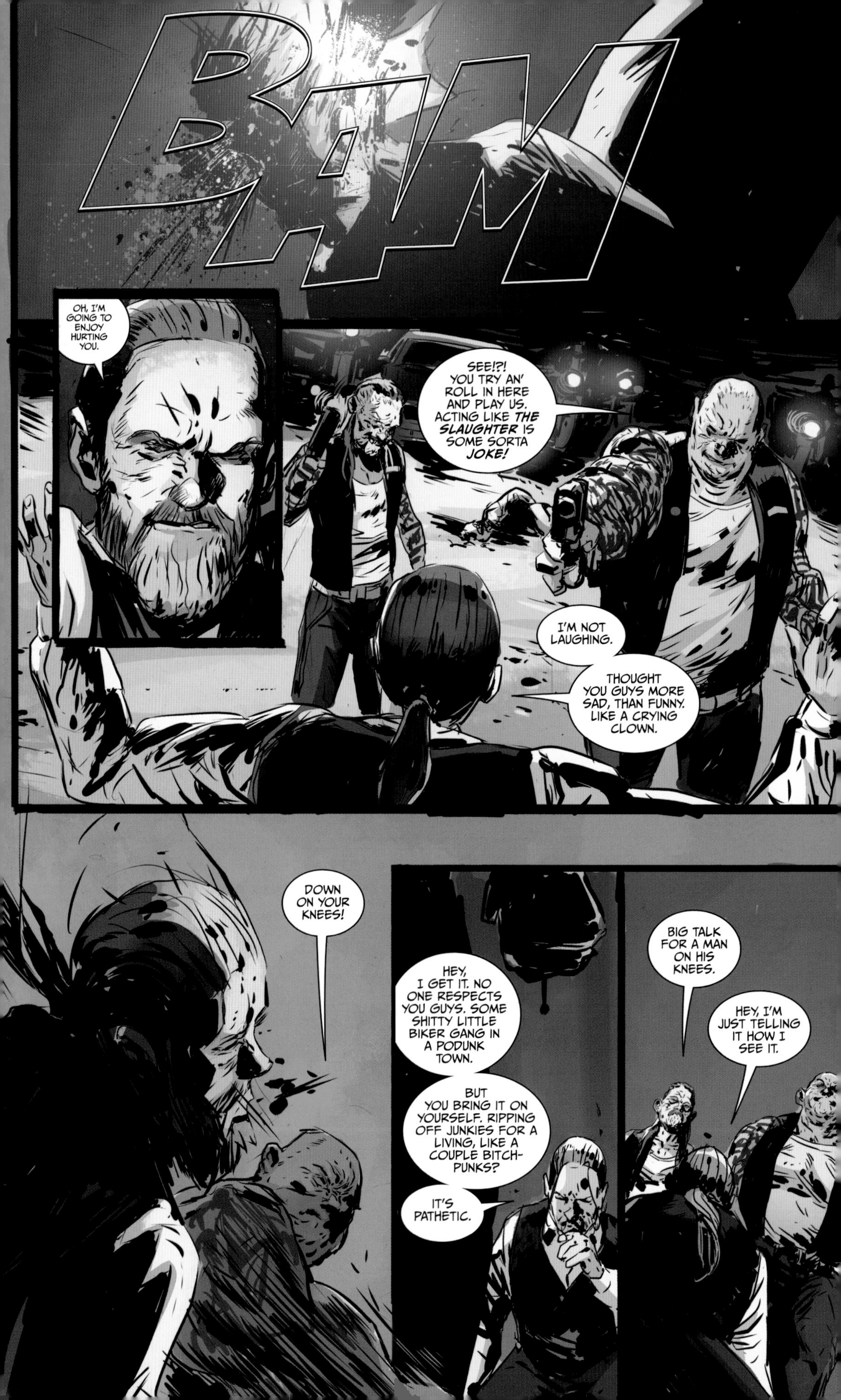
BAM
OH, I'M GOING TO ENJOY HURTING YOU.
SEE!?! YOU TRY AN' ROLL IN HERE AND PLAY US. ACTING LIKE THE SLAUGHTER IS SOME SORTA JOKE!
I'M NOT LAUGHING.
THOUGHT YOU GUYS MORE SAD, THAN FUNNY. LIKE A CRYING CLOWN.
DOWN ON YOUR KNEES!
HEY, I GET IT. NO ONE RESPECTS YOU GUYS. SOME SHITTY LITTLE BIKER GANG IN A PODUNK TOWN.
BUT YOU BRING IT ON YOURSELF. RIPPING OFF JUNKIES FOR A LIVING, LIKE A COUPLE BITCH-PUNKS?
IT'S PATHETIC.
BIG TALK FOR A MAN ON HIS KNEES.
HEY, I'M JUST TELLING IT HOW I SEE IT.

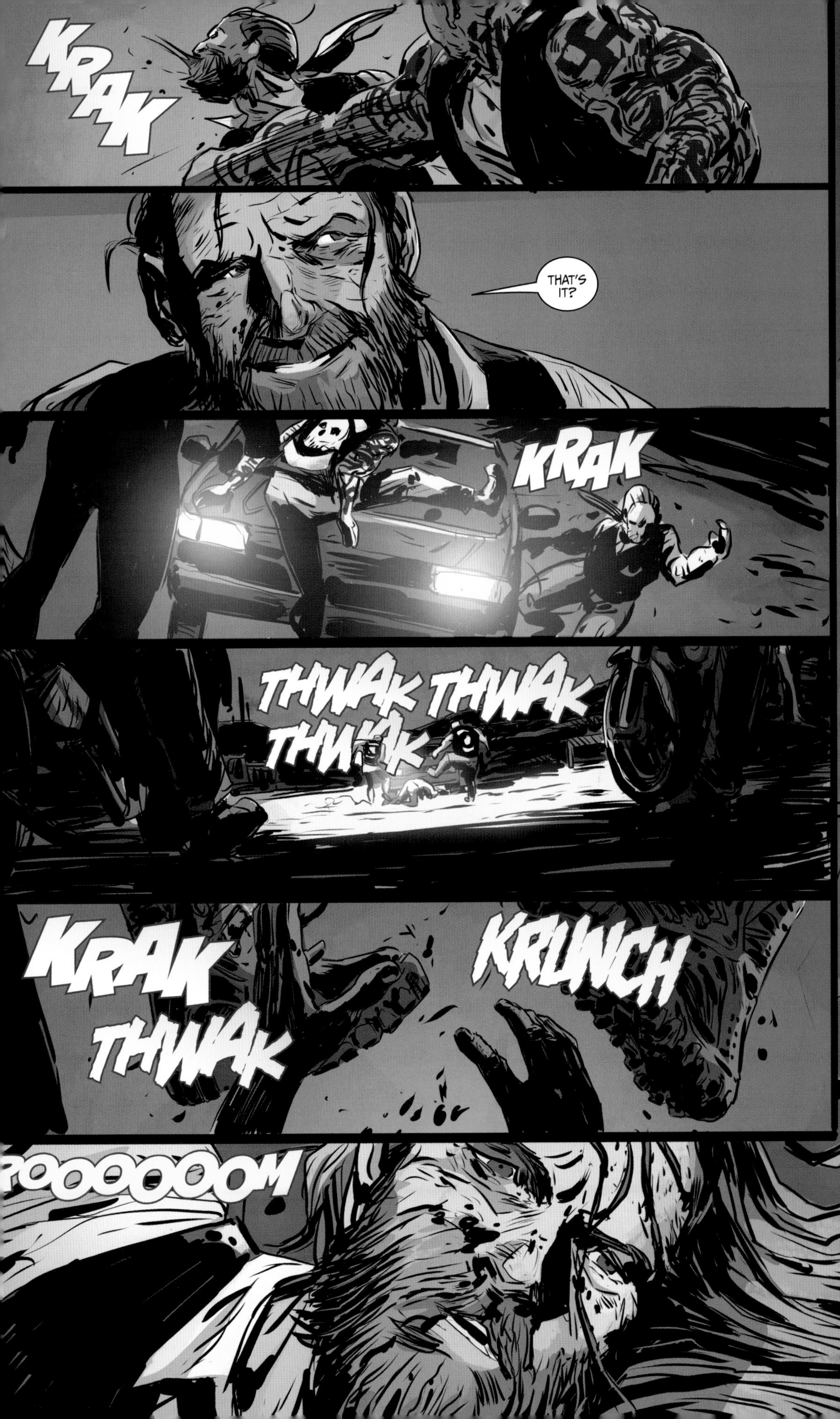
KRAK
THAT'S IT?
KRAK
THWAK THWAK
THWAK
KRAK
KRUNCH
THWAK
POOOOOOOM

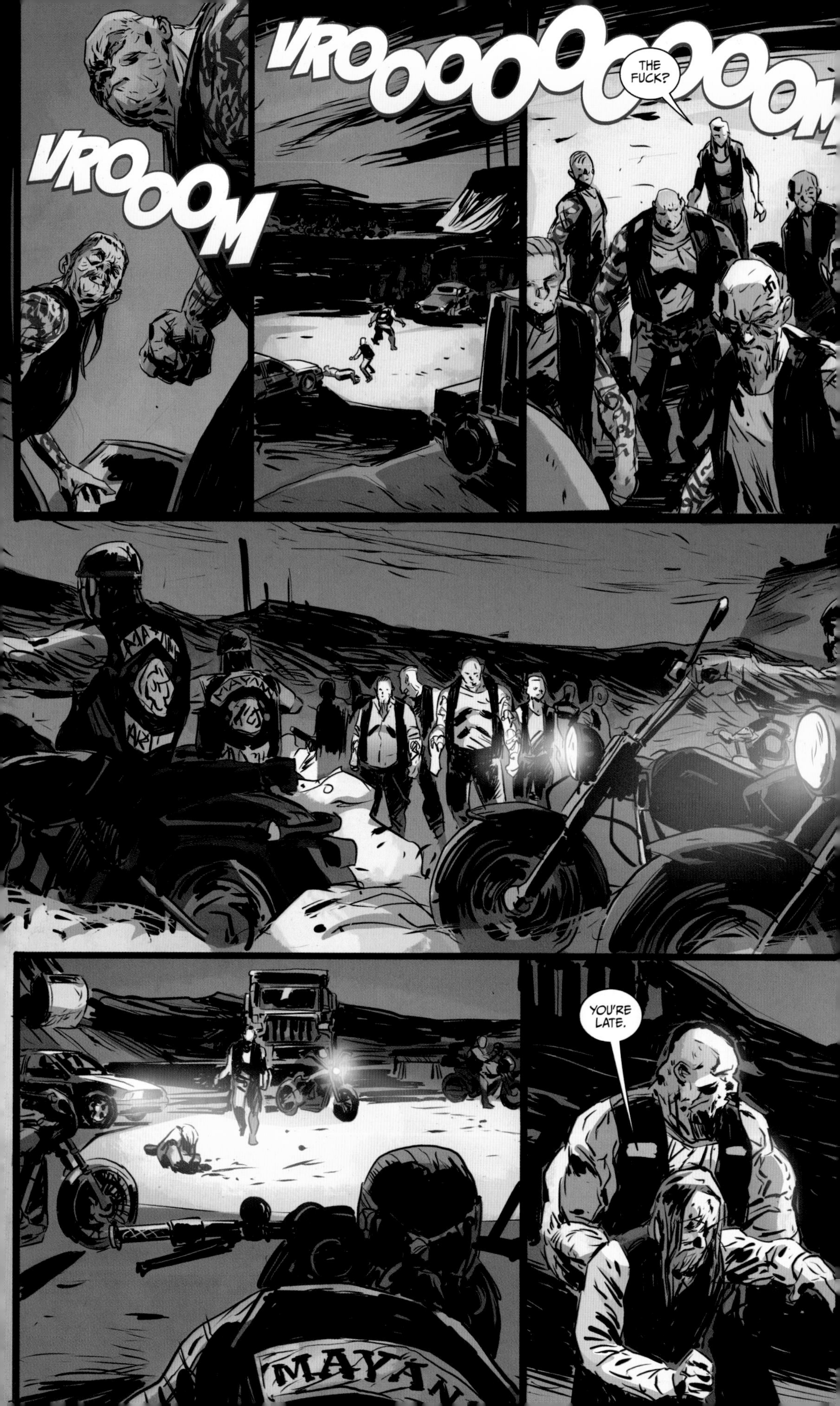
VROOOM
VROOOOOOOOOOM
THE FUCK?
MAYANS
YOU'RE LATE.
MAYAN

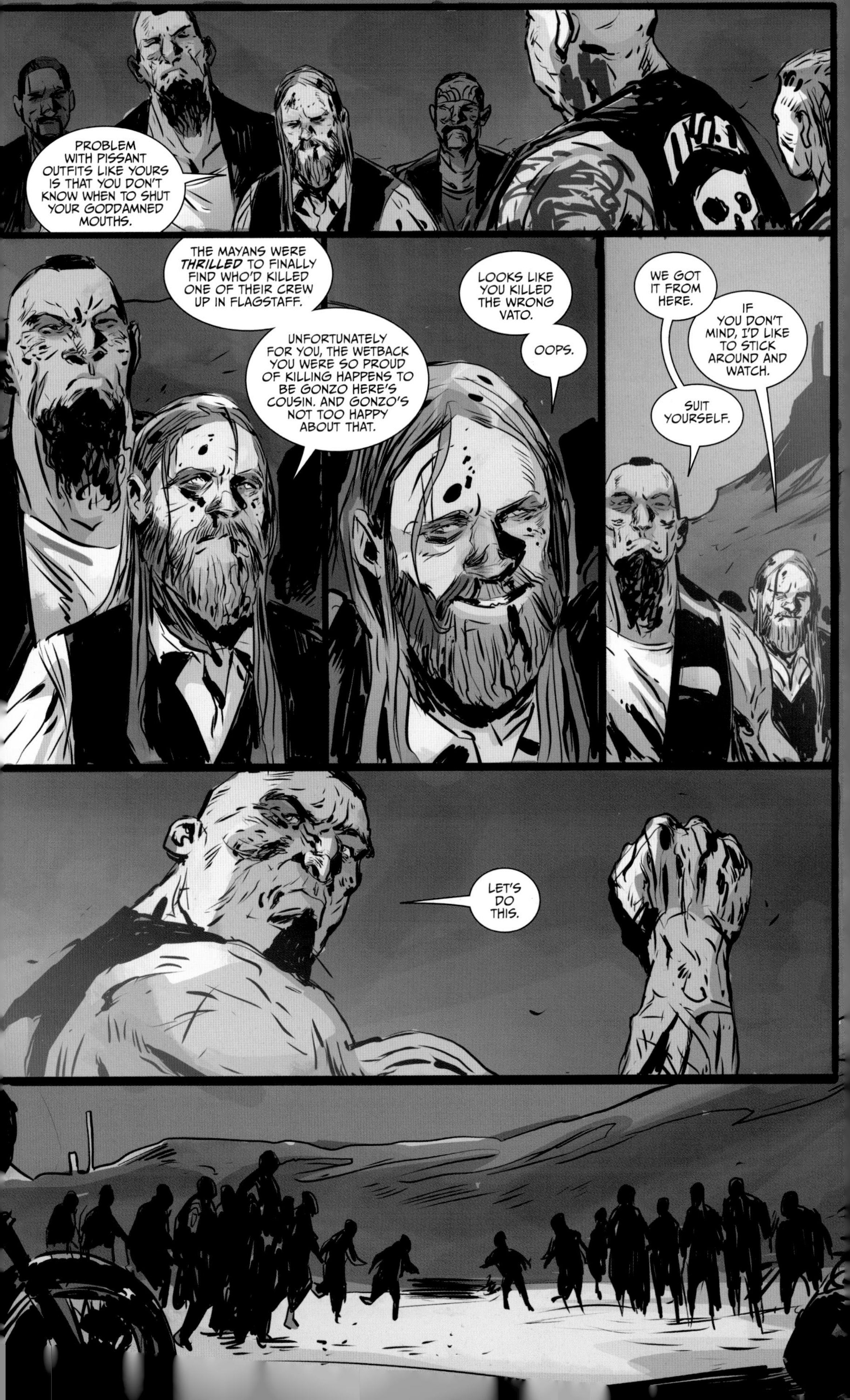
PROBLEM WITH PISSANT OUTFITS LIKE YOURS IS THAT YOU DON'T KNOW WHEN TO SHUT YOUR GODDAMNED MOUTHS.
THE MAYANS WERE *THRILLED* TO FINALLY FIND WHO'D KILLED ONE OF THEIR CREW UP IN FLAGSTAFF.
UNFORTUNATELY FOR YOU, THE WETBACK YOU WERE SO PROUD OF KILLING HAPPENS TO BE GONZO HERE'S COUSIN. AND GONZO'S NOT TOO HAPPY ABOUT THAT.
LOOKS LIKE YOU KILLED THE WRONG VATO.
OOPS.
WE GOT IT FROM HERE.
IF YOU DON'T MIND, I'D LIKE TO STICK AROUND AND WATCH.
SUIT YOURSELF.
LET'S DO THIS.

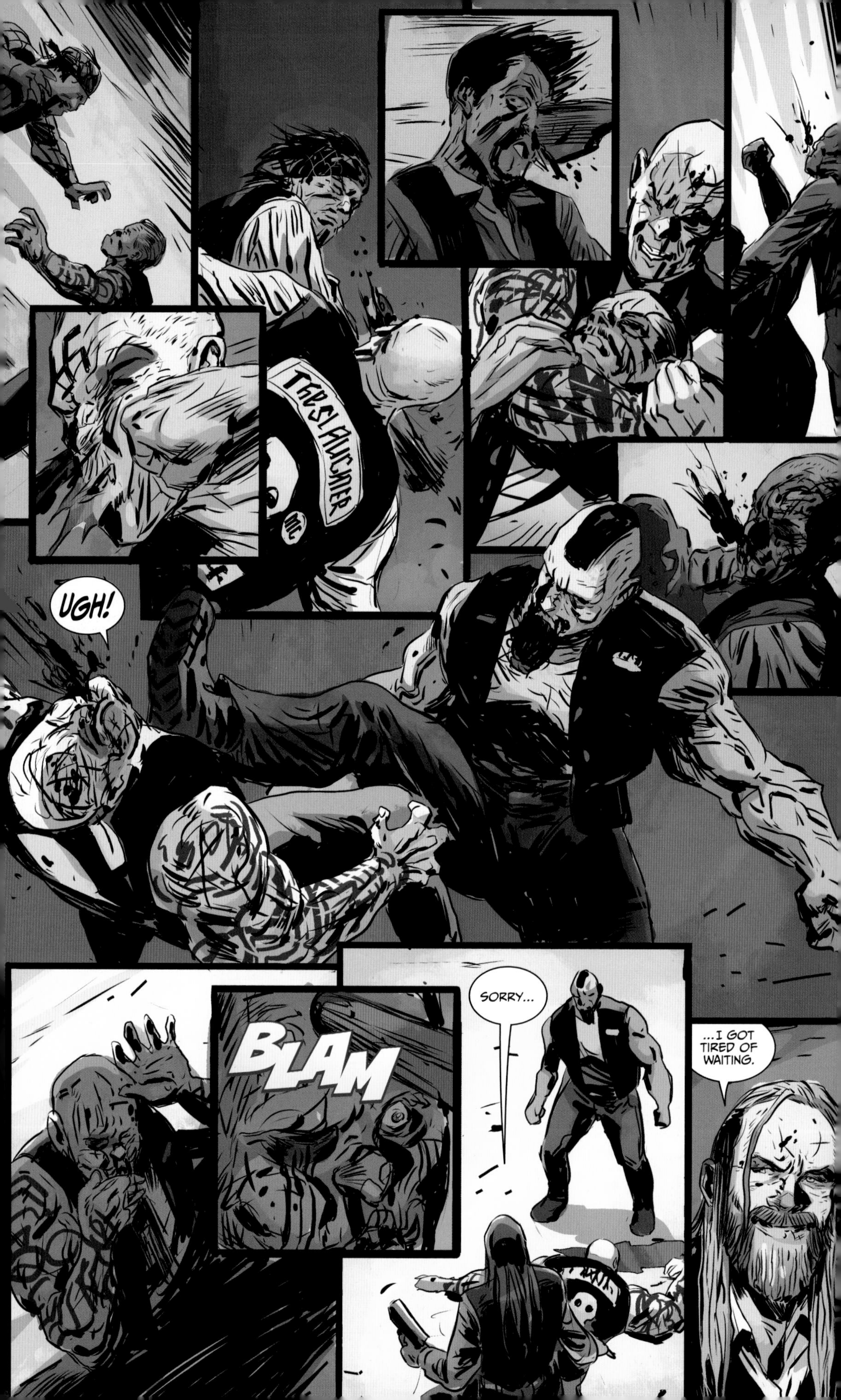

THE SLAUGHTER
MC
UGH!
BLAM
SORRY...
...I GOT TIRED OF WAITING.

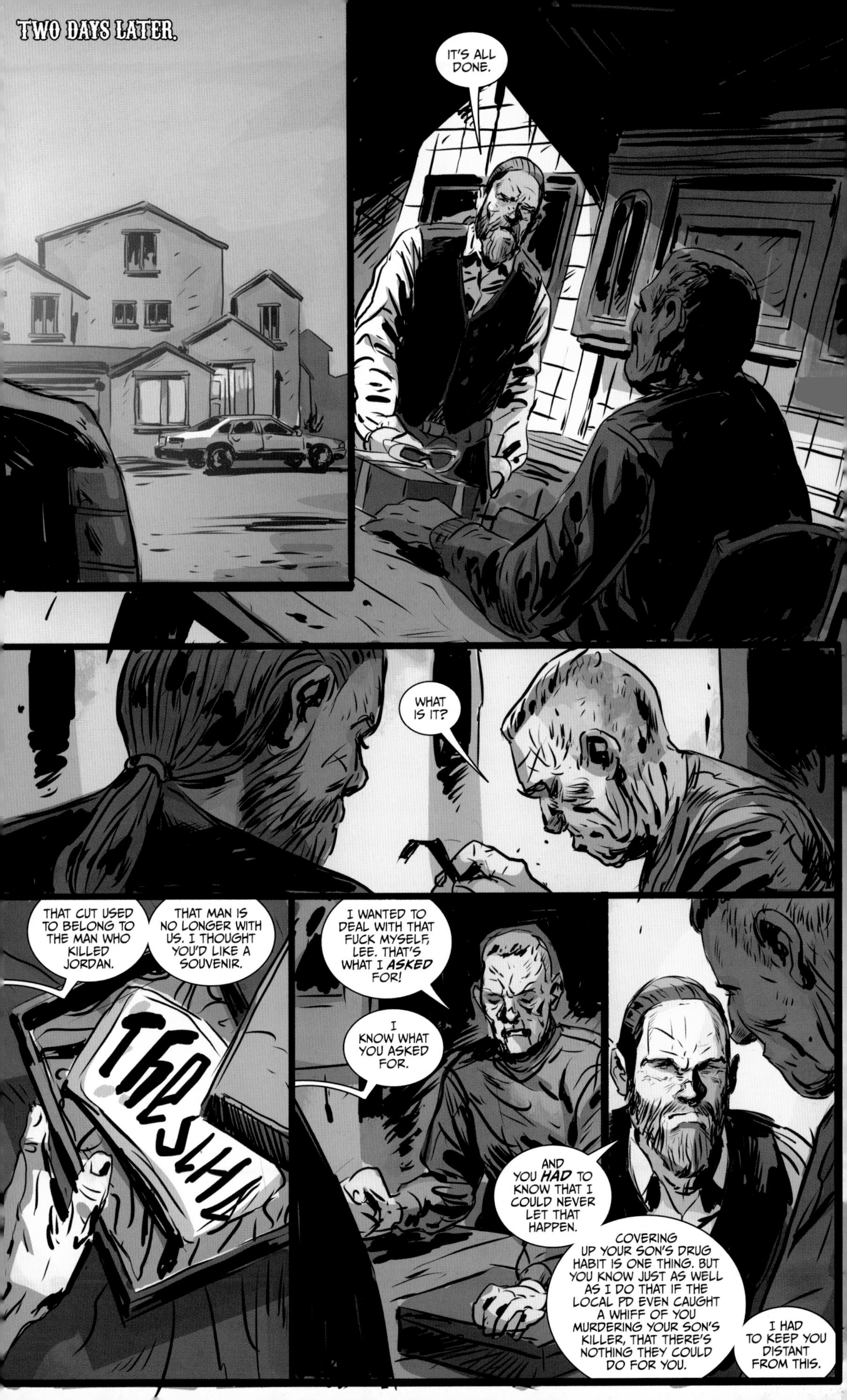
TWO DAYS LATER.
IT'S ALL DONE.
WHAT IS IT?
THAT CUT USED TO BELONG TO THE MAN WHO KILLED JORDAN.
THAT MAN IS NO LONGER WITH US. I THOUGHT YOU'D LIKE A SOUVENIR.
I WANTED TO DEAL WITH THAT FUCK MYSELF, LEE. THAT'S WHAT I ASKED FOR!
I KNOW WHAT YOU ASKED FOR.
AND YOU HAD TO KNOW THAT I COULD NEVER LET THAT HAPPEN.
COVERING UP YOUR SON'S DRUG HABIT IS ONE THING. BUT YOU KNOW JUST AS WELL AS I DO THAT IF THE LOCAL PD EVEN CAUGHT A WHIFF OF YOU MURDERING YOUR SON'S KILLER, THAT THERE'S NOTHING THEY COULD DO FOR YOU.
I HAD TO KEEP YOU DISTANT FROM THIS.

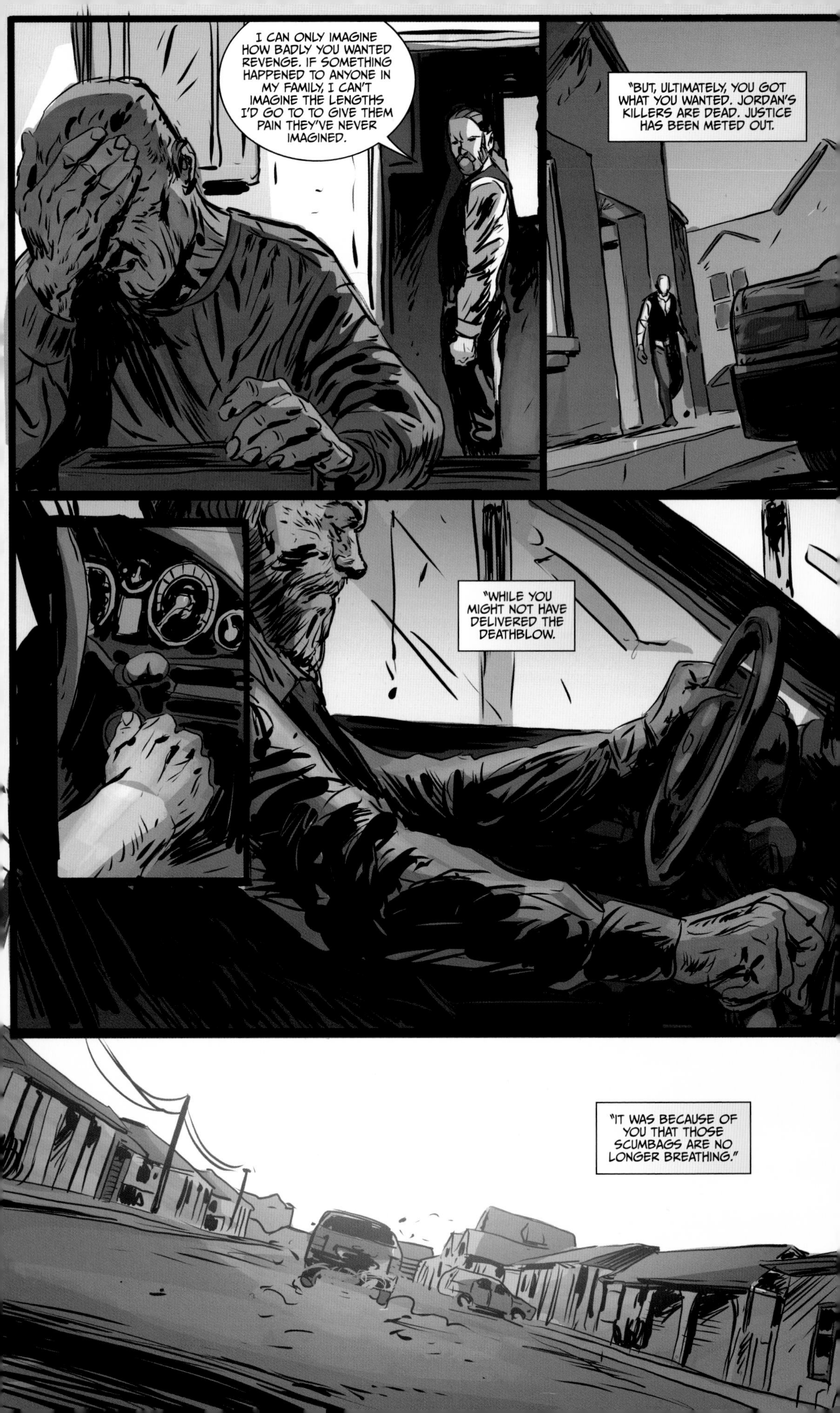
I CAN ONLY IMAGINE HOW BADLY YOU WANTED REVENGE. IF SOMETHING HAPPENED TO ANYONE IN MY FAMILY, I CAN'T IMAGINE THE LENGTHS I'D GO TO TO GIVE THEM PAIN THEY'VE NEVER IMAGINED.
"BUT, ULTIMATELY, YOU GOT WHAT YOU WANTED. JORDAN'S KILLERS ARE DEAD. JUSTICE HAS BEEN METED OUT.
"WHILE YOU MIGHT NOT HAVE DELIVERED THE DEATHBLOW.
"IT WAS BECAUSE OF YOU THAT THOSE SCUMBAGS ARE NO LONGER BREATHING."

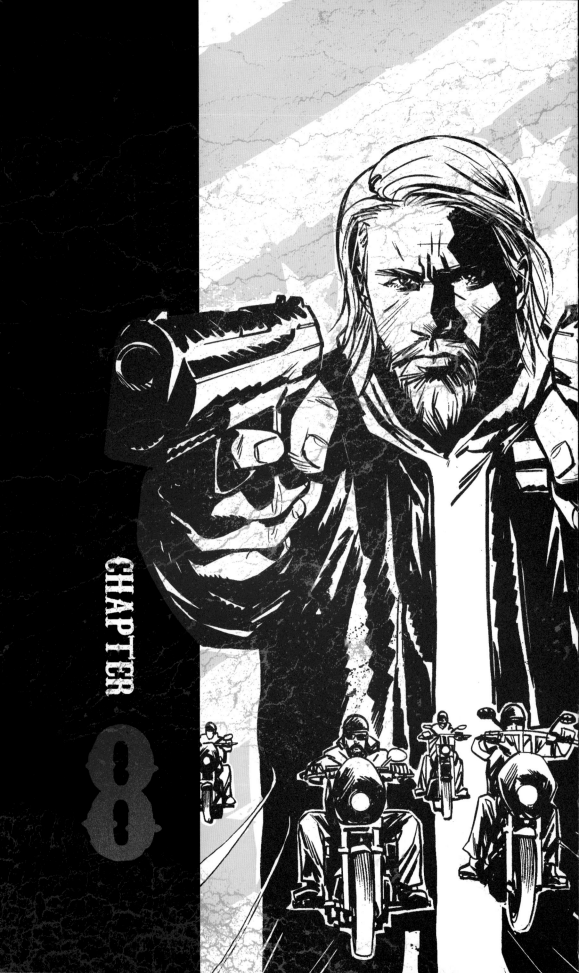

CHAPTER 8

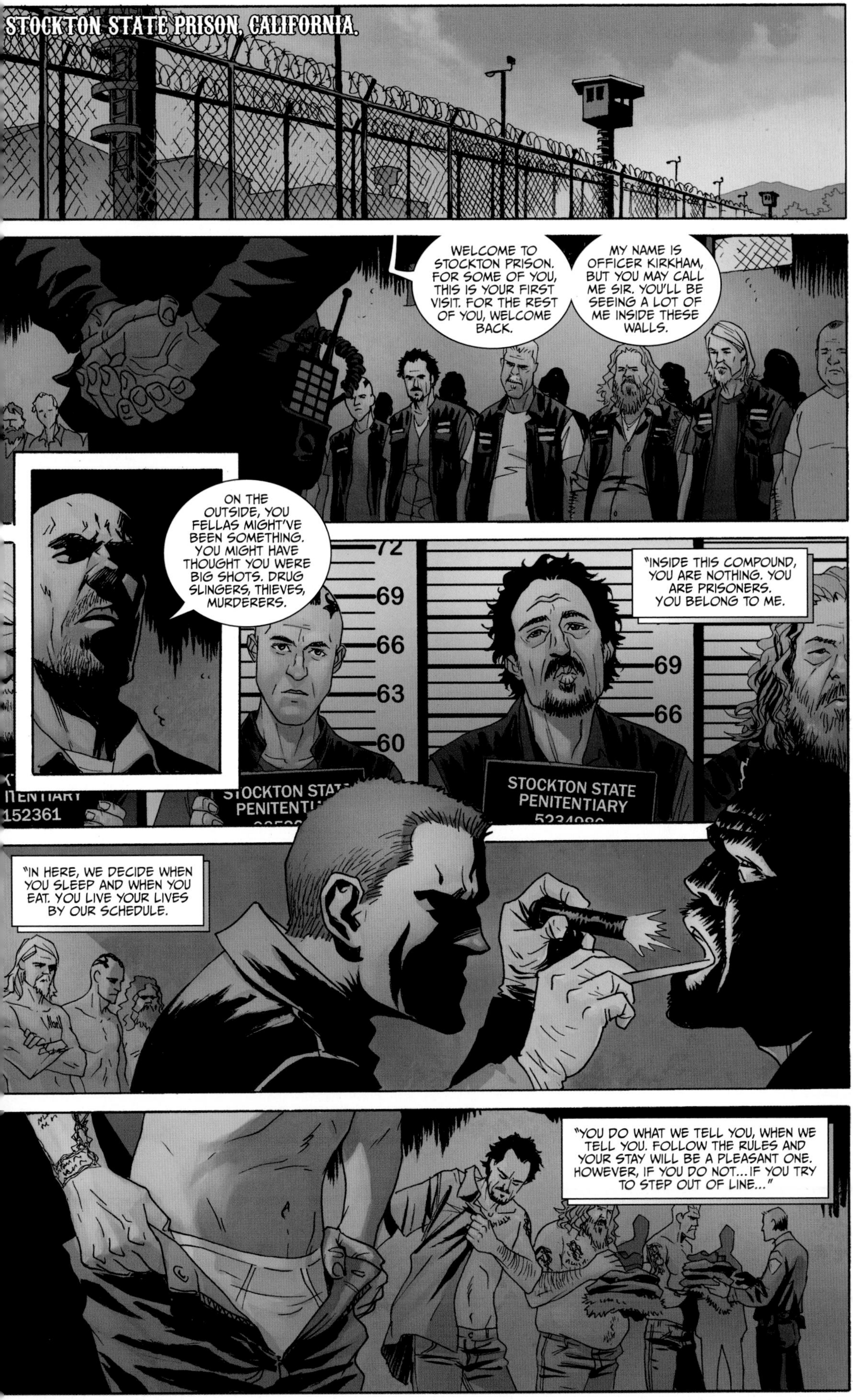
STOCKTON STATE PRISON, CALIFORNIA.
WELCOME TO STOCKTON PRISON. FOR SOME OF YOU, THIS IS YOUR FIRST VISIT. FOR THE REST OF YOU, WELCOME BACK.
MY NAME IS OFFICER KIRKHAM, BUT YOU MAY CALL ME SIR. YOU'LL BE SEEING A LOT OF ME INSIDE THESE WALLS.
ON THE OUTSIDE, YOU FELLAS MIGHT'VE BEEN SOMETHING. YOU MIGHT HAVE THOUGHT YOU WERE BIG SHOTS. DRUG SLINGERS, THIEVES, MURDERERS.
"INSIDE THIS COMPOUND, YOU ARE NOTHING. YOU ARE PRISONERS. YOU BELONG TO ME.
STOCKTON STATE PENITENTIARY
"IN HERE, WE DECIDE WHEN YOU SLEEP AND WHEN YOU EAT. YOU LIVE YOUR LIVES BY OUR SCHEDULE.
"YOU DO WHAT WE TELL YOU, WHEN WE TELL YOU. FOLLOW THE RULES AND YOUR STAY WILL BE A PLEASANT ONE. HOWEVER, IF YOU DO NOT... IF YOU TRY TO STEP OUT OF LINE..."

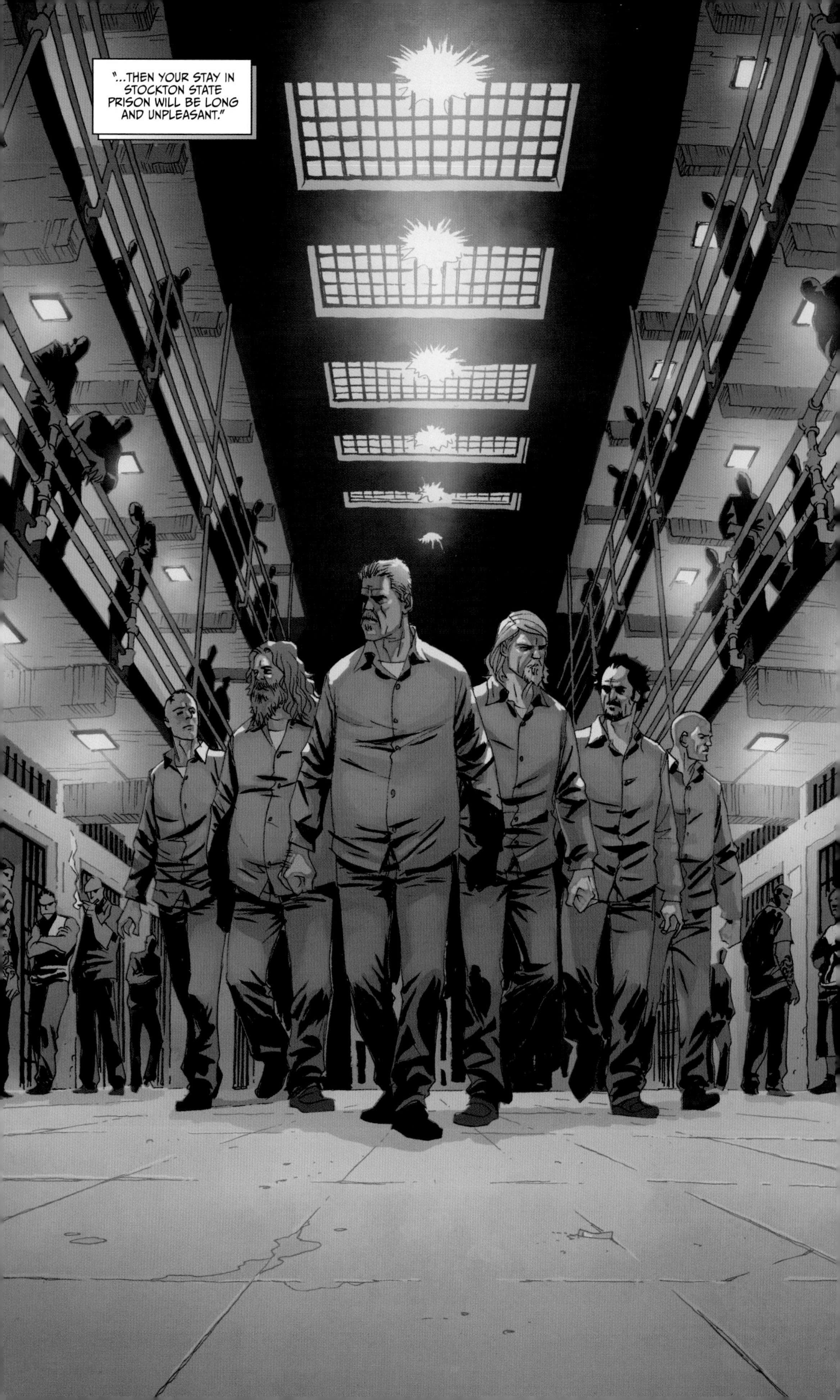
"...THEN YOUR STAY IN STOCKTON STATE PRISON WILL BE LONG AND UNPLEASANT."

MR. MORROW. A WORD, IF YOU PLEASE.

AH, WARDEN... I WAS JUST HEADED FOR MY SPA TREATMENT.

THE REST OF YOU BOYS KEEP ON MOVING.

YOU FELLAS GO ON. I'LL CATCH UP.

WHAT'S THIS ABOUT, WARDEN?

LET'S STEP INTO MY OFFICE.

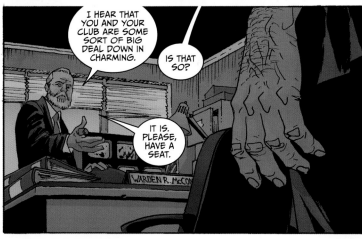

I HEAR THAT YOU AND YOUR CLUB ARE SOME SORT OF BIG DEAL DOWN IN CHARMING.

IS THAT SO?

IT IS. PLEASE, HAVE A SEAT.

I THOUGHT THAT MAYBE YOU AND I COULD HAVE A LITTLE CHAT ABOUT YOUR STAY HERE.

I UNDERSTAND THAT YOU'RE ALL ELIGIBLE FOR PAROLE AFTER 14 MONTHS. PROVIDED THAT THERE ARE NO INCIDENTS...

WE'RE JUST HERE TO DO OUR TIME. WE'RE NOT LOOKING FOR TROUBLE.

WELL THAT'S GOOD TO HEAR.

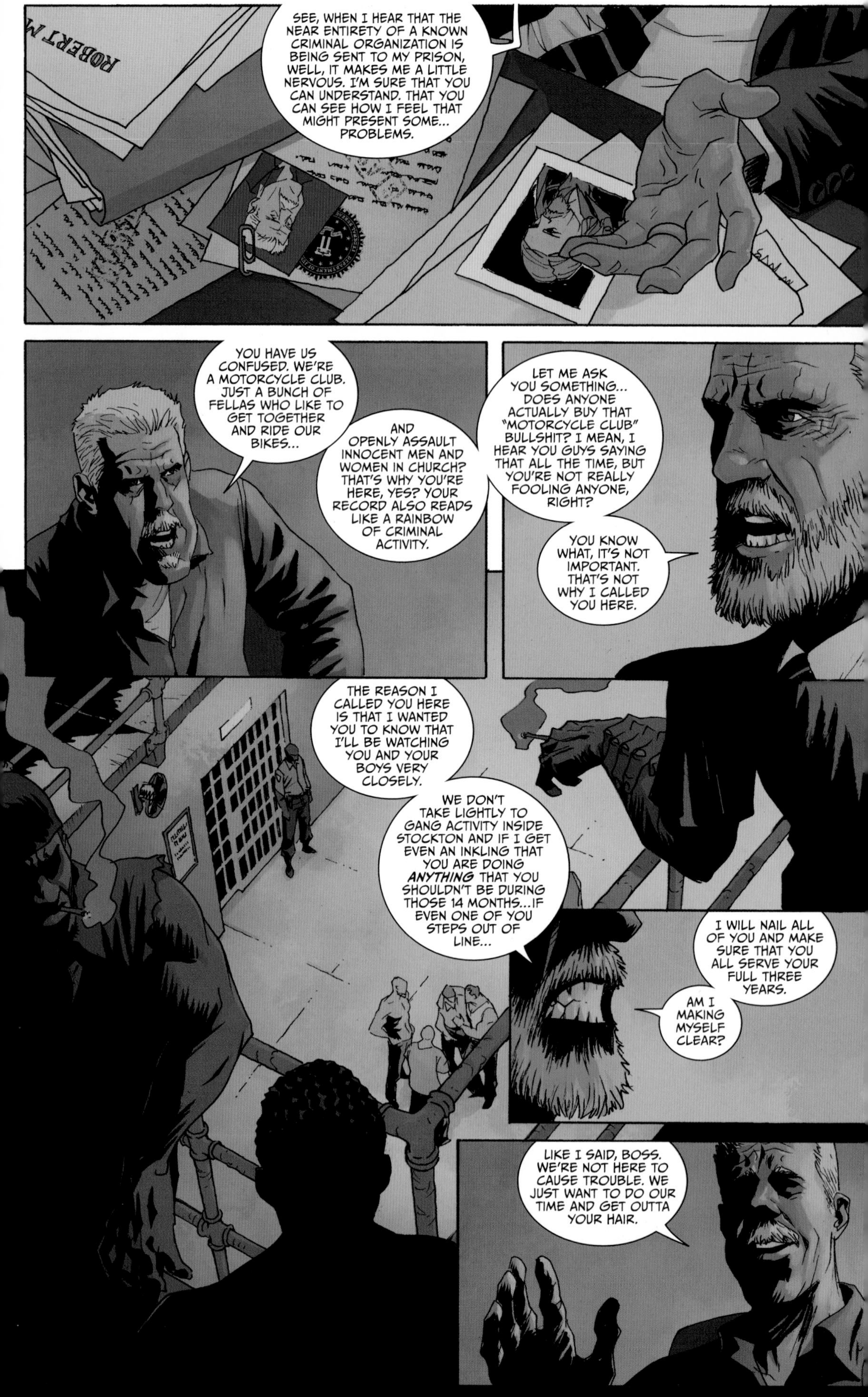

ROBERT M
SEE, WHEN I HEAR THAT THE NEAR ENTIRETY OF A KNOWN CRIMINAL ORGANIZATION IS BEING SENT TO MY PRISON, WELL, IT MAKES ME A LITTLE NERVOUS. I'M SURE THAT YOU CAN UNDERSTAND. THAT YOU CAN SEE HOW I FEEL THAT MIGHT PRESENT SOME... PROBLEMS.
YOU HAVE US CONFUSED. WE'RE A MOTORCYCLE CLUB. JUST A BUNCH OF FELLAS WHO LIKE TO GET TOGETHER AND RIDE OUR BIKES...
AND OPENLY ASSAULT INNOCENT MEN AND WOMEN IN CHURCH? THAT'S WHY YOU'RE HERE, YES? YOUR RECORD ALSO READS LIKE A RAINBOW OF CRIMINAL ACTIVITY.
LET ME ASK YOU SOMETHING... DOES ANYONE ACTUALLY BUY THAT "MOTORCYCLE CLUB" BULLSHIT? I MEAN, I HEAR YOU GUYS SAYING THAT ALL THE TIME, BUT YOU'RE NOT REALLY FOOLING ANYONE, RIGHT?
YOU KNOW WHAT, IT'S NOT IMPORTANT. THAT'S NOT WHY I CALLED YOU HERE.
THE REASON I CALLED YOU HERE IS THAT I WANTED YOU TO KNOW THAT I'LL BE WATCHING YOU AND YOUR BOYS VERY CLOSELY.
WE DON'T TAKE LIGHTLY TO GANG ACTIVITY INSIDE STOCKTON AND IF I GET EVEN AN INKLING THAT YOU ARE DOING *ANYTHING* THAT YOU SHOULDN'T BE DURING THOSE 14 MONTHS...IF EVEN ONE OF YOU STEPS OUT OF LINE...
I WILL NAIL ALL OF YOU AND MAKE SURE THAT YOU ALL SERVE YOUR FULL THREE YEARS.
AM I MAKING MYSELF CLEAR?
LIKE I SAID, BOSS. WE'RE NOT HERE TO CAUSE TROUBLE. WE JUST WANT TO DO OUR TIME AND GET OUTTA YOUR HAIR.

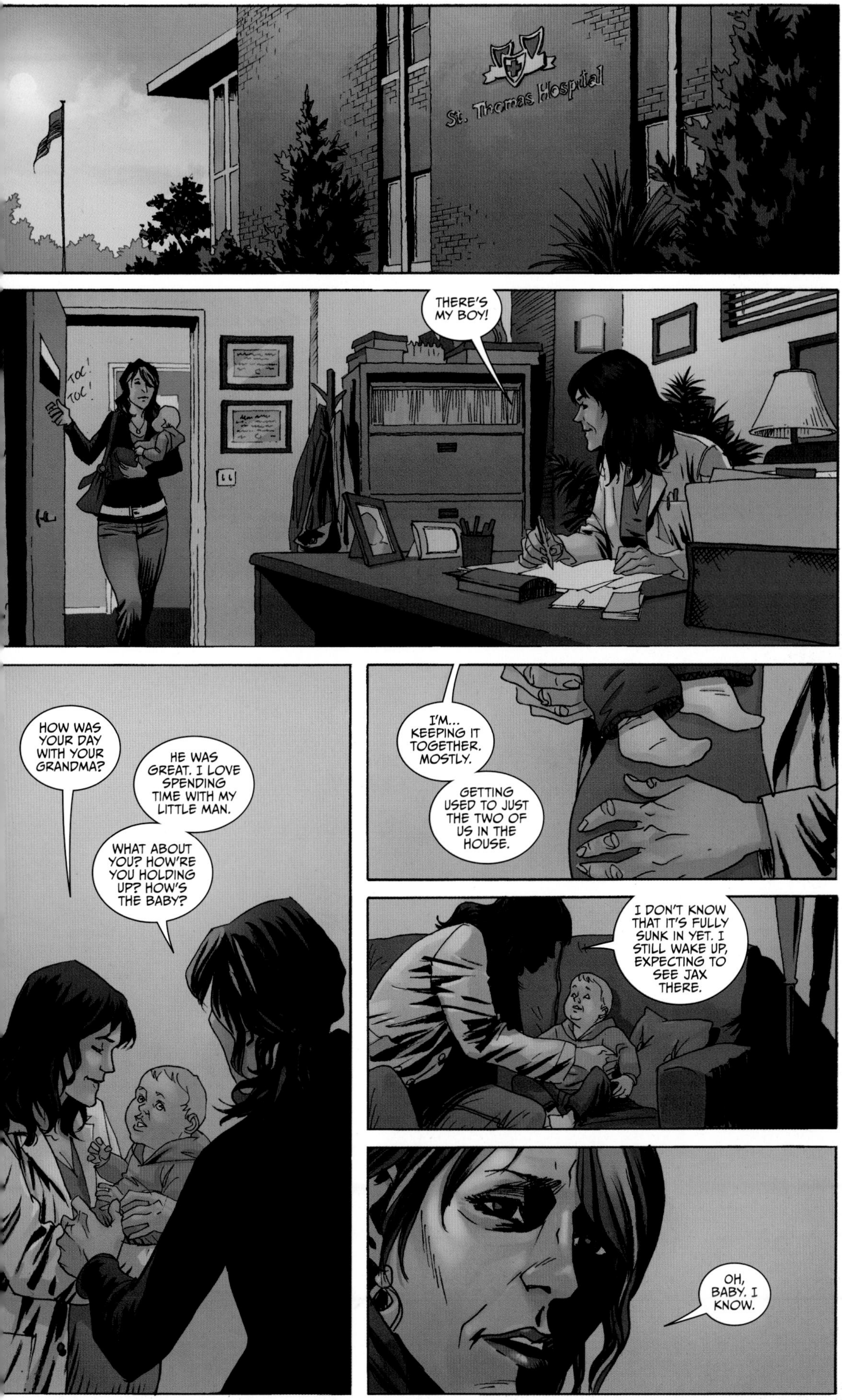
St. Thomas Hospital
TOC! TOC!
THERE'S MY BOY!
HOW WAS YOUR DAY WITH YOUR GRANDMA?
HE WAS GREAT. I LOVE SPENDING TIME WITH MY LITTLE MAN.
WHAT ABOUT YOU? HOW'RE YOU HOLDING UP? HOW'S THE BABY?
I'M... KEEPING IT TOGETHER. MOSTLY.
GETTING USED TO JUST THE TWO OF US IN THE HOUSE.
I DON'T KNOW THAT IT'S FULLY SUNK IN YET. I STILL WAKE UP, EXPECTING TO SEE JAX THERE.
OH, BABY. I KNOW.

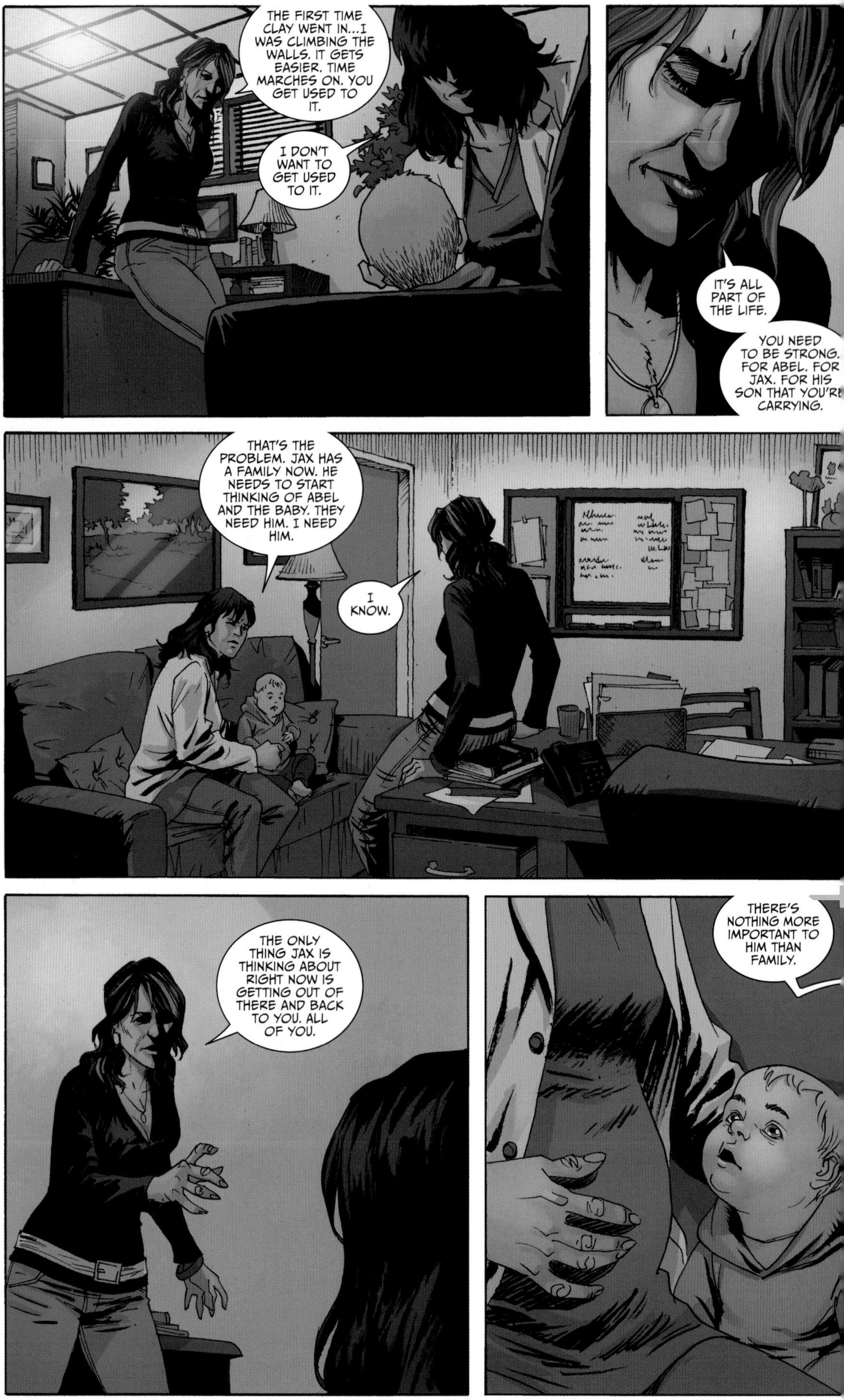
THE FIRST TIME CLAY WENT IN...I WAS CLIMBING THE WALLS. IT GETS EASIER. TIME MARCHES ON. YOU GET USED TO IT.
I DON'T WANT TO GET USED TO IT.
IT'S ALL PART OF THE LIFE.
YOU NEED TO BE STRONG. FOR ABEL. FOR JAX. FOR HIS SON THAT YOU'RE CARRYING.
THAT'S THE PROBLEM. JAX HAS A FAMILY NOW. HE NEEDS TO START THINKING OF ABEL AND THE BABY. THEY NEED HIM. I NEED HIM.
I KNOW.
THE ONLY THING JAX IS THINKING ABOUT RIGHT NOW IS GETTING OUT OF THERE AND BACK TO YOU. ALL OF YOU.
THERE'S NOTHING MORE IMPORTANT TO HIM THAN FAMILY.

HEY!

YOU ARE JAX TELLER, NO?

THE FUCK ARE YOU?

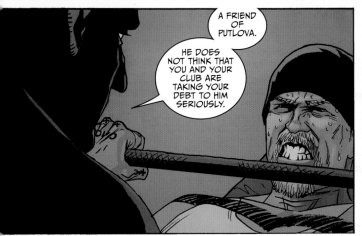

A FRIEND OF PUTLOVA.

HE DOES NOT THINK THAT YOU AND YOUR CLUB ARE TAKING YOUR DEBT TO HIM SERIOUSLY.

HOPEFULLY THIS WILL HELP YOU REALIZE HOW SERIOUS HE IS. HOW THIS IS NO JOKE.

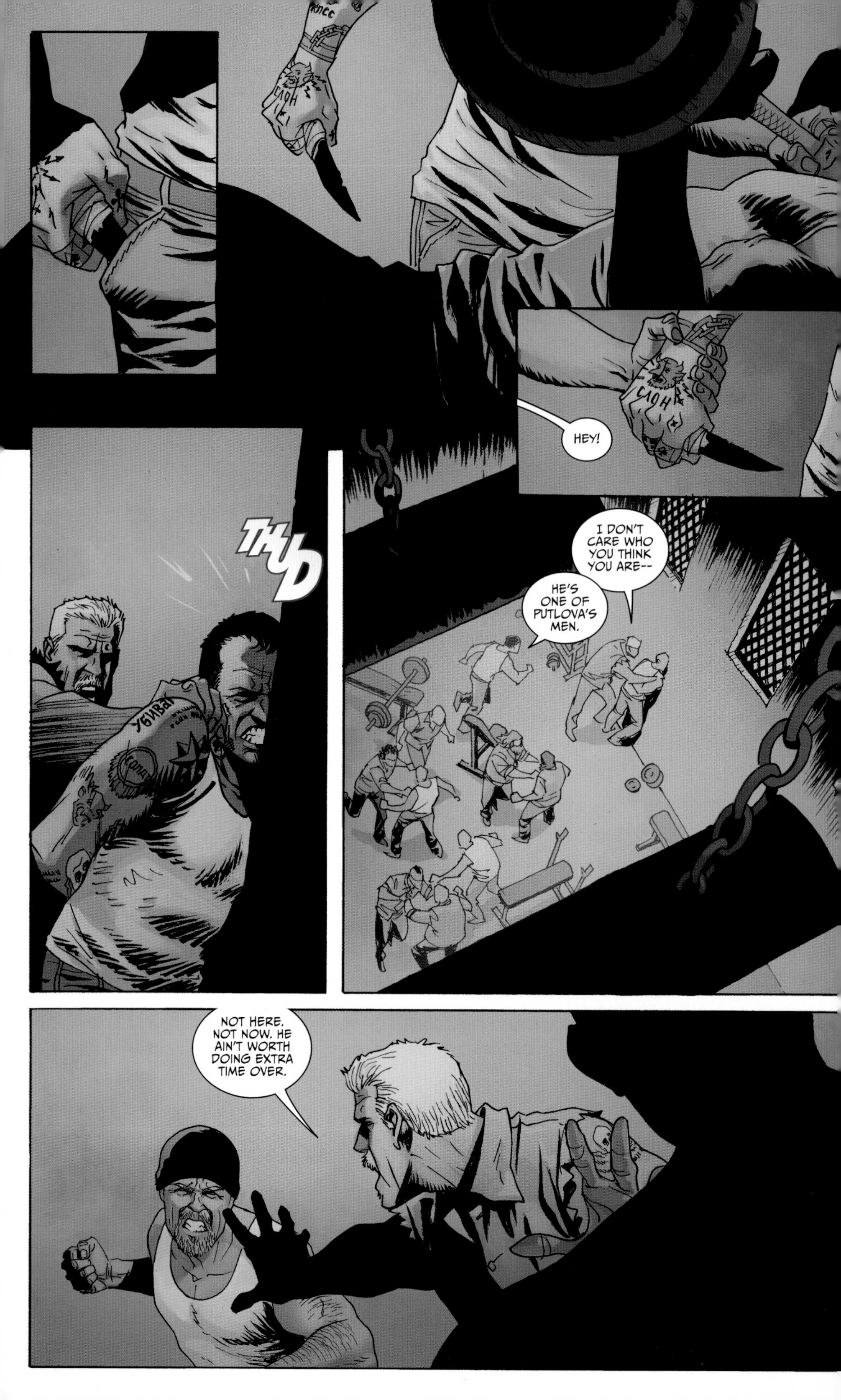
HEY!
THUD
I DON'T CARE WHO YOU THINK YOU ARE--
HE'S ONE OF PUTLOVA'S MEN.
NOT HERE. NOT NOW. HE AIN'T WORTH DOING EXTRA TIME OVER.

ARRRRGH!

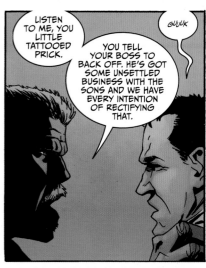

GUUUK

LISTEN TO ME, YOU LITTLE TATTOOED PRICK.

YOU TELL YOUR BOSS TO BACK OFF. HE'S GOT SOME UNSETTLED BUSINESS WITH THE SONS AND WE HAVE EVERY INTENTION OF RECTIFYING THAT.

WHY SHOULD HE BELIEVE YOU? YOU BETRAYED HIM ALREADY ONCE... YOU--

HEY! BREAK IT UP!

YOU'VE GOT THIRTY SECONDS TO BREAK IT UP AND DISPERSE. ONE SECOND LONGER, AND I MARCH YOUR ASSES TO THE HOLE.

HEY, OFFICER. WE WERE JUST--

TWENTY SECONDS.

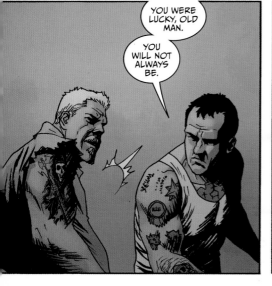

YOU WERE LUCKY, OLD MAN.

YOU WILL NOT ALWAYS BE.

YOU TOO, MORROW. GET A MOVE ON.

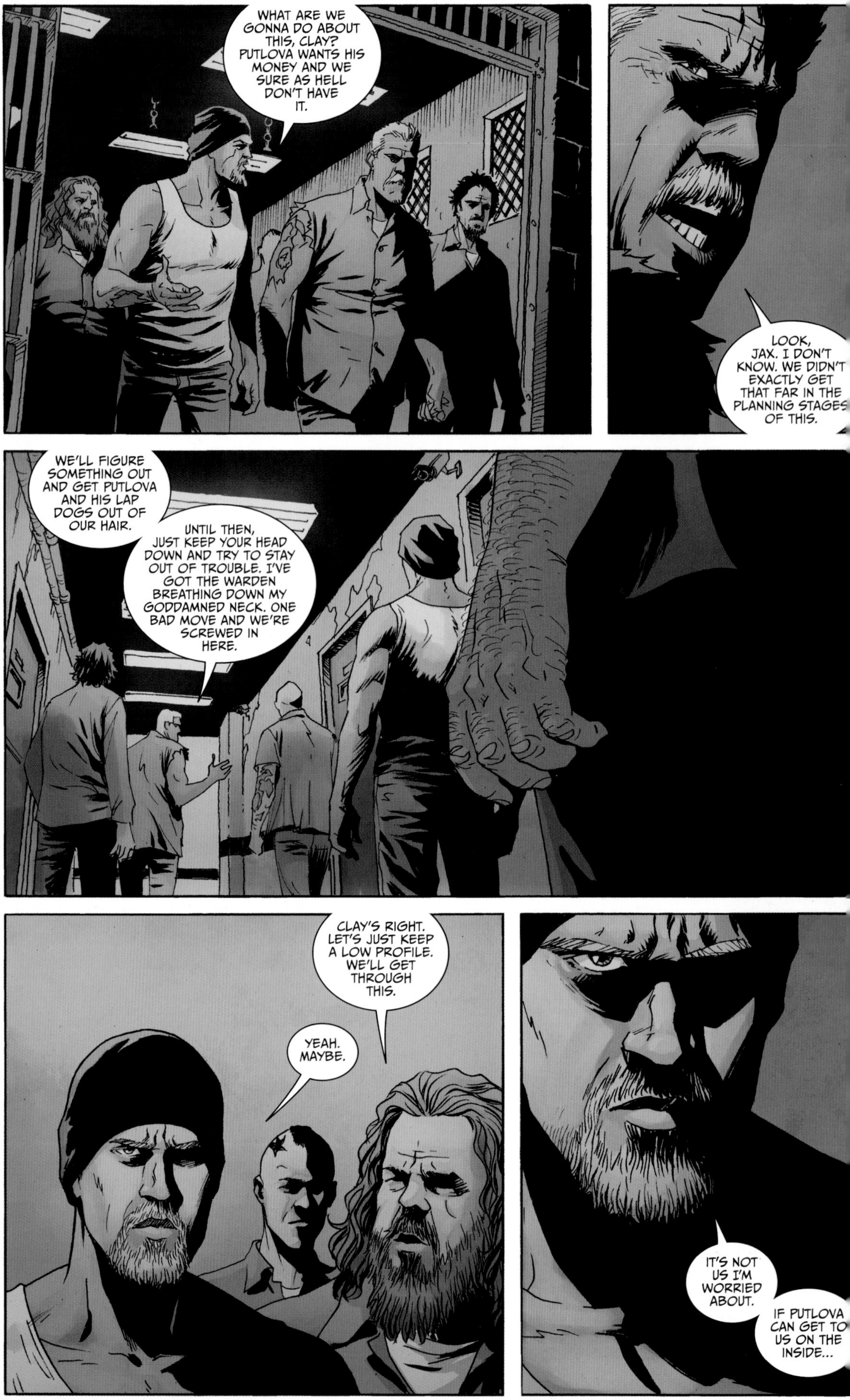
WHAT ARE WE GONNA DO ABOUT THIS, CLAY? PUTLOVA WANTS HIS MONEY AND WE SURE AS HELL DON'T HAVE IT.
LOOK, JAX. I DON'T KNOW. WE DIDN'T EXACTLY GET THAT FAR IN THE PLANNING STAGES OF THIS.
WE'LL FIGURE SOMETHING OUT AND GET PUTLOVA AND HIS LAP DOGS OUT OF OUR HAIR.
UNTIL THEN, JUST KEEP YOUR HEAD DOWN AND TRY TO STAY OUT OF TROUBLE. I'VE GOT THE WARDEN BREATHING DOWN MY GODDAMNED NECK. ONE BAD MOVE AND WE'RE SCREWED IN HERE.
CLAY'S RIGHT. LET'S JUST KEEP A LOW PROFILE. WE'LL GET THROUGH THIS.
YEAH. MAYBE.
IT'S NOT US I'M WORRIED ABOUT.
IF PUTLOVA CAN GET TO US ON THE INSIDE...

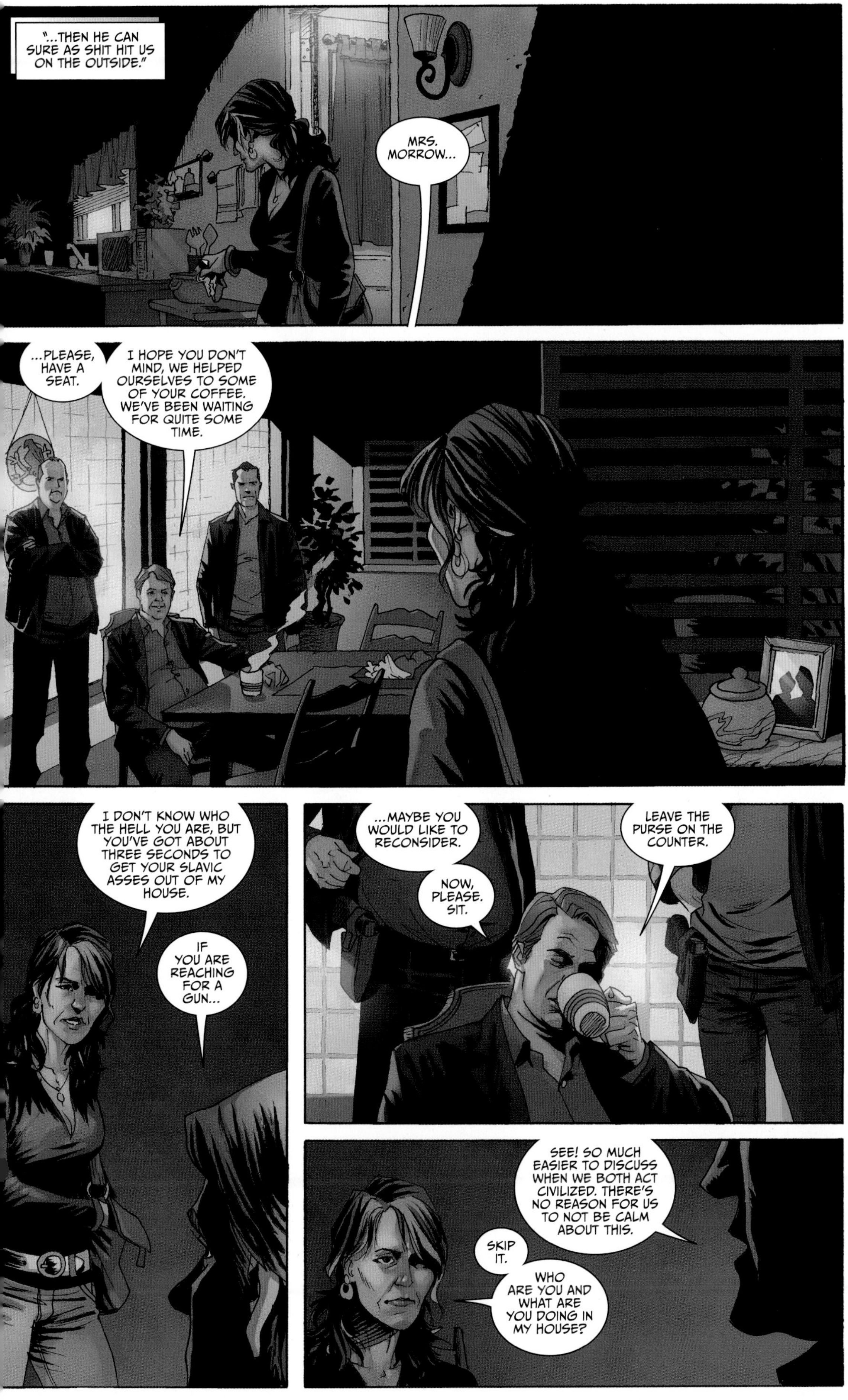

"...THEN HE CAN SURE AS SHIT HIT US ON THE OUTSIDE."
MRS. MORROW...
...PLEASE, HAVE A SEAT.
I HOPE YOU DON'T MIND, WE HELPED OURSELVES TO SOME OF YOUR COFFEE. WE'VE BEEN WAITING FOR QUITE SOME TIME.
I DON'T KNOW WHO THE HELL YOU ARE, BUT YOU'VE GOT ABOUT THREE SECONDS TO GET YOUR SLAVIC ASSES OUT OF MY HOUSE.
IF YOU ARE REACHING FOR A GUN...
...MAYBE YOU WOULD LIKE TO RECONSIDER.
LEAVE THE PURSE ON THE COUNTER.
NOW, PLEASE. SIT.
SEE! SO MUCH EASIER TO DISCUSS WHEN WE BOTH ACT CIVILIZED. THERE'S NO REASON FOR US TO NOT BE CALM ABOUT THIS.
SKIP IT.
WHO ARE YOU AND WHAT ARE YOU DOING IN MY HOUSE?

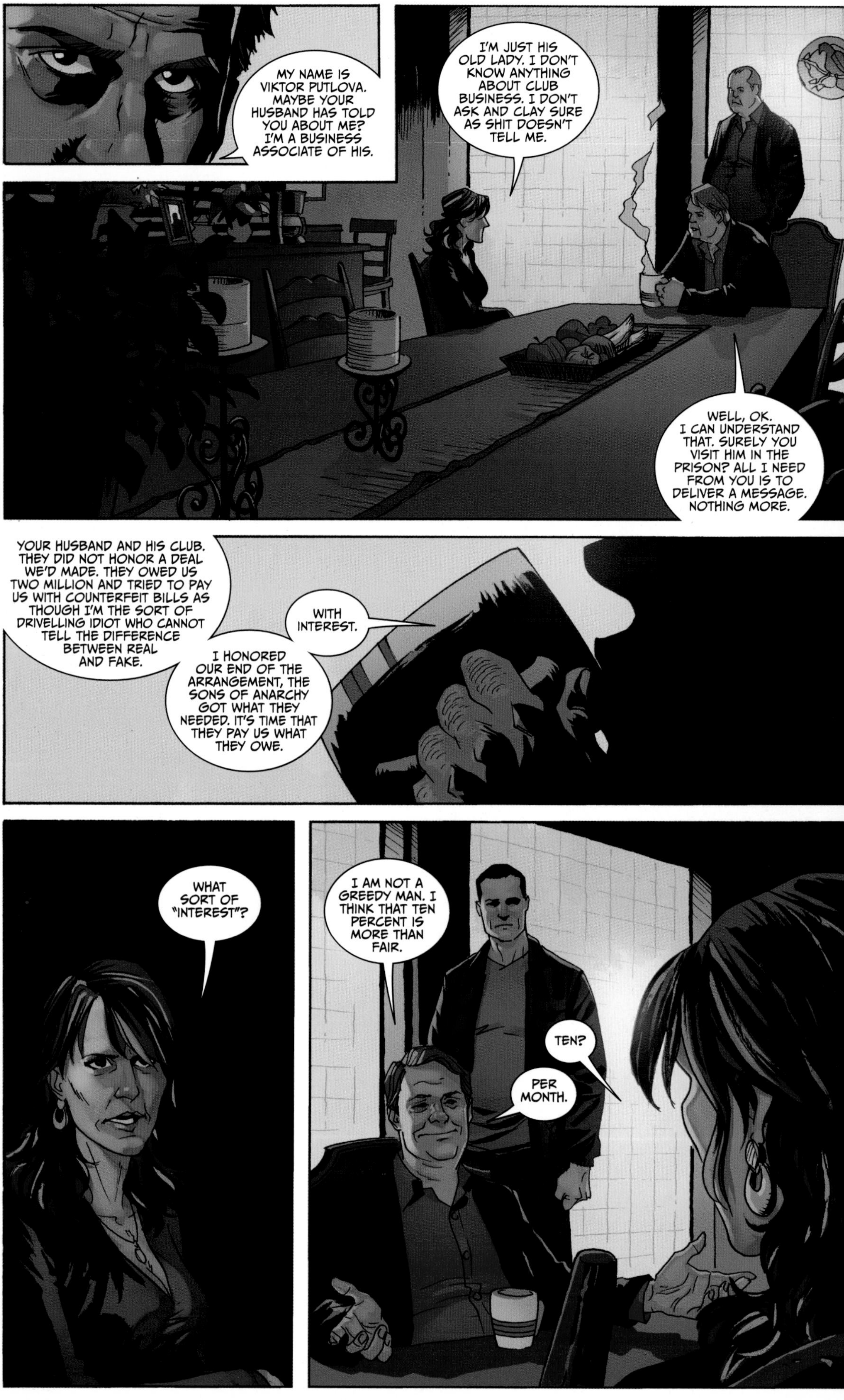
MY NAME IS VIKTOR PUTLOVA. MAYBE YOUR HUSBAND HAS TOLD YOU ABOUT ME? I'M A BUSINESS ASSOCIATE OF HIS.
I'M JUST HIS OLD LADY. I DON'T KNOW ANYTHING ABOUT CLUB BUSINESS. I DON'T ASK AND CLAY SURE AS SHIT DOESN'T TELL ME.
WELL, OK. I CAN UNDERSTAND THAT. SURELY YOU VISIT HIM IN THE PRISON? ALL I NEED FROM YOU IS TO DELIVER A MESSAGE. NOTHING MORE.
YOUR HUSBAND AND HIS CLUB. THEY DID NOT HONOR A DEAL WE'D MADE. THEY OWED US TWO MILLION AND TRIED TO PAY US WITH COUNTERFEIT BILLS AS THOUGH I'M THE SORT OF DRIVELLING IDIOT WHO CANNOT TELL THE DIFFERENCE BETWEEN REAL AND FAKE.
I HONORED OUR END OF THE ARRANGEMENT, THE SONS OF ANARCHY GOT WHAT THEY NEEDED. IT'S TIME THAT THEY PAY US WHAT THEY OWE.
WITH INTEREST.
WHAT SORT OF "INTEREST"?
I AM NOT A GREEDY MAN. I THINK THAT TEN PERCENT IS MORE THAN FAIR.
TEN?
PER MONTH.

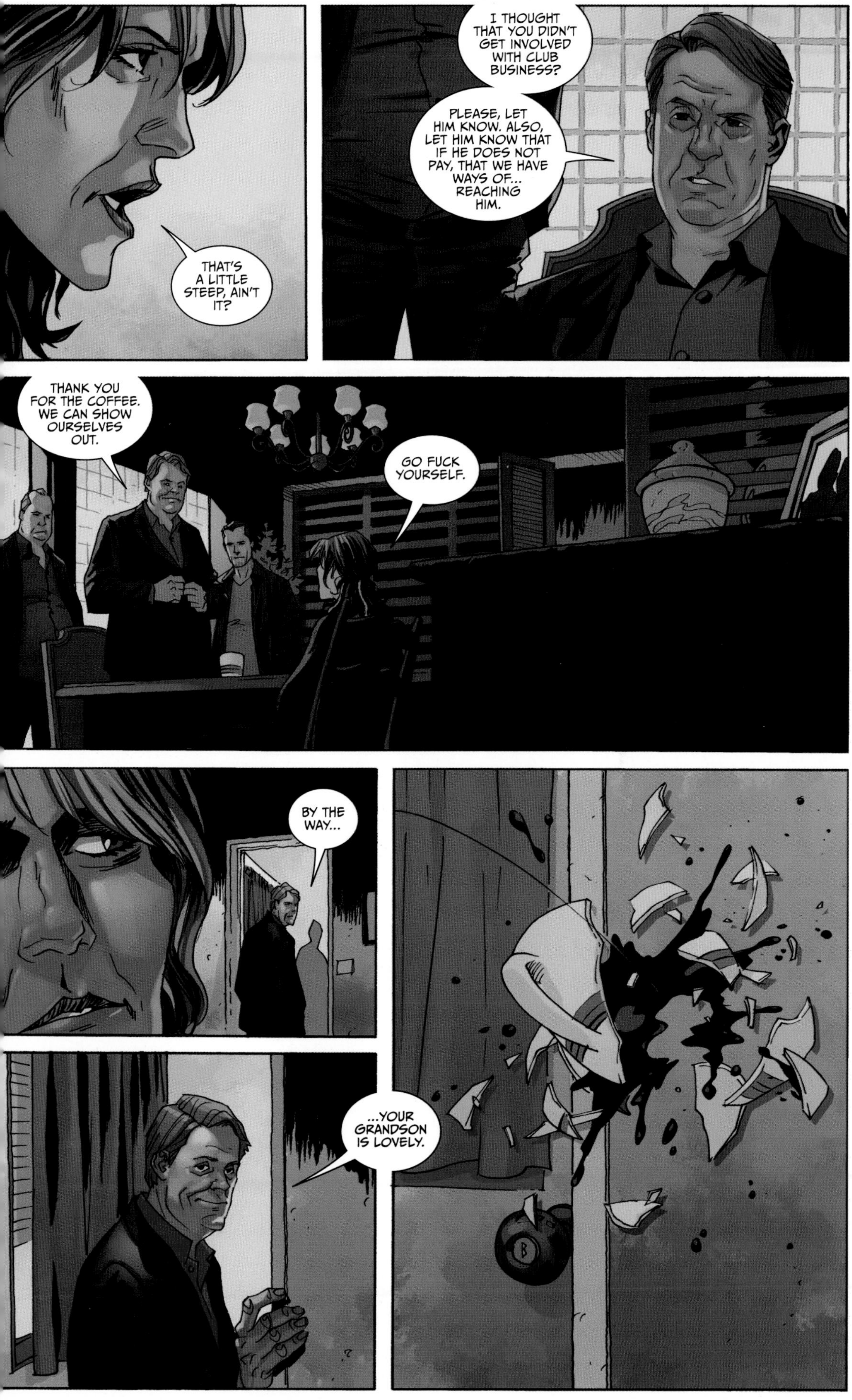
THAT'S A LITTLE STEEP, AIN'T IT?
I THOUGHT THAT YOU DIDN'T GET INVOLVED WITH CLUB BUSINESS?
PLEASE, LET HIM KNOW. ALSO, LET HIM KNOW THAT IF HE DOES NOT PAY, THAT WE HAVE WAYS OF... REACHING HIM.
THANK YOU FOR THE COFFEE. WE CAN SHOW OURSELVES OUT.
GO FUCK YOURSELF.
BY THE WAY...
...YOUR GRANDSON IS LOVELY.

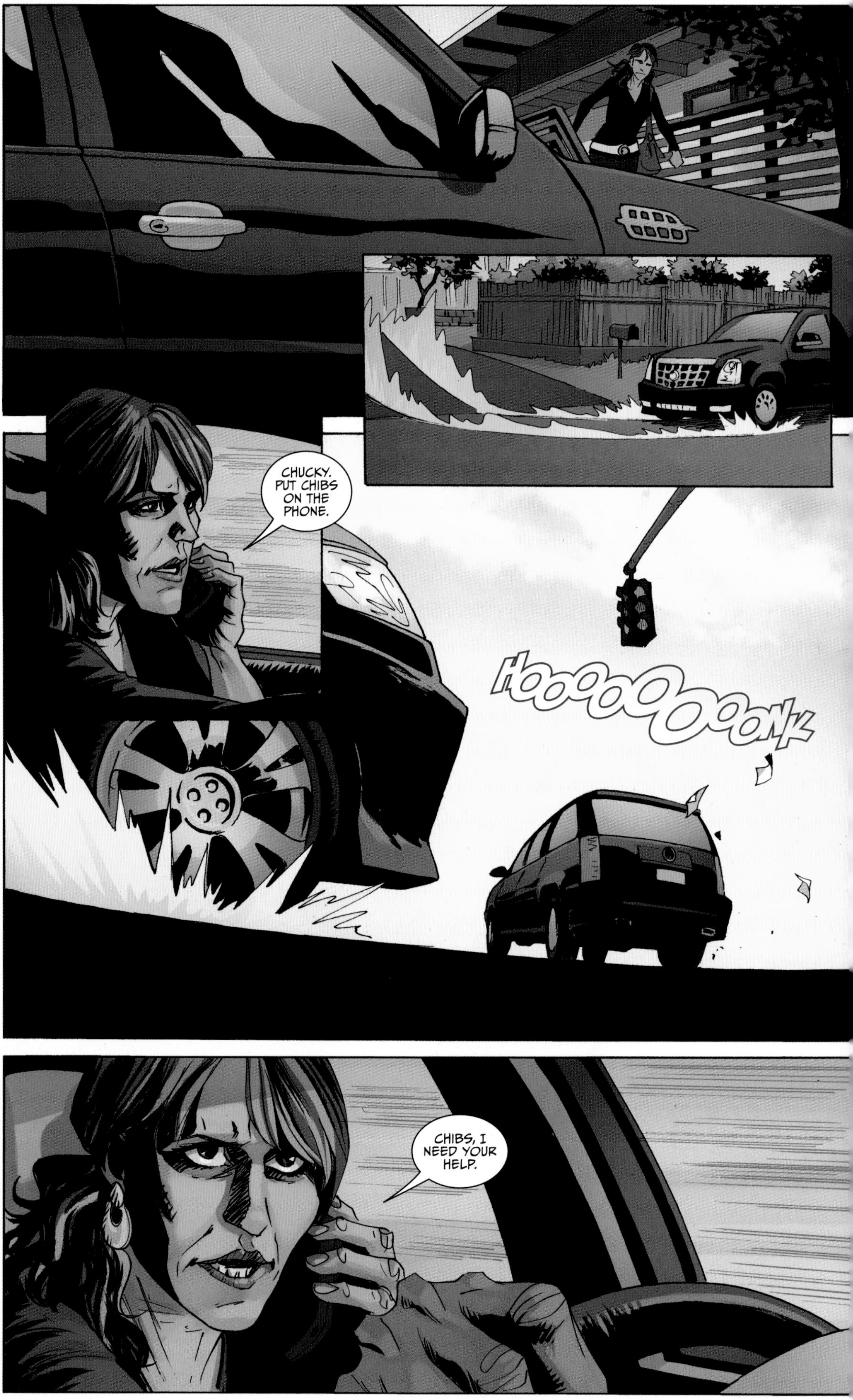
CHUCKY. PUT CHIBS ON THE PHONE.
HOOOOOOOOONK
CHIBS, I NEED YOUR HELP.

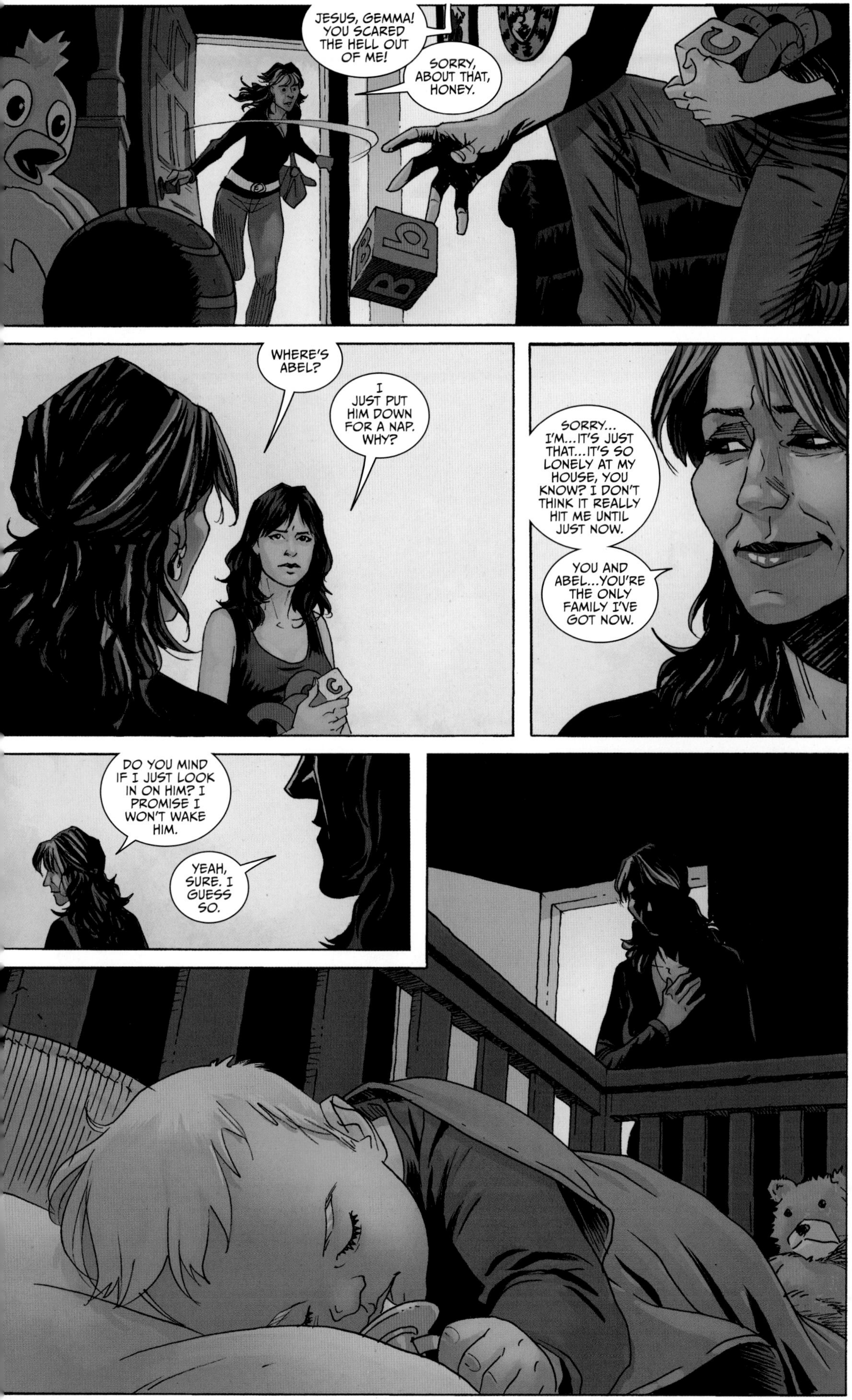
JESUS, GEMMA! YOU SCARED THE HELL OUT OF ME!
SORRY, ABOUT THAT, HONEY.
WHERE'S ABEL?
I JUST PUT HIM DOWN FOR A NAP. WHY?
SORRY... I'M...IT'S JUST THAT...IT'S SO LONELY AT MY HOUSE, YOU KNOW? I DON'T THINK IT REALLY HIT ME UNTIL JUST NOW.
YOU AND ABEL...YOU'RE THE ONLY FAMILY I'VE GOT NOW.
DO YOU MIND IF I JUST LOOK IN ON HIM? I PROMISE I WON'T WAKE HIM.
YEAH, SURE. I GUESS SO.

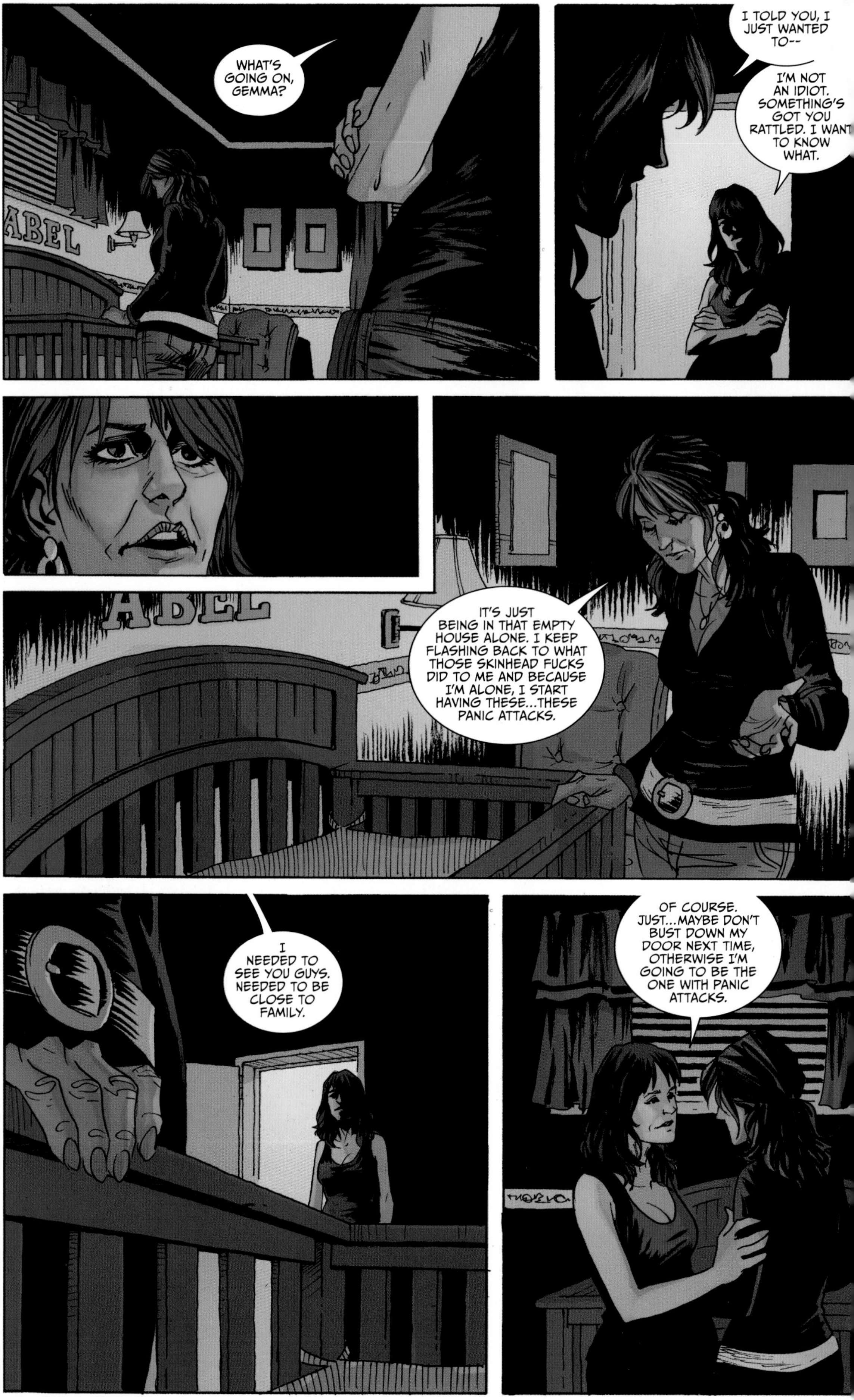

WHAT'S GOING ON, GEMMA?
I TOLD YOU, I JUST WANTED TO--
I'M NOT AN IDIOT. SOMETHING'S GOT YOU RATTLED. I WANT TO KNOW WHAT.
ABEL
IT'S JUST BEING IN THAT EMPTY HOUSE ALONE. I KEEP FLASHING BACK TO WHAT THOSE SKINHEAD FUCKS DID TO ME AND BECAUSE I'M ALONE, I START HAVING THESE...THESE PANIC ATTACKS.
I NEEDED TO SEE YOU GUYS. NEEDED TO BE CLOSE TO FAMILY.
OF COURSE. JUST...MAYBE DON'T BUST DOWN MY DOOR NEXT TIME, OTHERWISE I'M GOING TO BE THE ONE WITH PANIC ATTACKS.

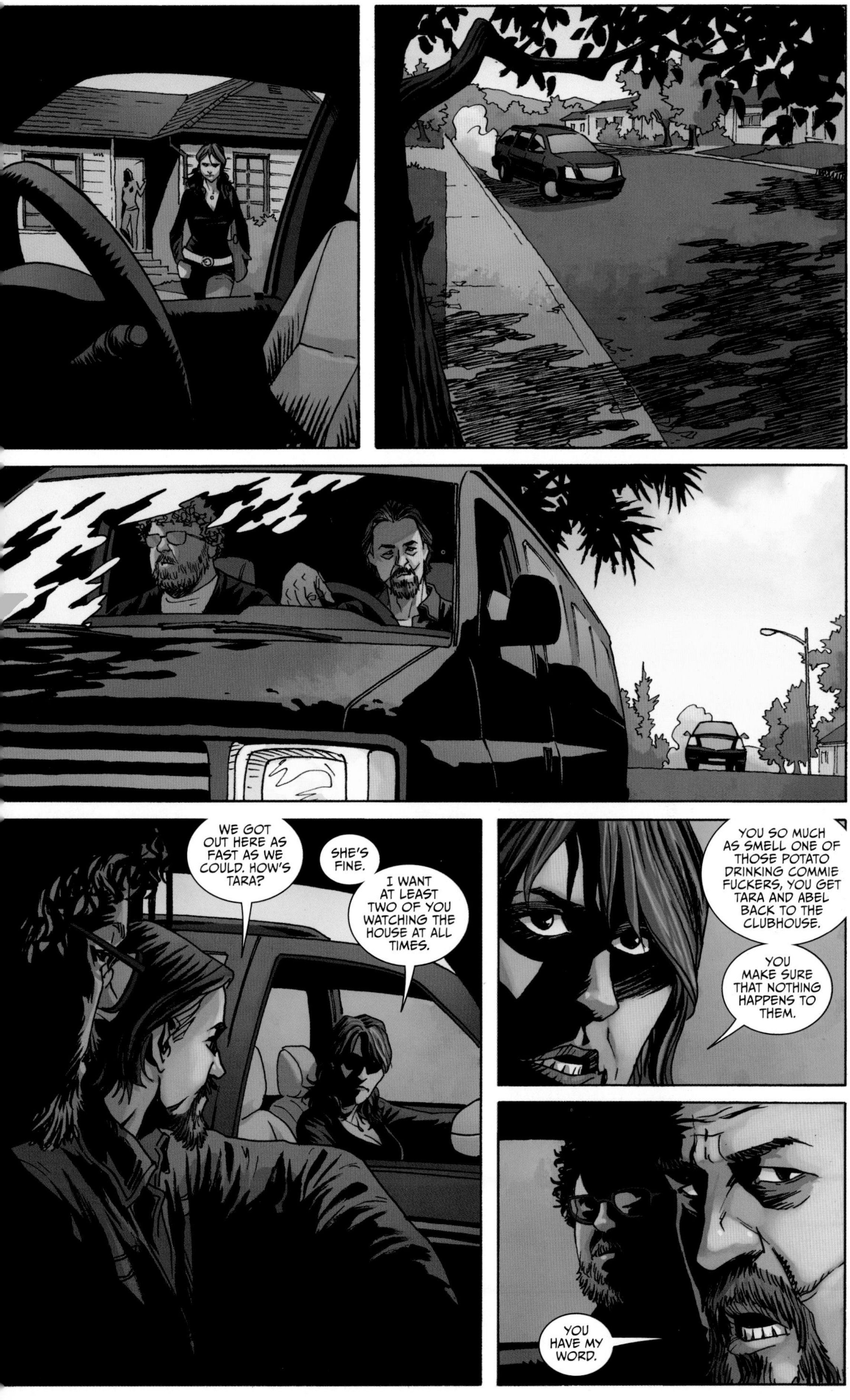

WE GOT OUT HERE AS FAST AS WE COULD. HOW'S TARA?
SHE'S FINE.
I WANT AT LEAST TWO OF YOU WATCHING THE HOUSE AT ALL TIMES.
YOU SO MUCH AS SMELL ONE OF THOSE POTATO DRINKING COMMIE FUCKERS, YOU GET TARA AND ABEL BACK TO THE CLUBHOUSE.
YOU MAKE SURE THAT NOTHING HAPPENS TO THEM.
YOU HAVE MY WORD.

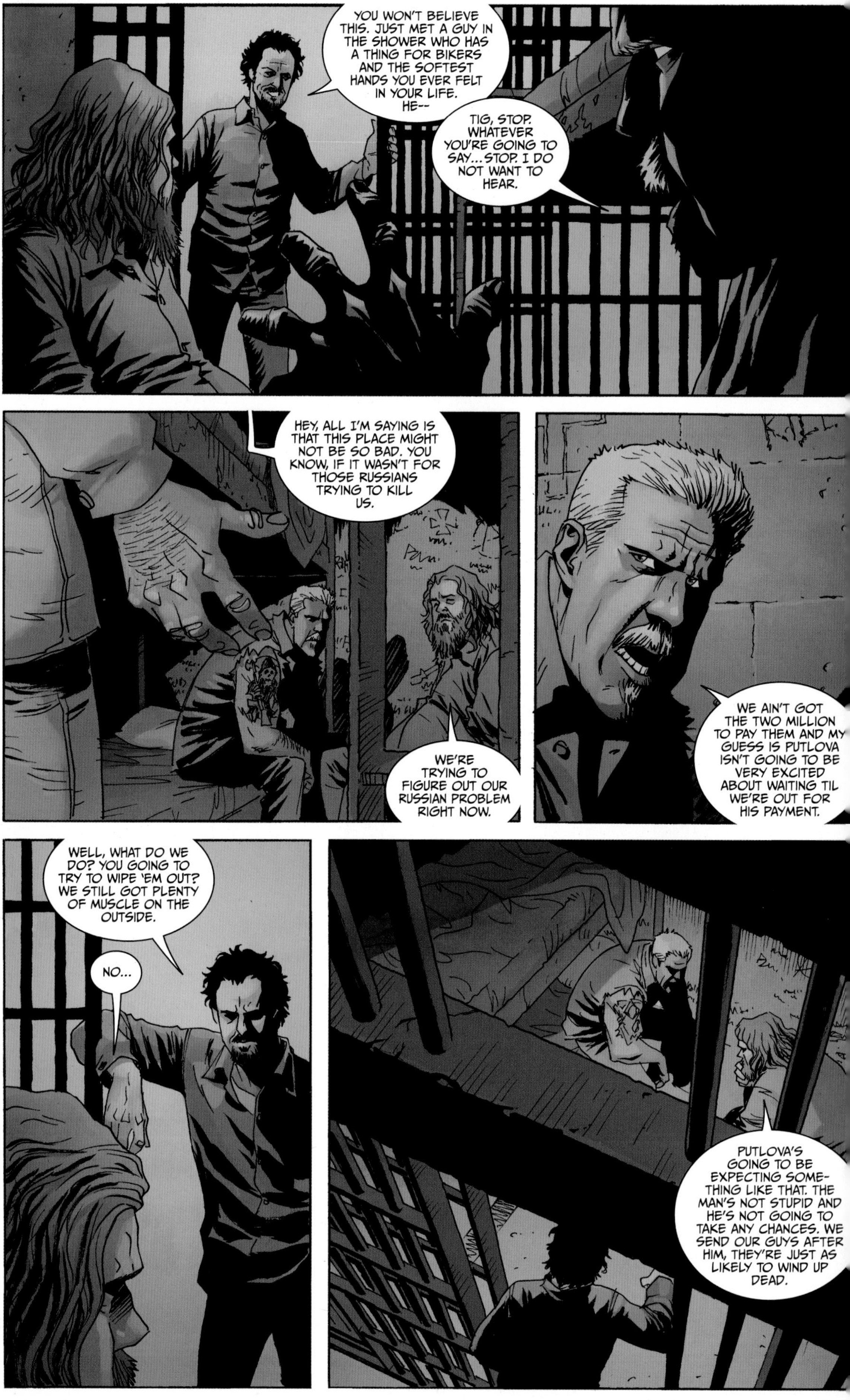
YOU WON'T BELIEVE THIS. JUST MET A GUY IN THE SHOWER WHO HAS A THING FOR BIKERS AND THE SOFTEST HANDS YOU EVER FELT IN YOUR LIFE. HE--
TIG, STOP. WHATEVER YOU'RE GOING TO SAY... STOP. I DO NOT WANT TO HEAR.
HEY, ALL I'M SAYING IS THAT THIS PLACE MIGHT NOT BE SO BAD. YOU KNOW, IF IT WASN'T FOR THOSE RUSSIANS TRYING TO KILL US.
WE'RE TRYING TO FIGURE OUT OUR RUSSIAN PROBLEM RIGHT NOW.
WE AIN'T GOT THE TWO MILLION TO PAY THEM AND MY GUESS IS PUTLOVA ISN'T GOING TO BE VERY EXCITED ABOUT WAITING TIL WE'RE OUT FOR HIS PAYMENT.
WELL, WHAT DO WE DO? YOU GOING TO TRY TO WIPE 'EM OUT? WE STILL GOT PLENTY OF MUSCLE ON THE OUTSIDE.
NO...
PUTLOVA'S GOING TO BE EXPECTING SOME-THING LIKE THAT. THE MAN'S NOT STUPID AND HE'S NOT GOING TO TAKE ANY CHANCES. WE SEND OUR GUYS AFTER HIM, THEY'RE JUST AS LIKELY TO WIND UP DEAD.

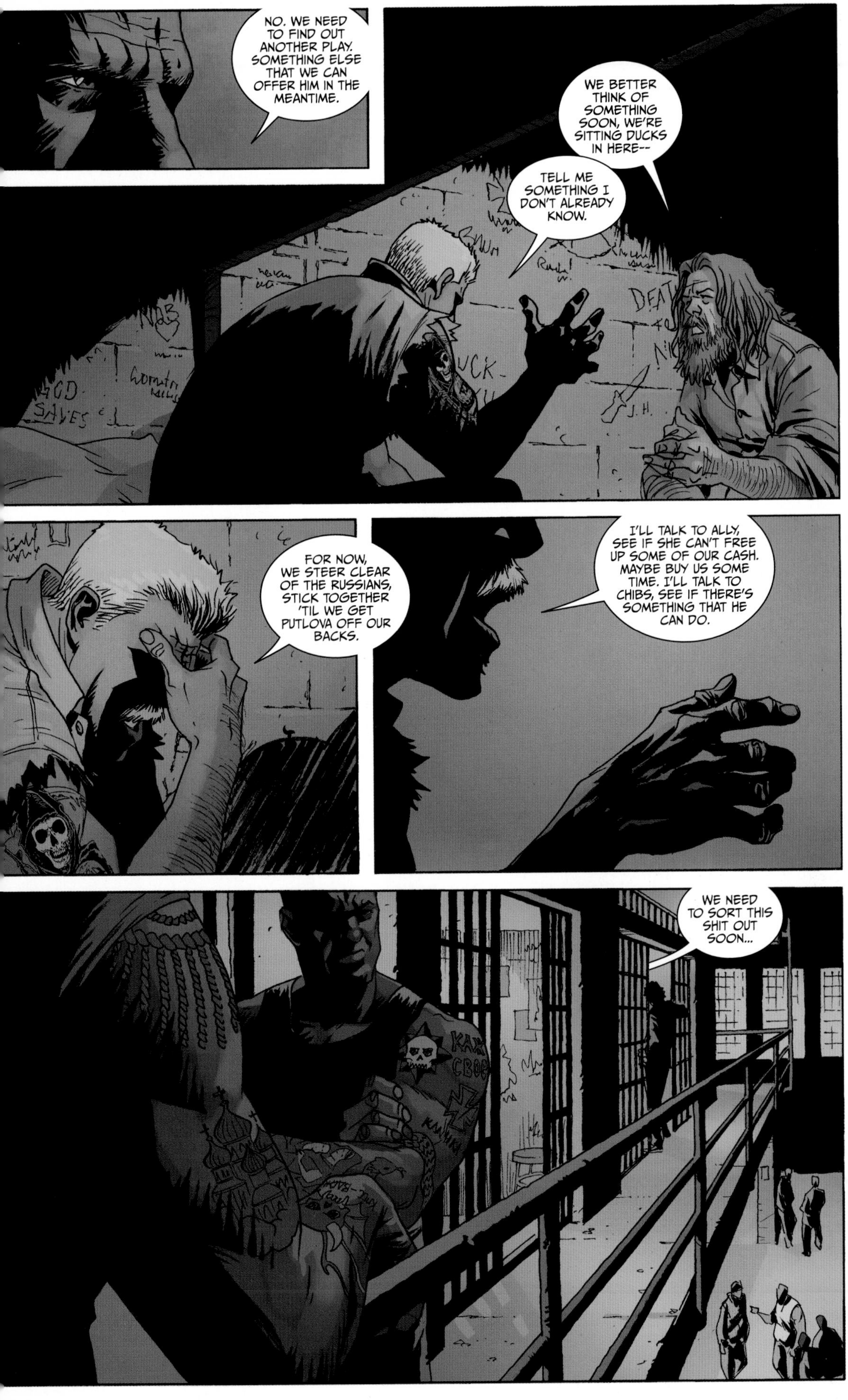

NO. WE NEED TO FIND OUT ANOTHER PLAY. SOMETHING ELSE THAT WE CAN OFFER HIM IN THE MEANTIME.
WE BETTER THINK OF SOMETHING SOON, WE'RE SITTING DUCKS IN HERE--
TELL ME SOMETHING I DON'T ALREADY KNOW.
FOR NOW, WE STEER CLEAR OF THE RUSSIANS, STICK TOGETHER 'TIL WE GET PUTLOVA OFF OUR BACKS.
I'LL TALK TO ALLY, SEE IF SHE CAN'T FREE UP SOME OF OUR CASH. MAYBE BUY US SOME TIME. I'LL TALK TO CHIBS, SEE IF THERE'S SOMETHING THAT HE CAN DO.
WE NEED TO SORT THIS SHIT OUT SOON...

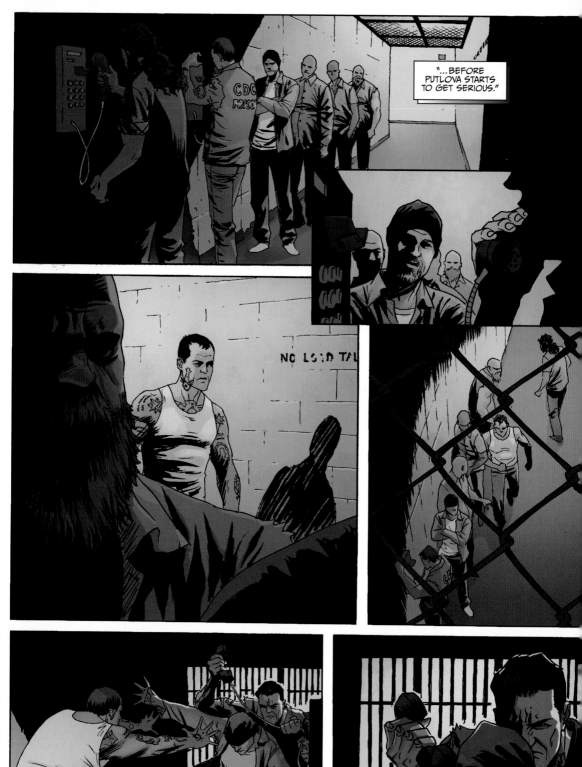

"...BEFORE PUTLOVA STARTS TO GET SERIOUS."

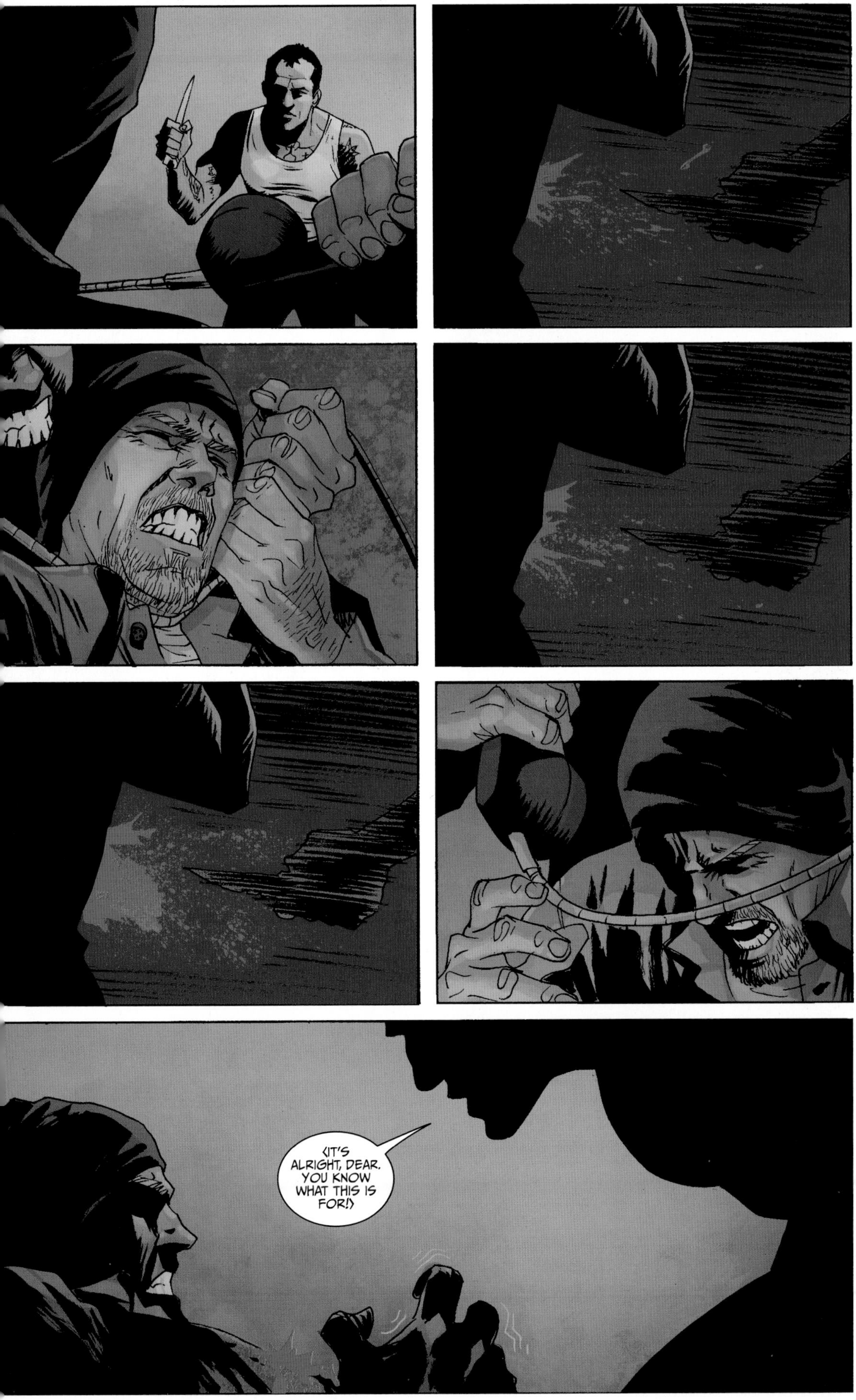
<IT'S ALRIGHT, DEAR. YOU KNOW WHAT THIS IS FOR!>

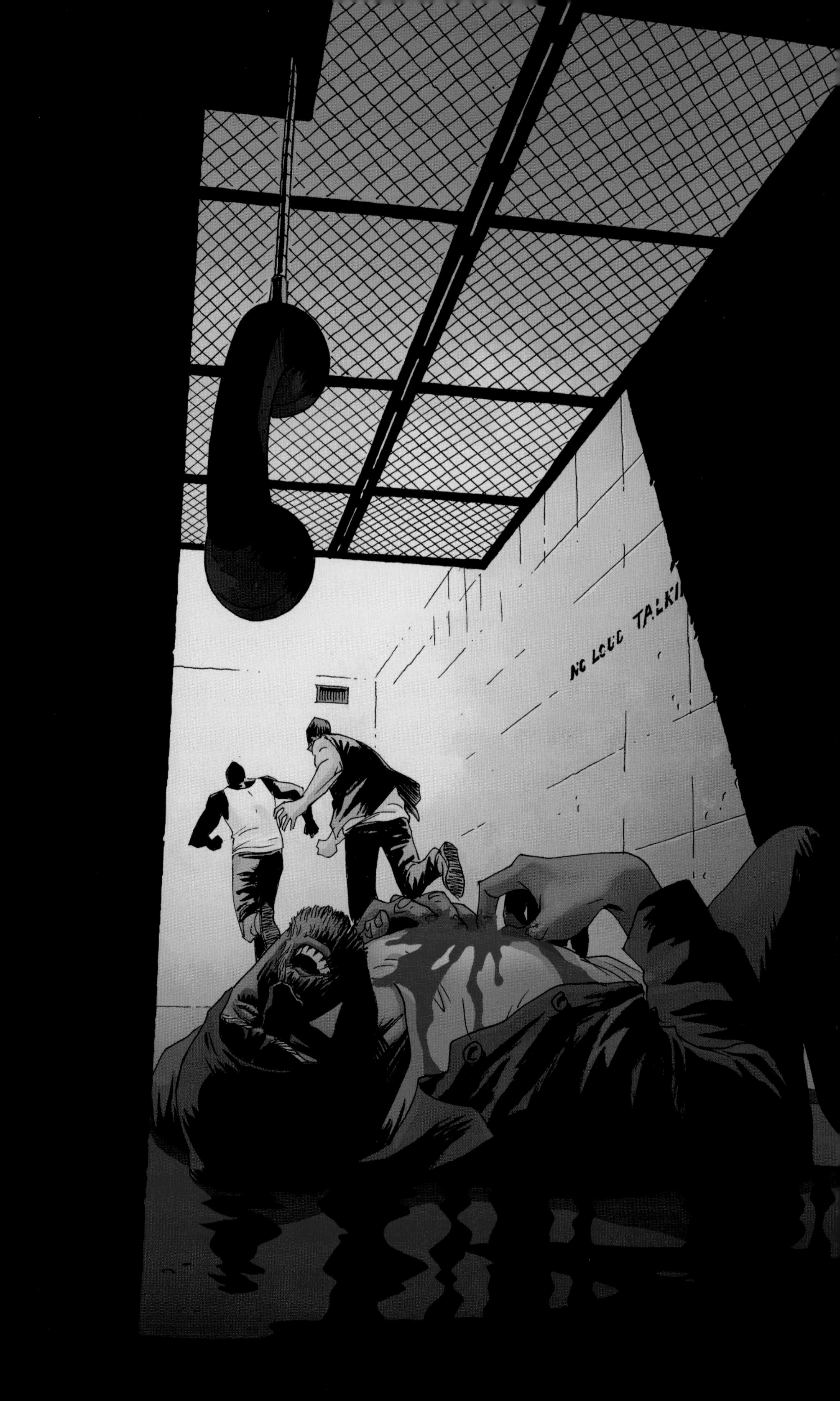
NO LOUD TALKI

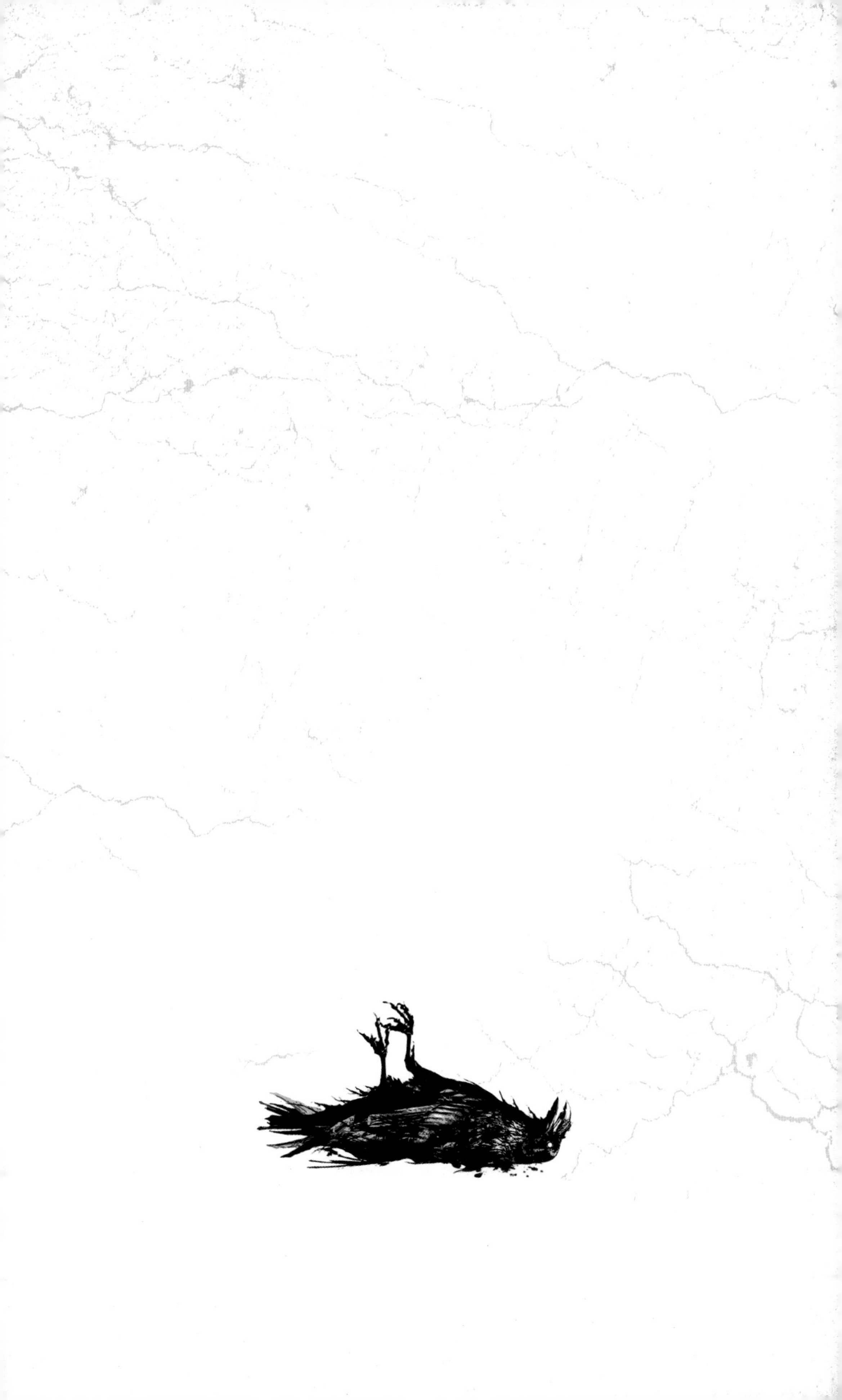

CHAPTER 9

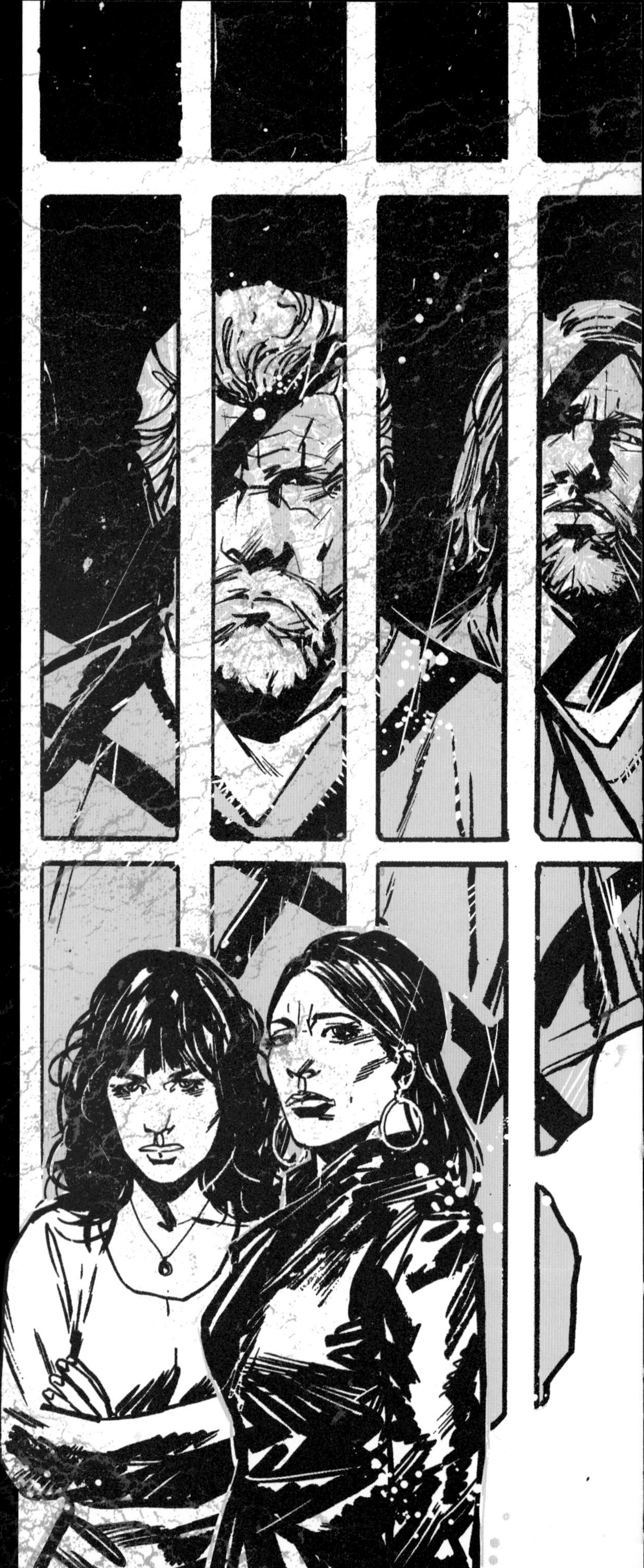

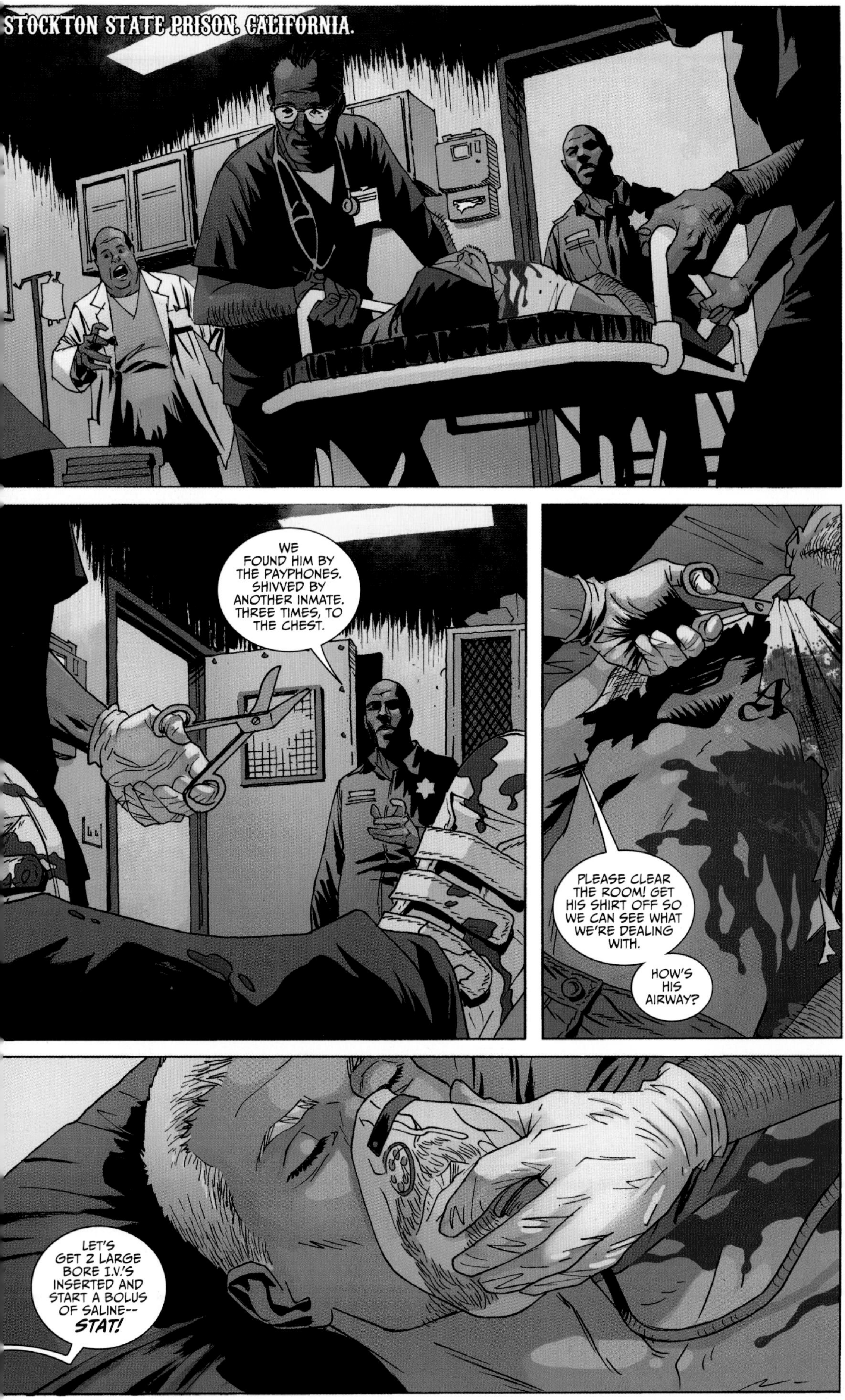
STOCKTON STATE PRISON, CALIFORNIA.
WE FOUND HIM BY THE PAYPHONES. SHIVVED BY ANOTHER INMATE. THREE TIMES, TO THE CHEST.
PLEASE CLEAR THE ROOM! GET HIS SHIRT OFF SO WE CAN SEE WHAT WE'RE DEALING WITH.
HOW'S HIS AIRWAY?
LET'S GET 2 LARGE BORE I.V.'S INSERTED AND START A BOLUS OF SALINE-- STAT!

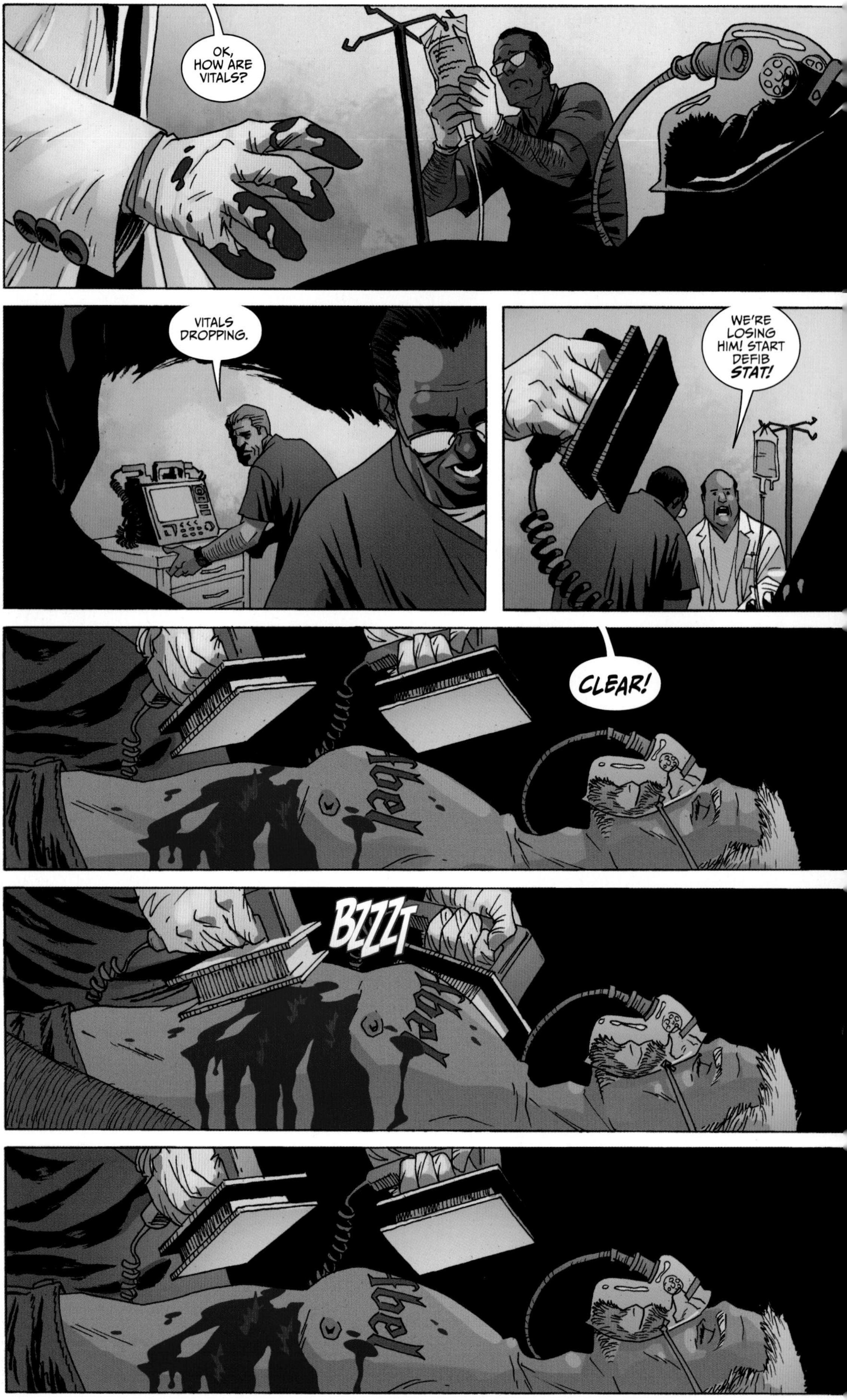
OK, HOW ARE VITALS?
VITALS DROPPING.
WE'RE LOSING HIM! START DEFIB STAT!
CLEAR!
BZZZT

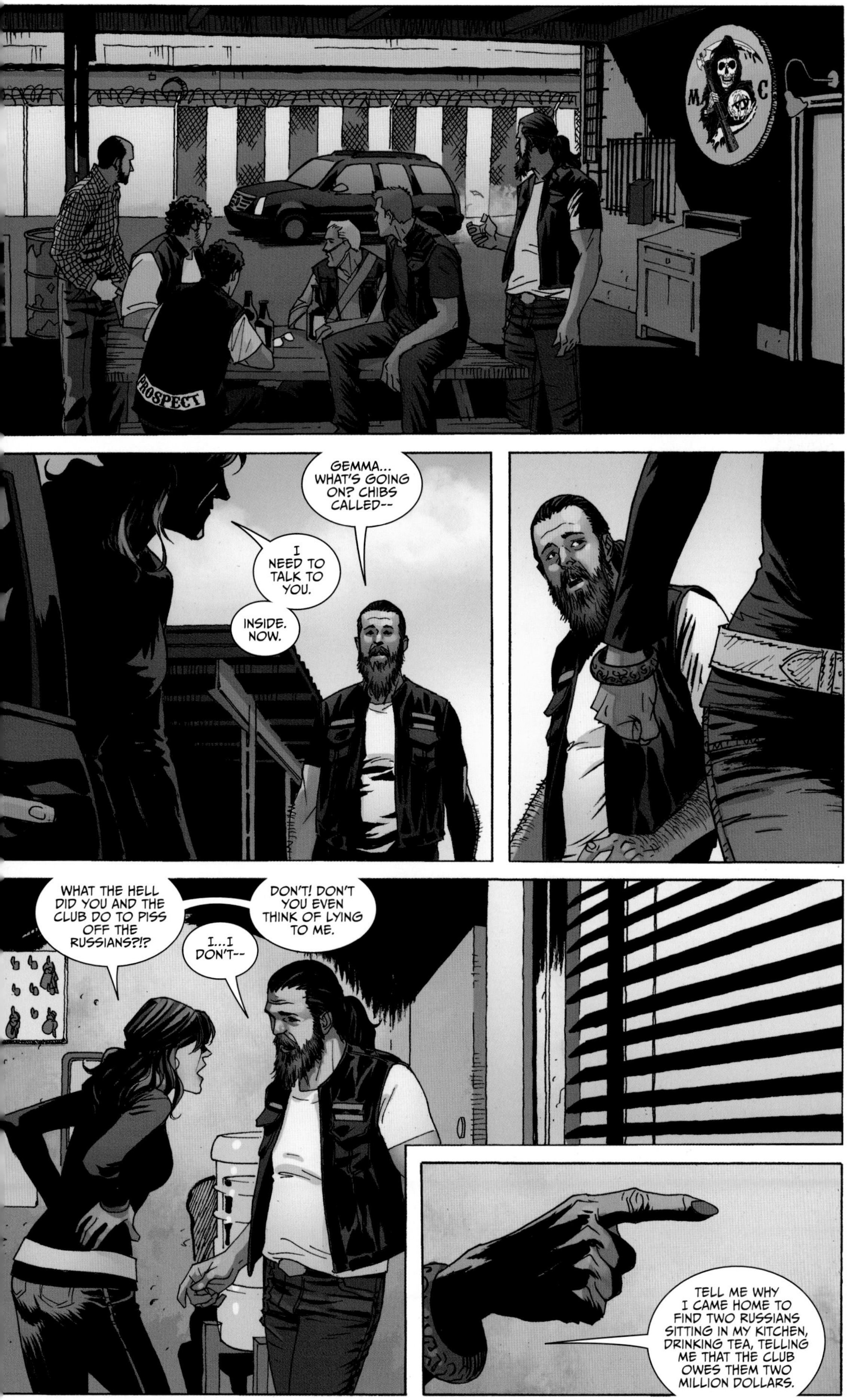
PROSPECT
GEMMA... WHAT'S GOING ON? CHIBS CALLED--
I NEED TO TALK TO YOU.
INSIDE. NOW.
WHAT THE HELL DID YOU AND THE CLUB DO TO PISS OFF THE RUSSIANS?!?
I...I DON'T--
DON'T! DON'T YOU EVEN THINK OF LYING TO ME.
TELL ME WHY I CAME HOME TO FIND TWO RUSSIANS SITTING IN MY KITCHEN, DRINKING TEA, TELLING ME THAT THE CLUB OWES THEM TWO MILLION DOLLARS.

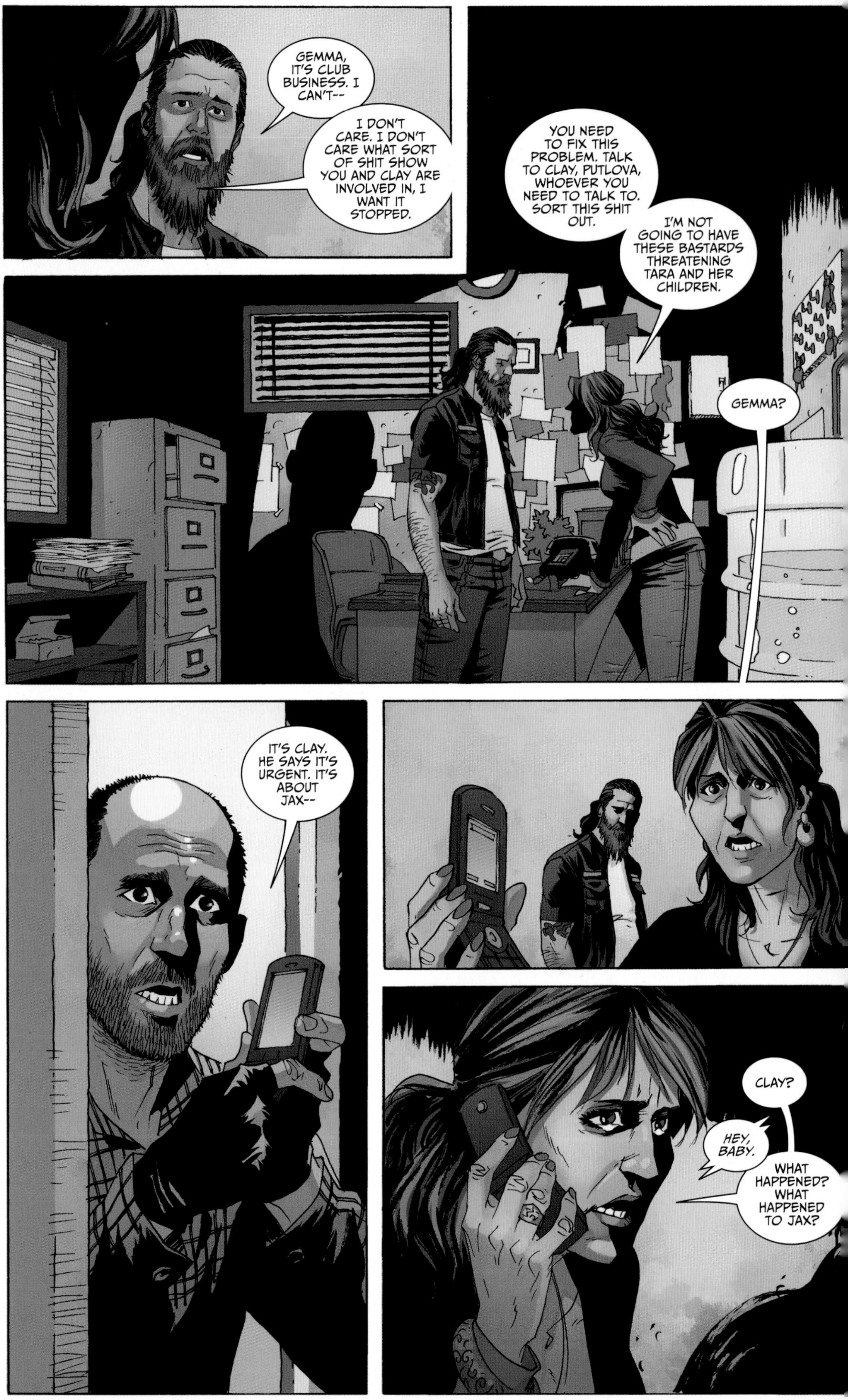
GEMMA, IT'S CLUB BUSINESS. I CAN'T--
I DON'T CARE. I DON'T CARE WHAT SORT OF SHIT SHOW YOU AND CLAY ARE INVOLVED IN, I WANT IT STOPPED.
YOU NEED TO FIX THIS PROBLEM. TALK TO CLAY, PUTLOVA, WHOEVER YOU NEED TO TALK TO. SORT THIS SHIT OUT.
I'M NOT GOING TO HAVE THESE BASTARDS THREATENING TARA AND HER CHILDREN.
GEMMA?
IT'S CLAY. HE SAYS IT'S URGENT. IT'S ABOUT JAX--
CLAY?
HEY, BABY.
WHAT HAPPENED? WHAT HAPPENED TO JAX?

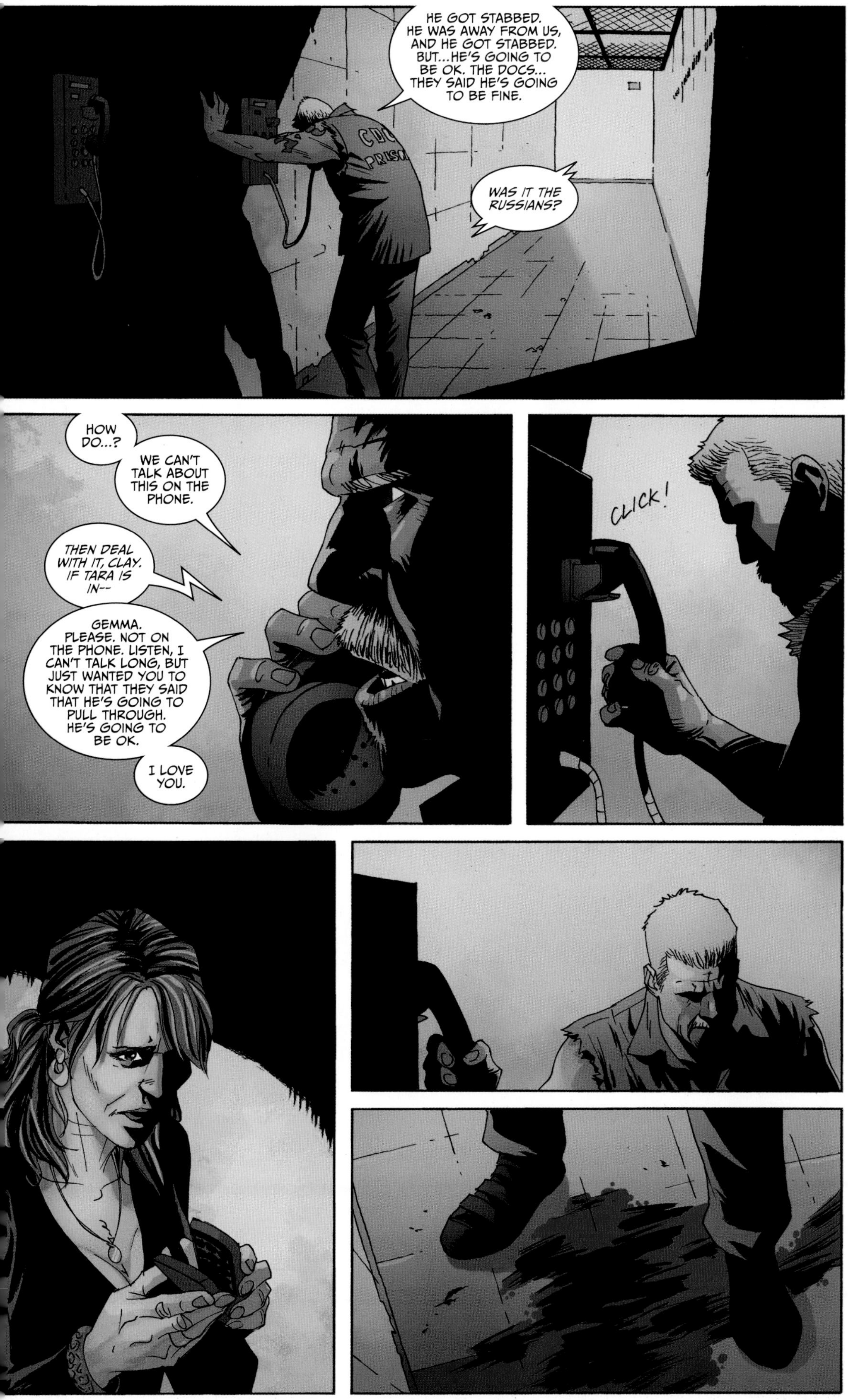
HE GOT STABBED. HE WAS AWAY FROM US, AND HE GOT STABBED. BUT...HE'S GOING TO BE OK. THE DOCS... THEY SAID HE'S GOING TO BE FINE.
WAS IT THE RUSSIANS?
HOW DO...?
WE CAN'T TALK ABOUT THIS ON THE PHONE.
THEN DEAL WITH IT, CLAY. IF TARA IS IN--
GEMMA. PLEASE. NOT ON THE PHONE. LISTEN, I CAN'T TALK LONG, BUT JUST WANTED YOU TO KNOW THAT THEY SAID THAT HE'S GOING TO PULL THROUGH. HE'S GOING TO BE OK.
I LOVE YOU.
CLICK!

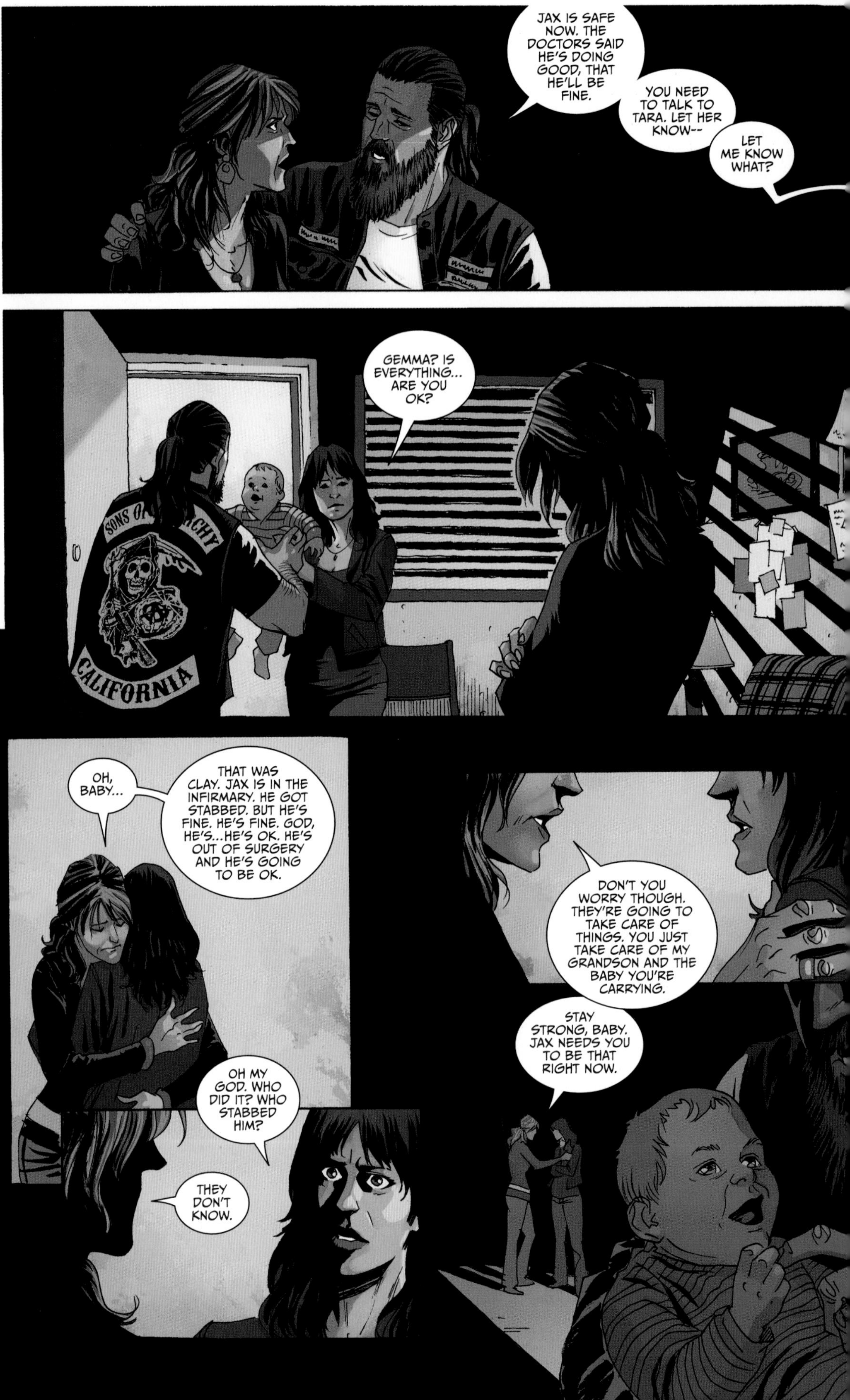
JAX IS SAFE NOW. THE DOCTORS SAID HE'S DOING GOOD, THAT HE'LL BE FINE.
YOU NEED TO TALK TO TARA. LET HER KNOW--
LET ME KNOW WHAT?
GEMMA? IS EVERYTHING... ARE YOU OK?
SONS OF ANARCHY
CALIFORNIA
OH, BABY...
THAT WAS CLAY. JAX IS IN THE INFIRMARY. HE GOT STABBED. BUT HE'S FINE. HE'S FINE. GOD, HE'S...HE'S OK. HE'S OUT OF SURGERY AND HE'S GOING TO BE OK.
OH MY GOD. WHO DID IT? WHO STABBED HIM?
THEY DON'T KNOW.
DON'T YOU WORRY THOUGH. THEY'RE GOING TO TAKE CARE OF THINGS. YOU JUST TAKE CARE OF MY GRANDSON AND THE BABY YOU'RE CARRYING.
STAY STRONG, BABY. JAX NEEDS YOU TO BE THAT RIGHT NOW.

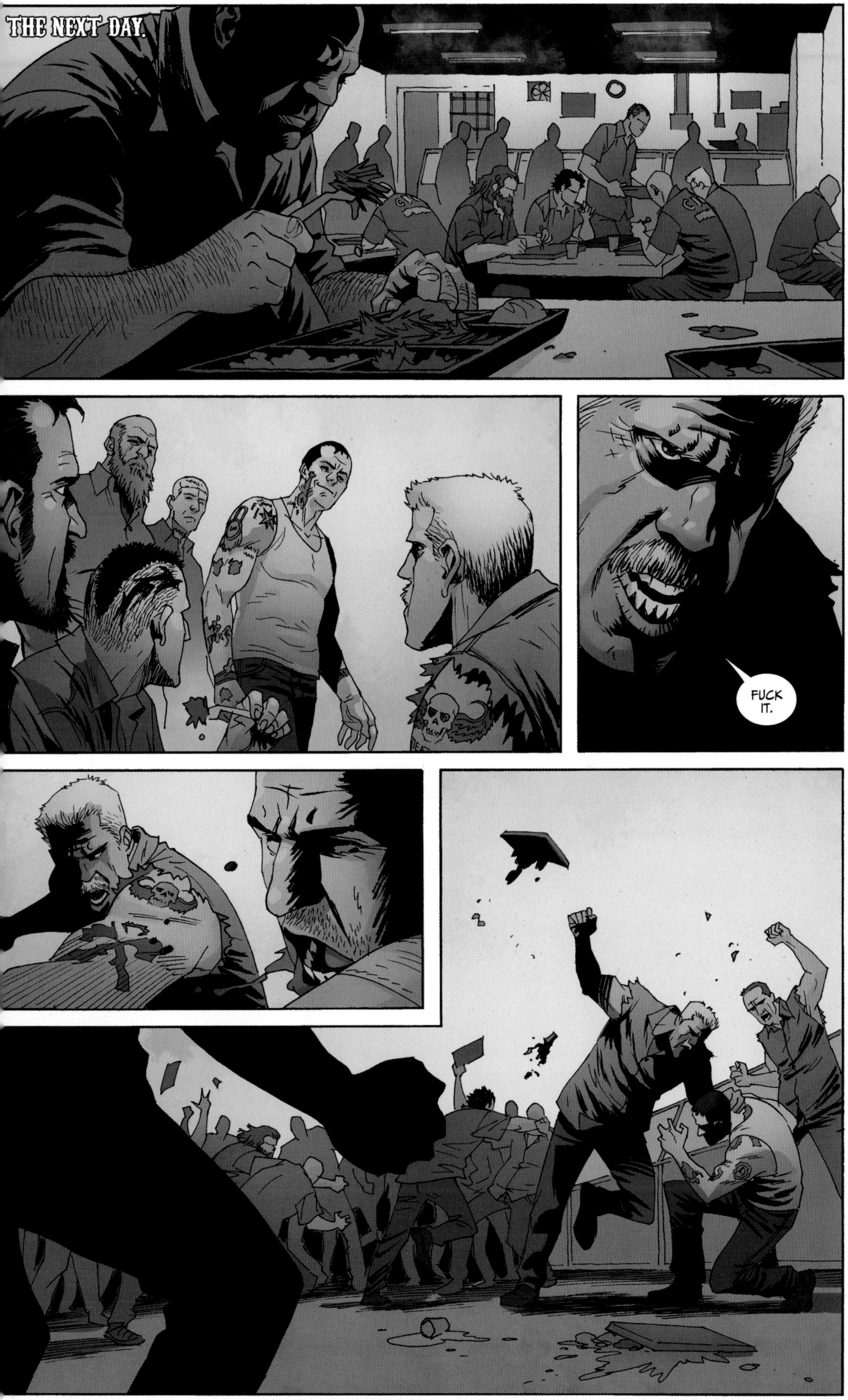
THE NEXT DAY.
FUCK IT.

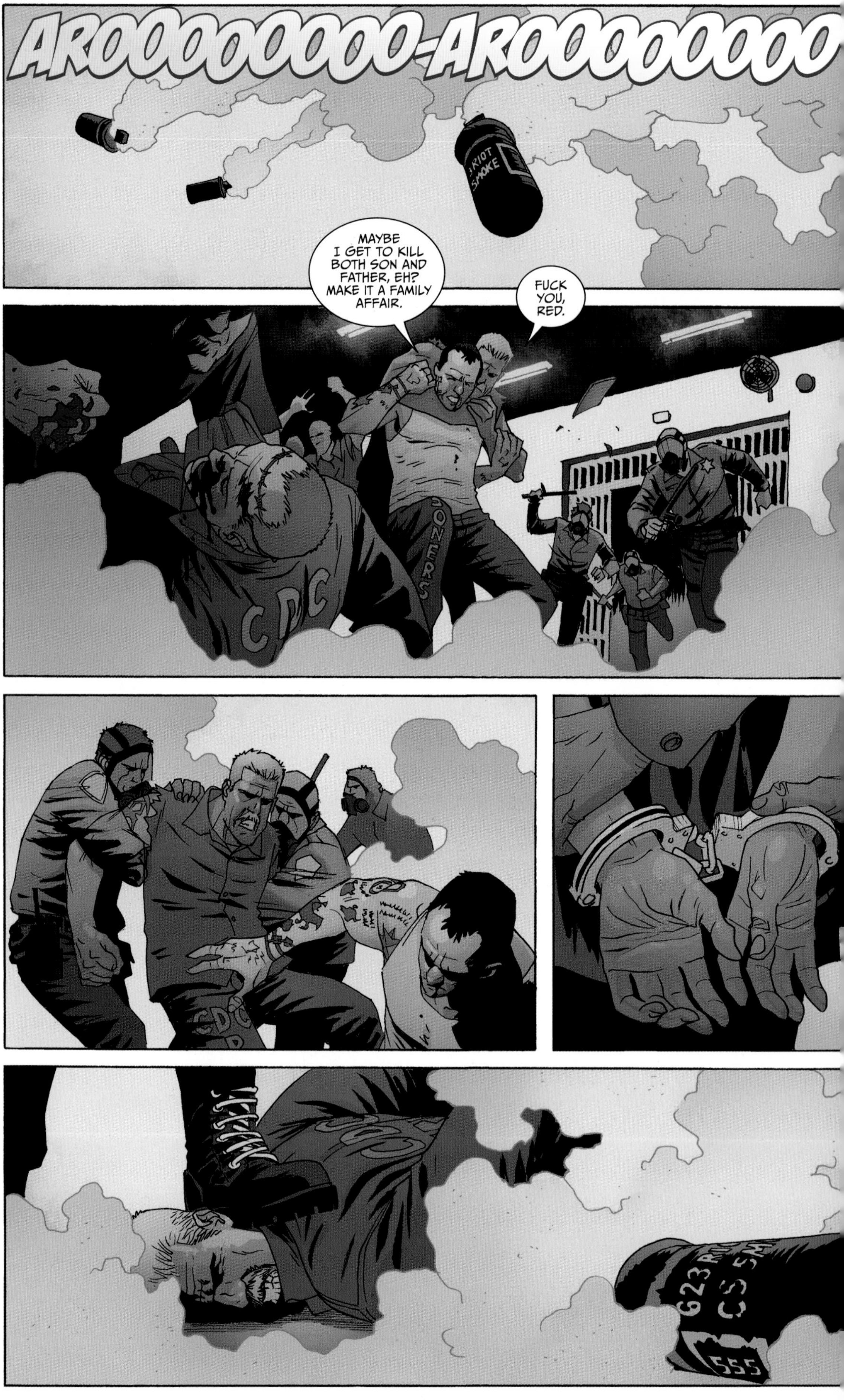
AROOOOOOOO-AROOOOOOOO
3 RIOT SMOKE
MAYBE I GET TO KILL BOTH SON AND FATHER, EH? MAKE IT A FAMILY AFFAIR.
FUCK YOU, RED.
CDC

WEEKS LATER.

CLACK

RISE AND SHINE, MORROW. LOCKDOWN'S BEEN LIFTED. WE'RE TAKING YOU BACK TO GEN POP.

AND JUST WHEN I WAS GETTING USED TO THE PEACE AND QUIET.

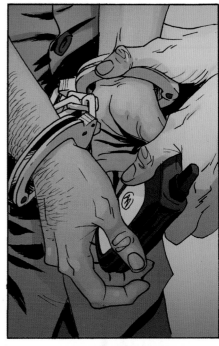

APPRECIATE YOU LOOKING OUT.

JUST MAKE SURE TO REMOVE THE SIM CARD AND FLUSH IT BEFORE YOU GET RID OF THE PHONE.

HOW YOU FEELING?

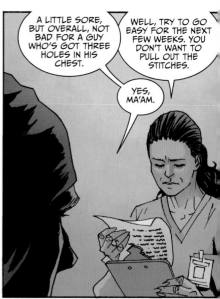

A LITTLE SORE, BUT OVERALL, NOT BAD FOR A GUY WHO'S GOT THREE HOLES IN HIS CHEST.

WELL, TRY TO GO EASY FOR THE NEXT FEW WEEKS. YOU DON'T WANT TO PULL OUT THE STITCHES.

YES, MA'AM.

ANY SIGN OF INFECTION--

YOU'LL BE THE FIRST TO KNOW.

I TAKE IT YOU'RE MY ESCORT?

JUST HERE TO MAKE SURE NO ONE ELSE STABS YOU ON THE WAY BACK TO YOUR CELL.

MY HERO.

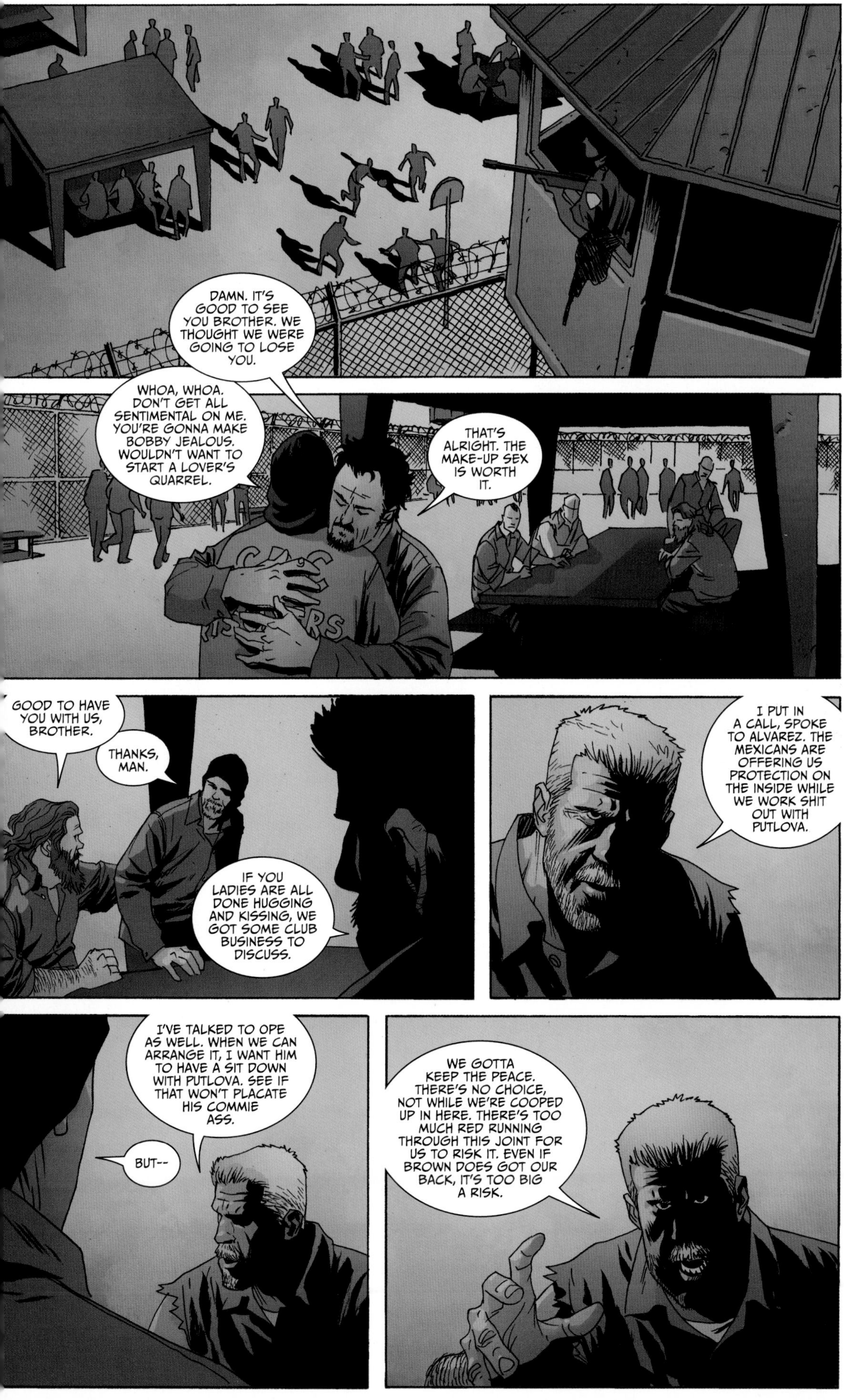
DAMN. IT'S GOOD TO SEE YOU BROTHER. WE THOUGHT WE WERE GOING TO LOSE YOU.
WHOA, WHOA. DON'T GET ALL SENTIMENTAL ON ME. YOU'RE GONNA MAKE BOBBY JEALOUS. WOULDN'T WANT TO START A LOVER'S QUARREL.
THAT'S ALRIGHT. THE MAKE-UP SEX IS WORTH IT.
GOOD TO HAVE YOU WITH US, BROTHER.
THANKS, MAN.
IF YOU LADIES ARE ALL DONE HUGGING AND KISSING, WE GOT SOME CLUB BUSINESS TO DISCUSS.
I PUT IN A CALL, SPOKE TO ALVAREZ. THE MEXICANS ARE OFFERING US PROTECTION ON THE INSIDE WHILE WE WORK SHIT OUT WITH PUTLOVA.
I'VE TALKED TO OPE AS WELL. WHEN WE CAN ARRANGE IT, I WANT HIM TO HAVE A SIT DOWN WITH PUTLOVA. SEE IF THAT WON'T PLACATE HIS COMMIE ASS.
BUT--
WE GOTTA KEEP THE PEACE. THERE'S NO CHOICE, NOT WHILE WE'RE COOPED UP IN HERE. THERE'S TOO MUCH RED RUNNING THROUGH THIS JOINT FOR US TO RISK IT. EVEN IF BROWN DOES GOT OUR BACK, IT'S TOO BIG A RISK.

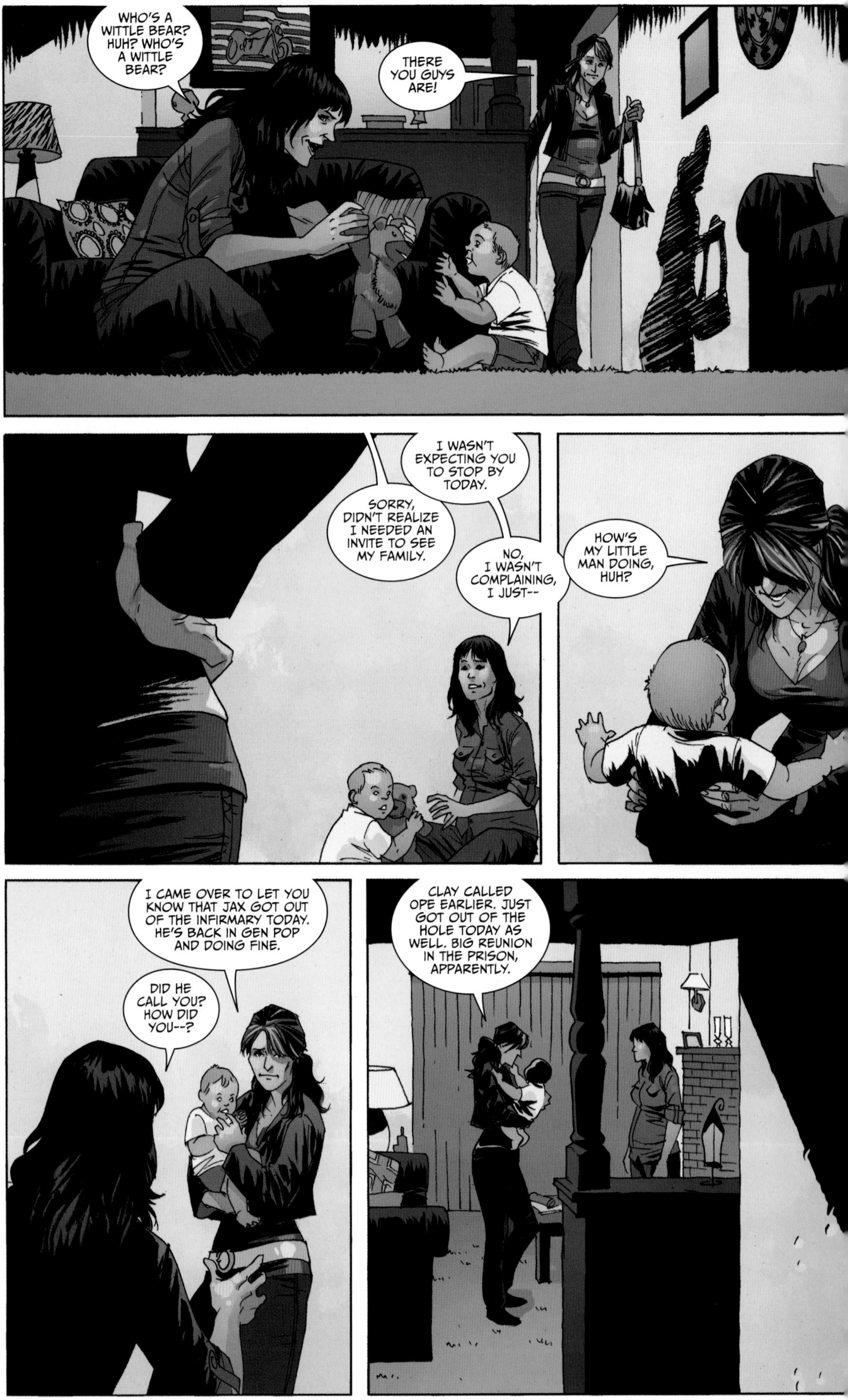
WHO'S A WITTLE BEAR? HUH? WHO'S A WITTLE BEAR?
THERE YOU GUYS ARE!
I WASN'T EXPECTING YOU TO STOP BY TODAY.
SORRY, DIDN'T REALIZE I NEEDED AN INVITE TO SEE MY FAMILY.
NO, I WASN'T COMPLAINING, I JUST--
HOW'S MY LITTLE MAN DOING, HUH?
I CAME OVER TO LET YOU KNOW THAT JAX GOT OUT OF THE INFIRMARY TODAY. HE'S BACK IN GEN POP AND DOING FINE.
DID HE CALL YOU? HOW DID YOU--?
CLAY CALLED OPE EARLIER. JUST GOT OUT OF THE HOLE TODAY AS WELL. BIG REUNION IN THE PRISON, APPARENTLY.

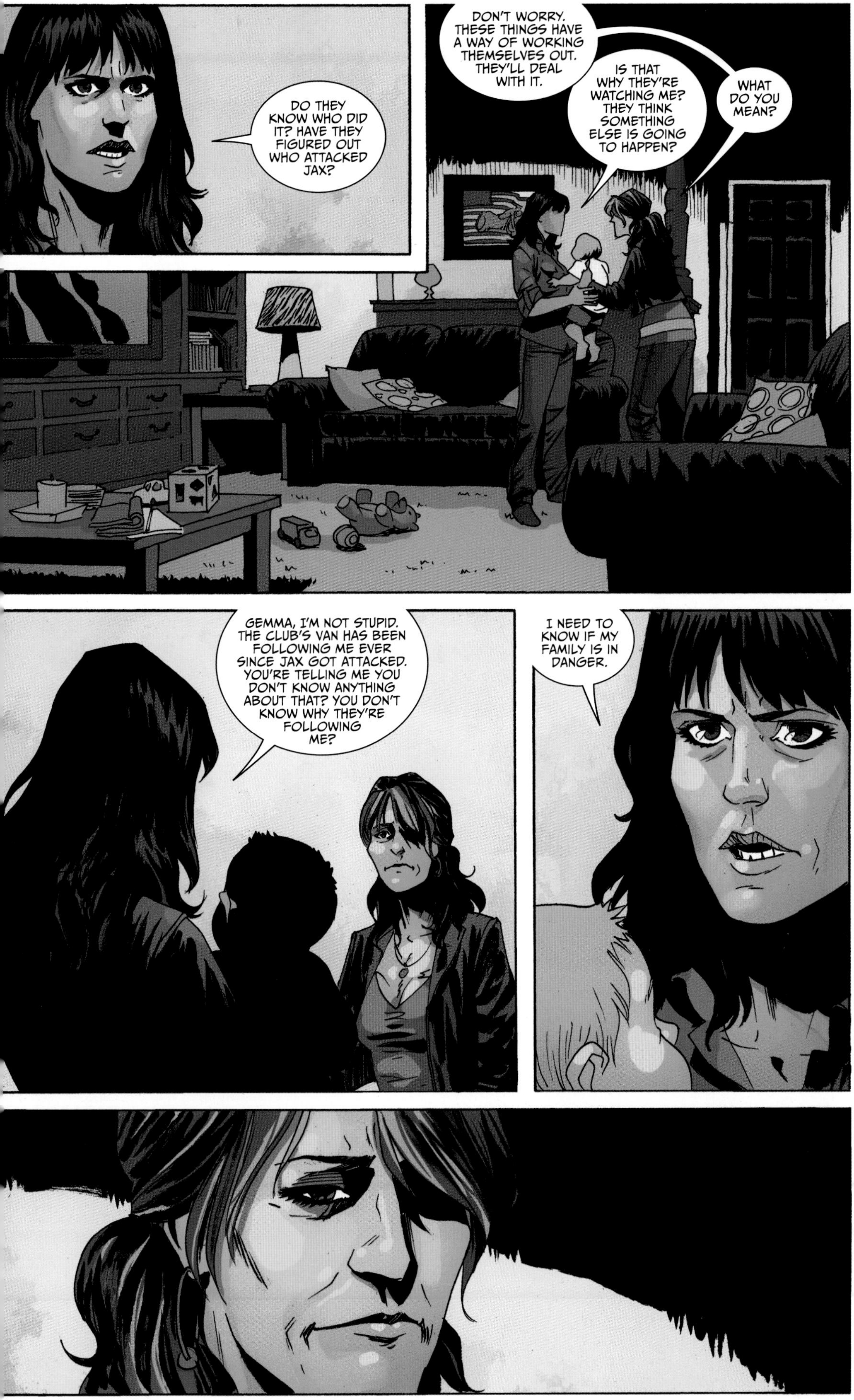

DO THEY KNOW WHO DID IT? HAVE THEY FIGURED OUT WHO ATTACKED JAX?
DON'T WORRY. THESE THINGS HAVE A WAY OF WORKING THEMSELVES OUT. THEY'LL DEAL WITH IT.
IS THAT WHY THEY'RE WATCHING ME? THEY THINK SOMETHING ELSE IS GOING TO HAPPEN?
WHAT DO YOU MEAN?
GEMMA, I'M NOT STUPID. THE CLUB'S VAN HAS BEEN FOLLOWING ME EVER SINCE JAX GOT ATTACKED. YOU'RE TELLING ME YOU DON'T KNOW ANYTHING ABOUT THAT? YOU DON'T KNOW WHY THEY'RE FOLLOWING ME?
I NEED TO KNOW IF MY FAMILY IS IN DANGER.

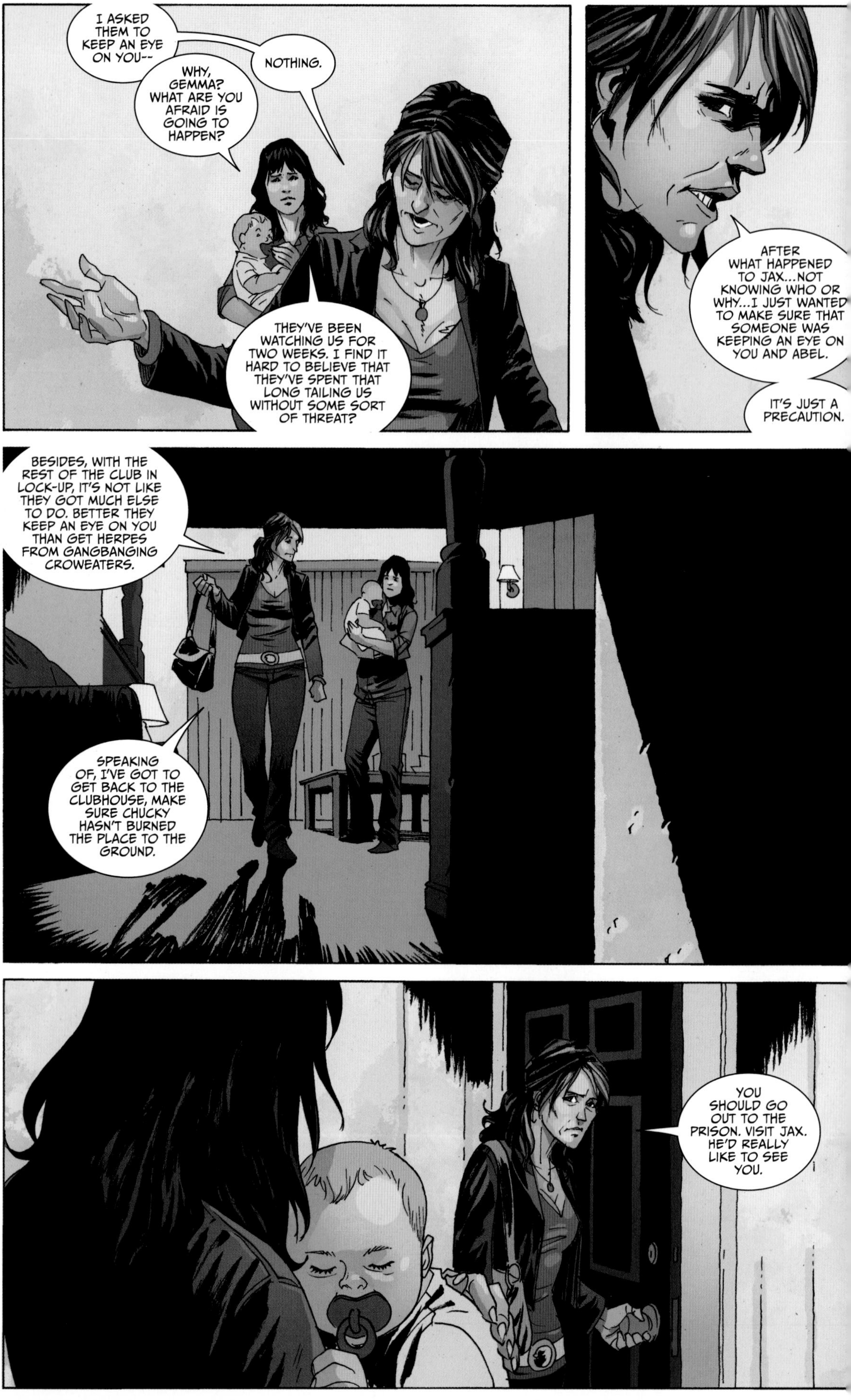
I ASKED THEM TO KEEP AN EYE ON YOU--
WHY, GEMMA? WHAT ARE YOU AFRAID IS GOING TO HAPPEN?
NOTHING.
THEY'VE BEEN WATCHING US FOR TWO WEEKS. I FIND IT HARD TO BELIEVE THAT THEY'VE SPENT THAT LONG TAILING US WITHOUT SOME SORT OF THREAT?
AFTER WHAT HAPPENED TO JAX...NOT KNOWING WHO OR WHY...I JUST WANTED TO MAKE SURE THAT SOMEONE WAS KEEPING AN EYE ON YOU AND ABEL.
IT'S JUST A PRECAUTION.
BESIDES, WITH THE REST OF THE CLUB IN LOCK-UP, IT'S NOT LIKE THEY GOT MUCH ELSE TO DO. BETTER THEY KEEP AN EYE ON YOU THAN GET HERPES FROM GANGBANGING CROWEATERS.
SPEAKING OF, I'VE GOT TO GET BACK TO THE CLUBHOUSE, MAKE SURE CHUCKY HASN'T BURNED THE PLACE TO THE GROUND.
YOU SHOULD GO OUT TO THE PRISON. VISIT JAX. HE'D REALLY LIKE TO SEE YOU.

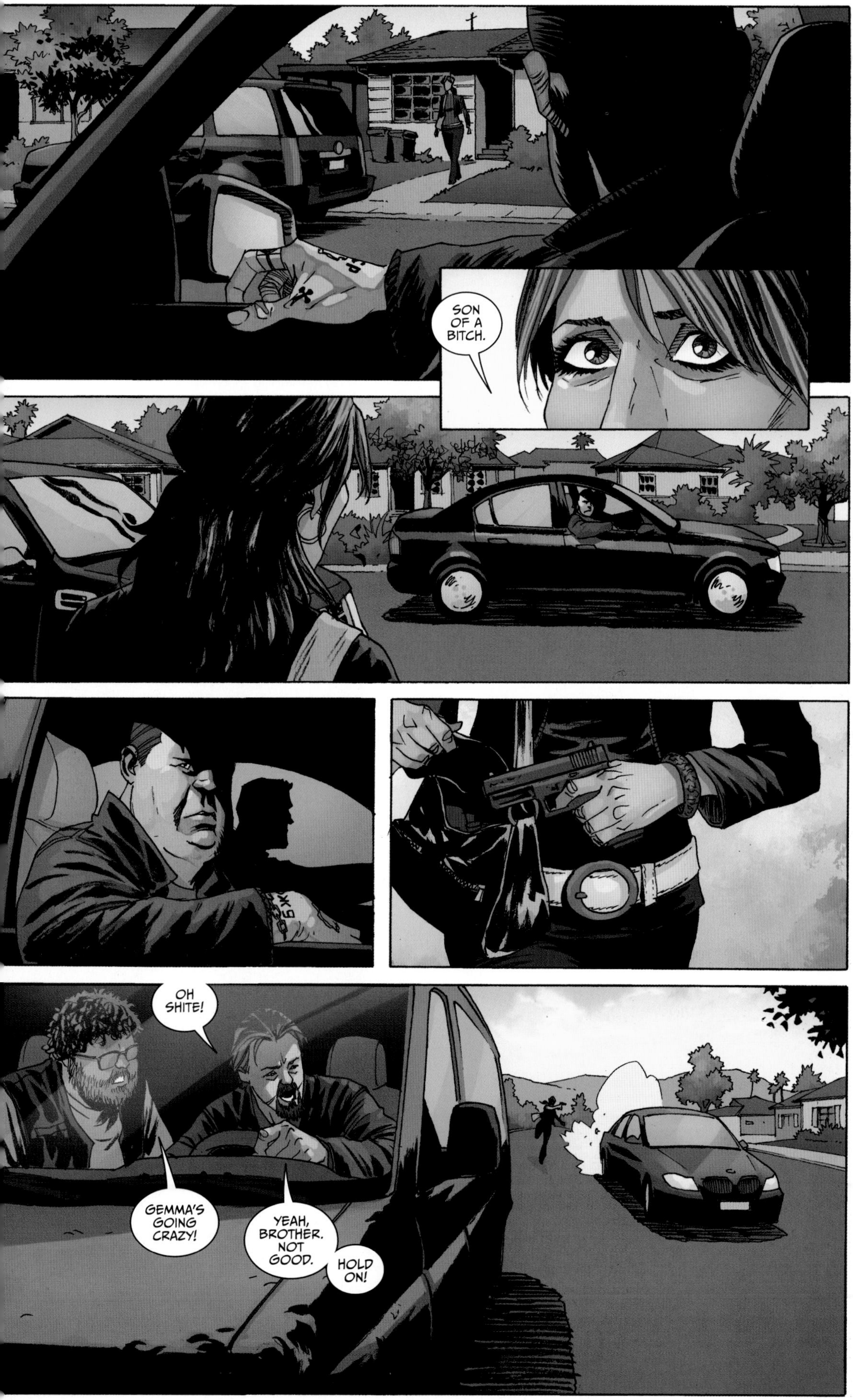
SON OF A BITCH.
OH SHITE!
GEMMA'S GOING CRAZY!
YEAH, BROTHER. NOT GOOD.
HOLD ON!

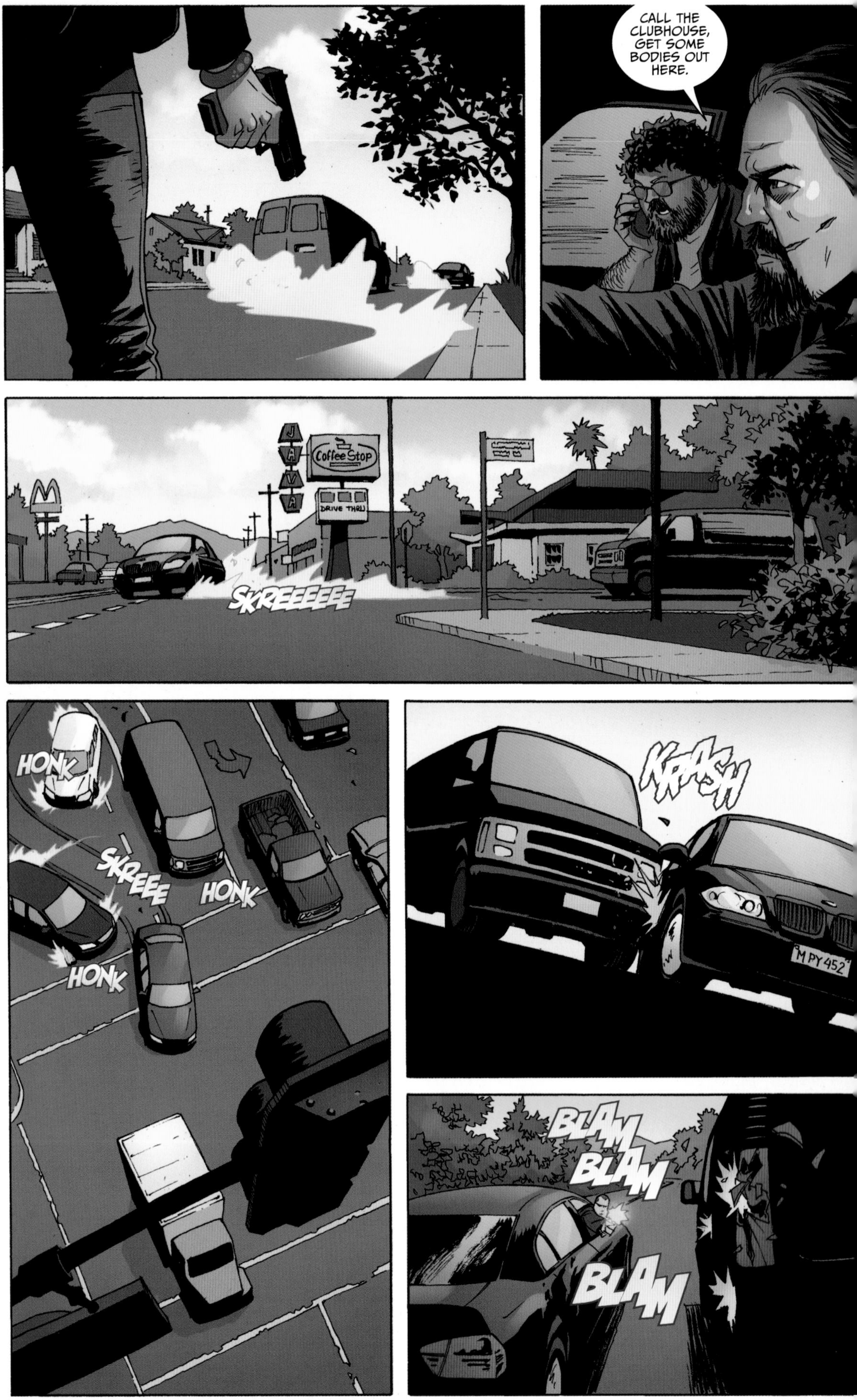
CALL THE CLUBHOUSE, GET SOME BODIES OUT HERE.
JAVA
Coffee Stop
DRIVE THRU
SKREEEEEE
HONK
SKREEE
HONK
HONK
KRASH
M PY 452
BLAM
BLAM
BLAM

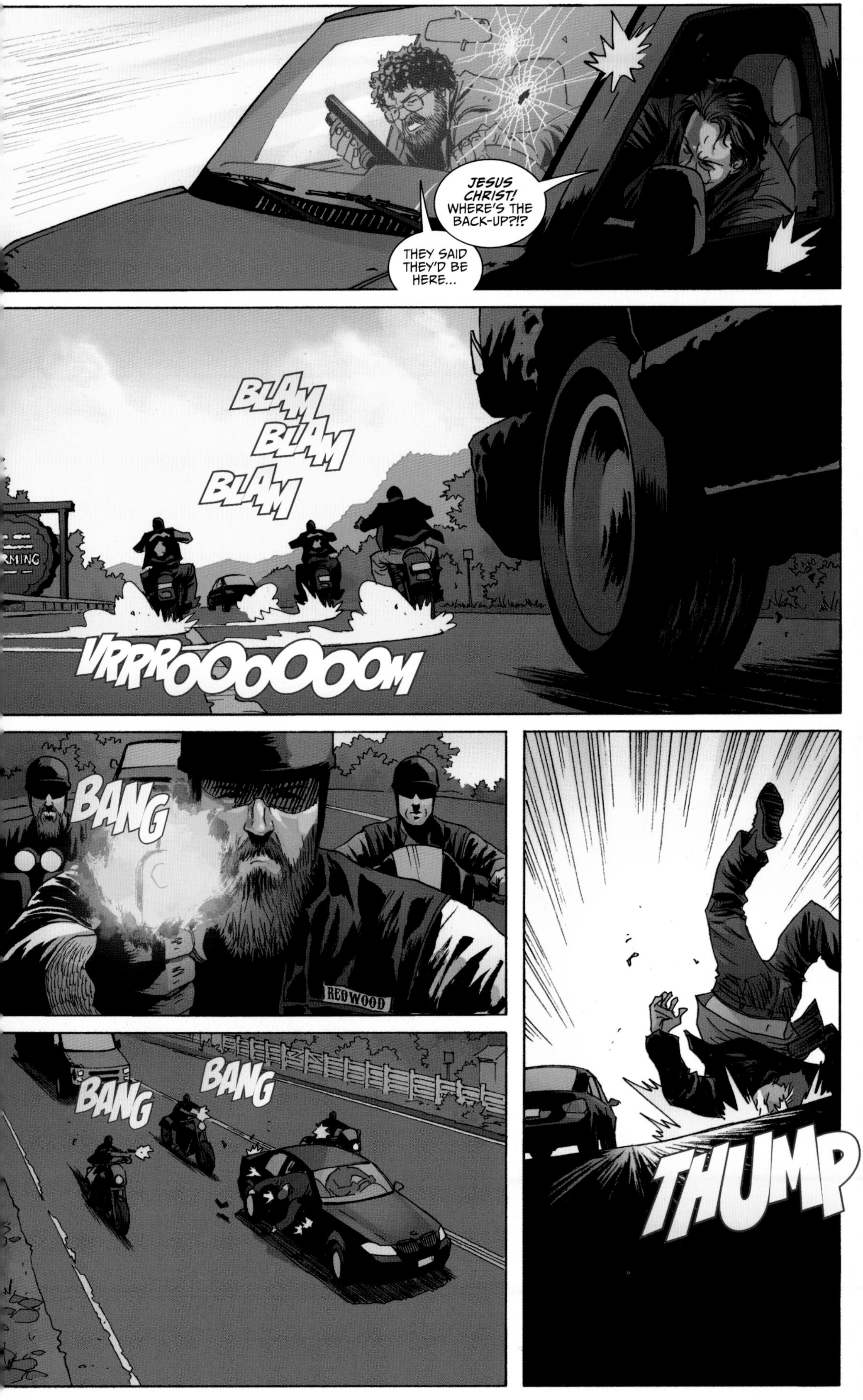
JESUS CHRIST! WHERE'S THE BACK-UP?!?
THEY SAID THEY'D BE HERE...
BLAM
BLAM
BLAM
RMING
VRRROOOOOOM
BANG
REDWOOD
BANG
BANG
THUMP

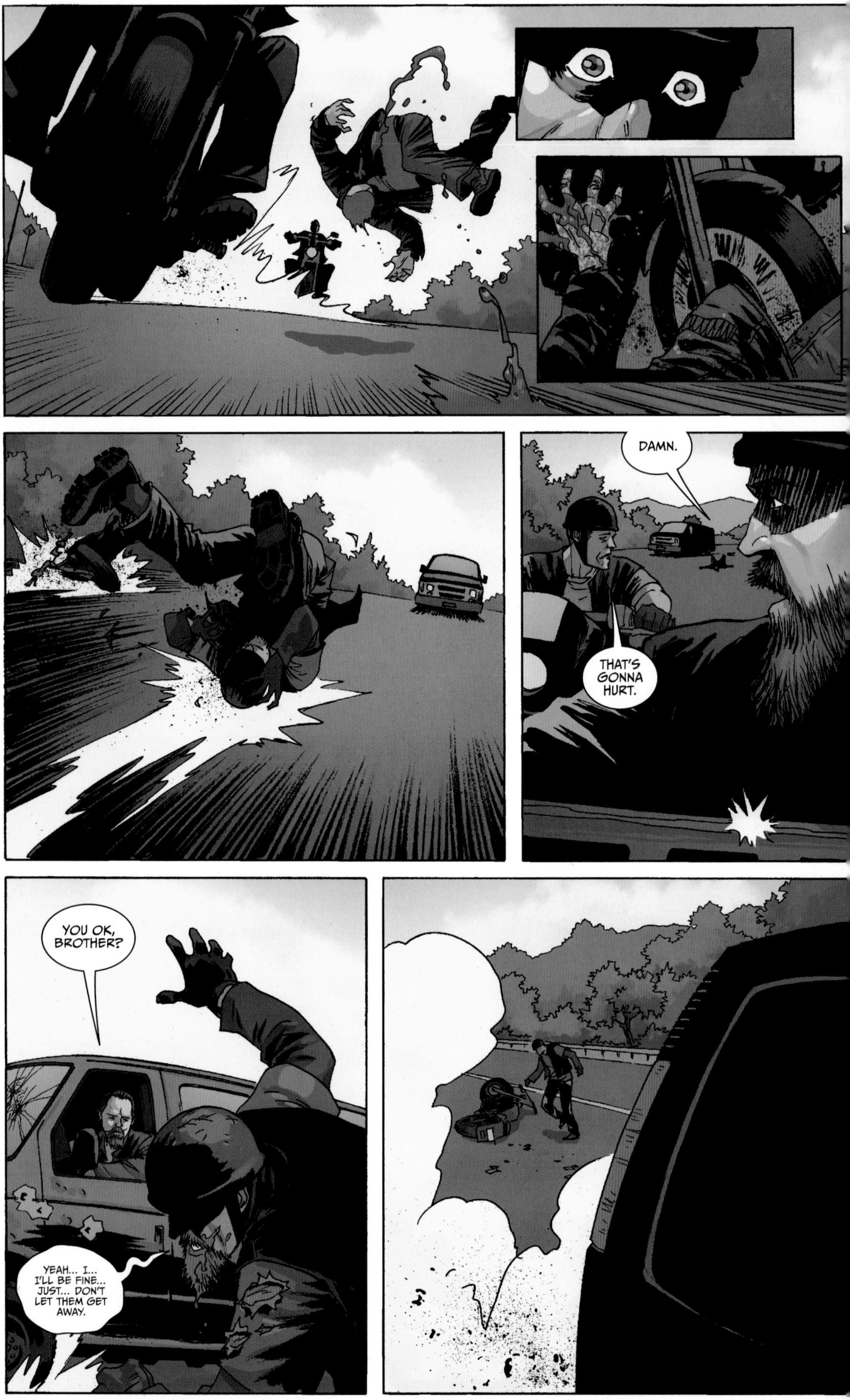
DAMN.
THAT'S GONNA HURT.
YOU OK, BROTHER?
YEAH... I... I'LL BE FINE... JUST... DON'T LET THEM GET AWAY.

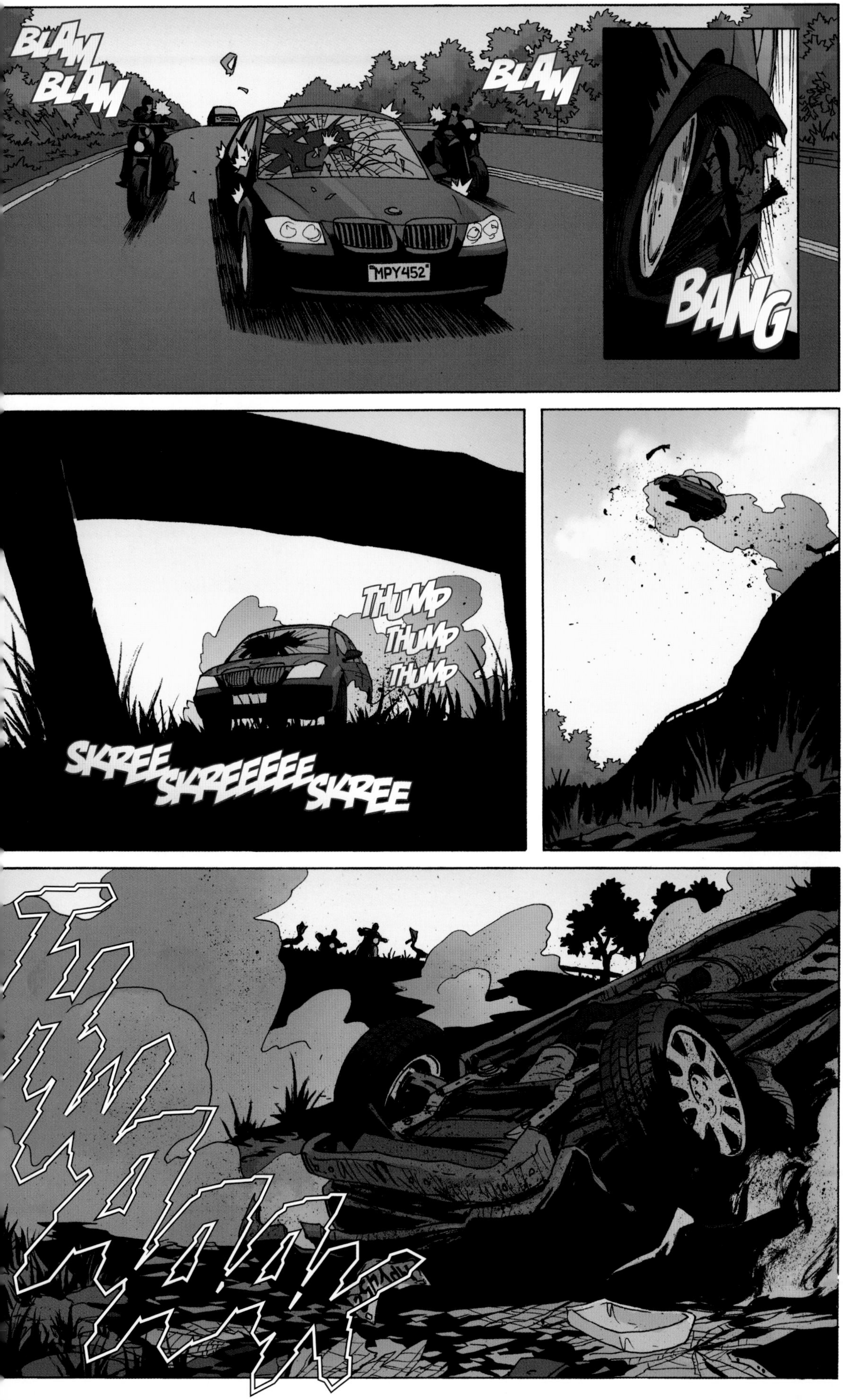
BLAM
BLAM
BLAM
MPY452
BANG
THUMP
THUMP
THUMP
SKREE
SKREEEEEE
SKREE

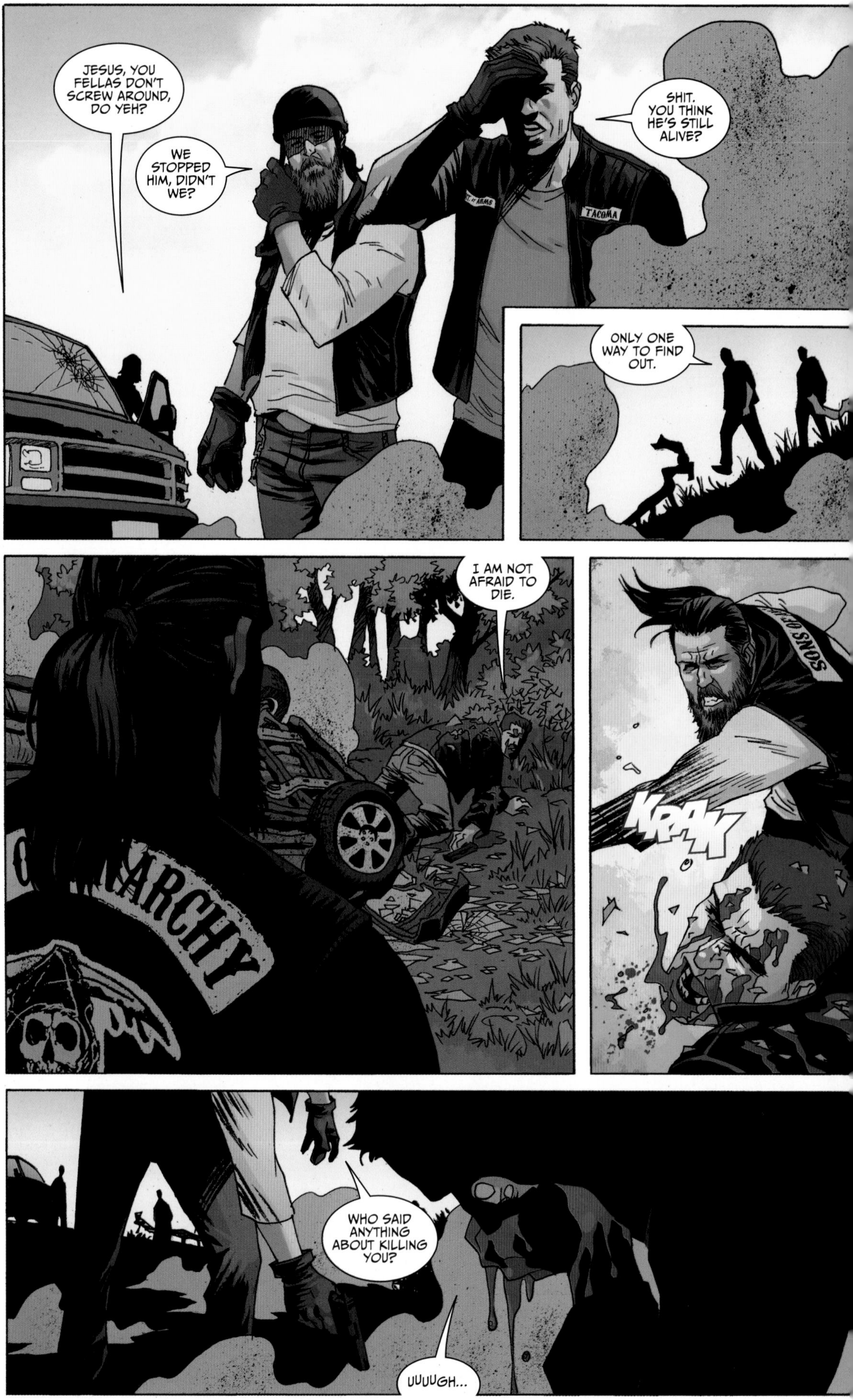
JESUS, YOU FELLAS DON'T SCREW AROUND, DO YEH?
WE STOPPED HIM, DIDN'T WE?
SHIT. YOU THINK HE'S STILL ALIVE?
TACOMA
ONLY ONE WAY TO FIND OUT.
I AM NOT AFRAID TO DIE.
SONS OF ANARCHY
KRAK
WHO SAID ANYTHING ABOUT KILLING YOU?
UUUUGH...

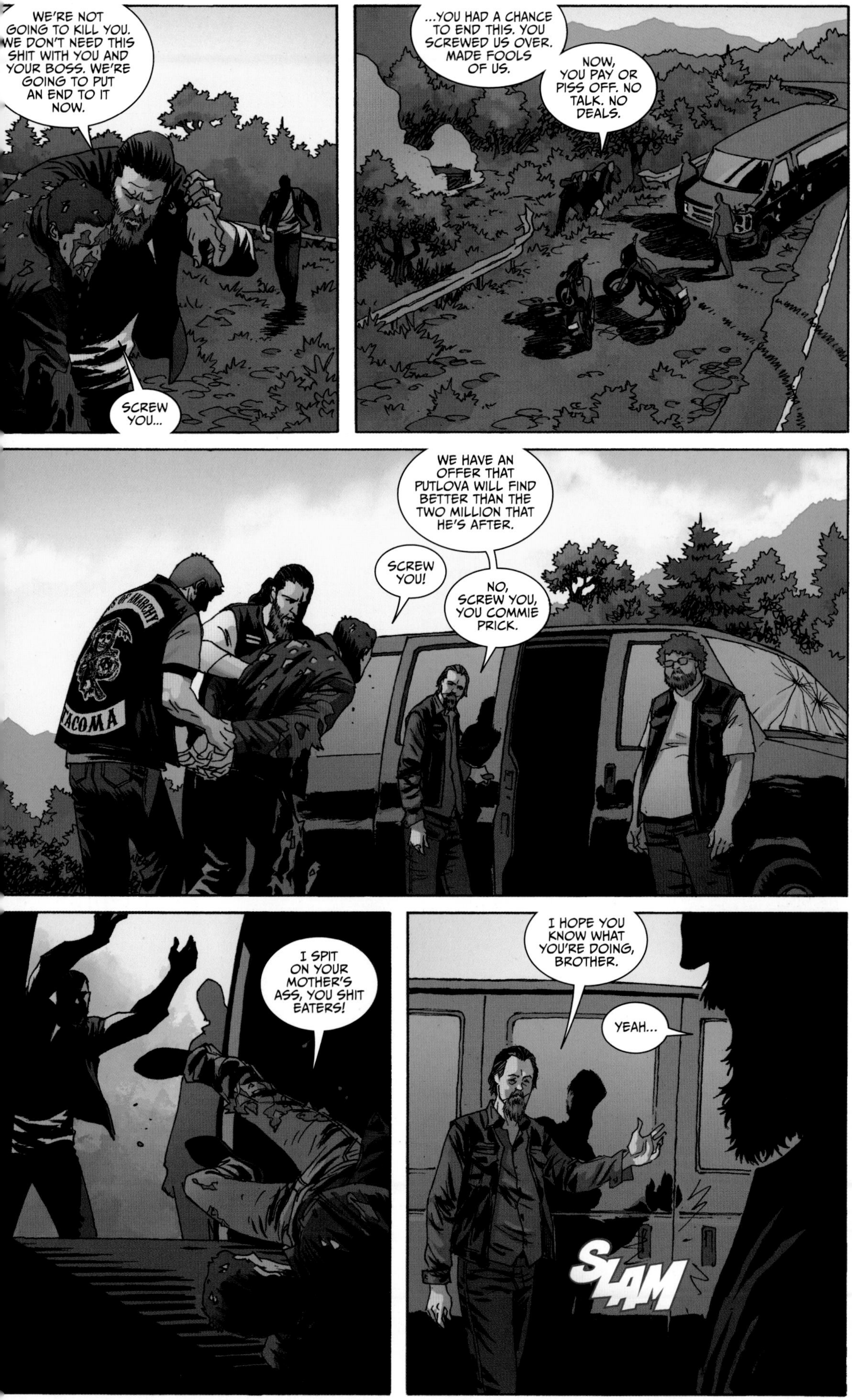
WE'RE NOT GOING TO KILL YOU. WE DON'T NEED THIS SHIT WITH YOU AND YOUR BOSS. WE'RE GOING TO PUT AN END TO IT NOW.
SCREW YOU...
...YOU HAD A CHANCE TO END THIS. YOU SCREWED US OVER. MADE FOOLS OF US.
NOW, YOU PAY OR PISS OFF. NO TALK. NO DEALS.
WE HAVE AN OFFER THAT PUTLOVA WILL FIND BETTER THAN THE TWO MILLION THAT HE'S AFTER.
SCREW YOU!
NO, SCREW YOU, YOU COMMIE PRICK.
TACOMA
I SPIT ON YOUR MOTHER'S ASS, YOU SHIT EATERS!
I HOPE YOU KNOW WHAT YOU'RE DOING, BROTHER.
YEAH...
SLAM

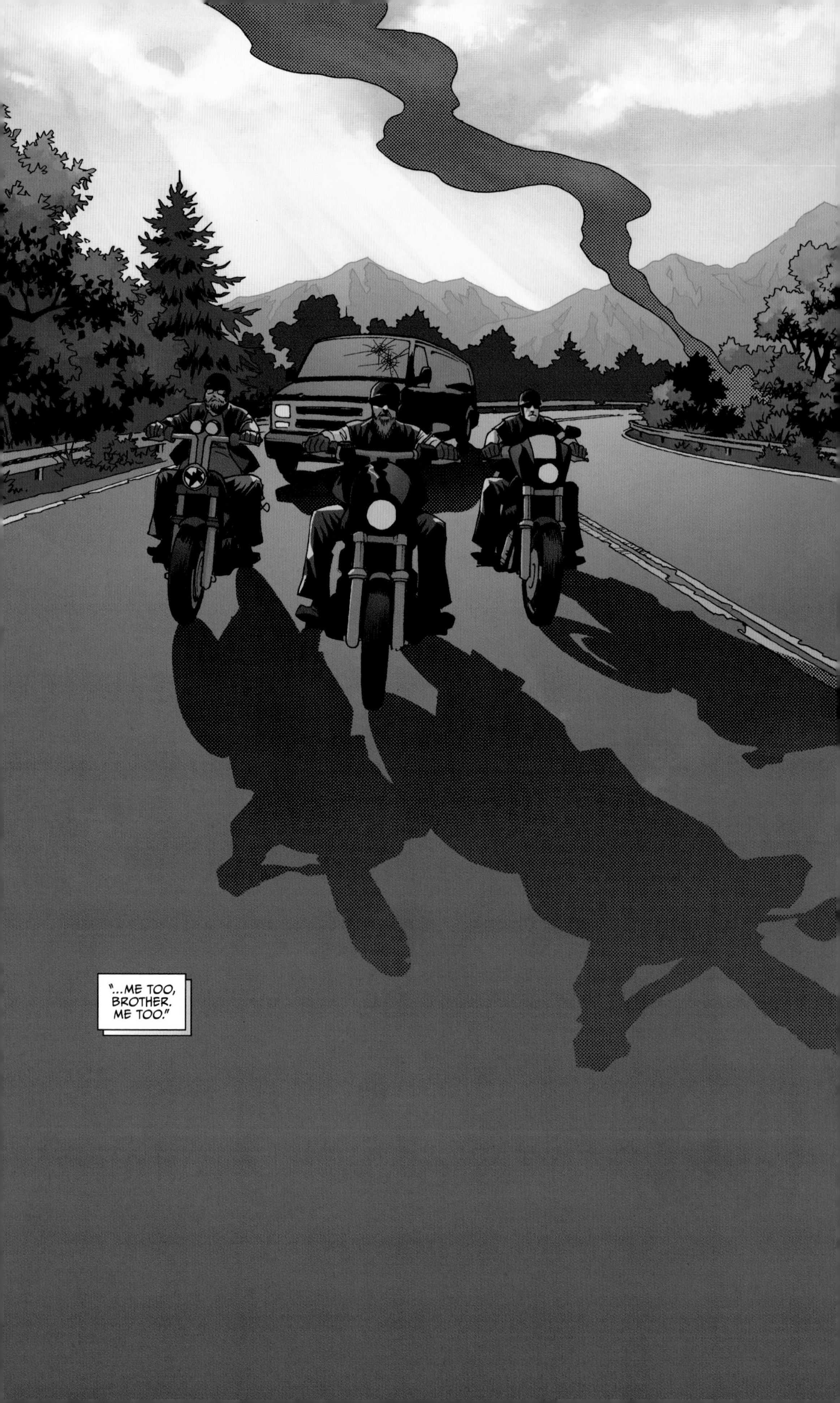
"...ME TOO, BROTHER. ME TOO."

CHAPTER 10

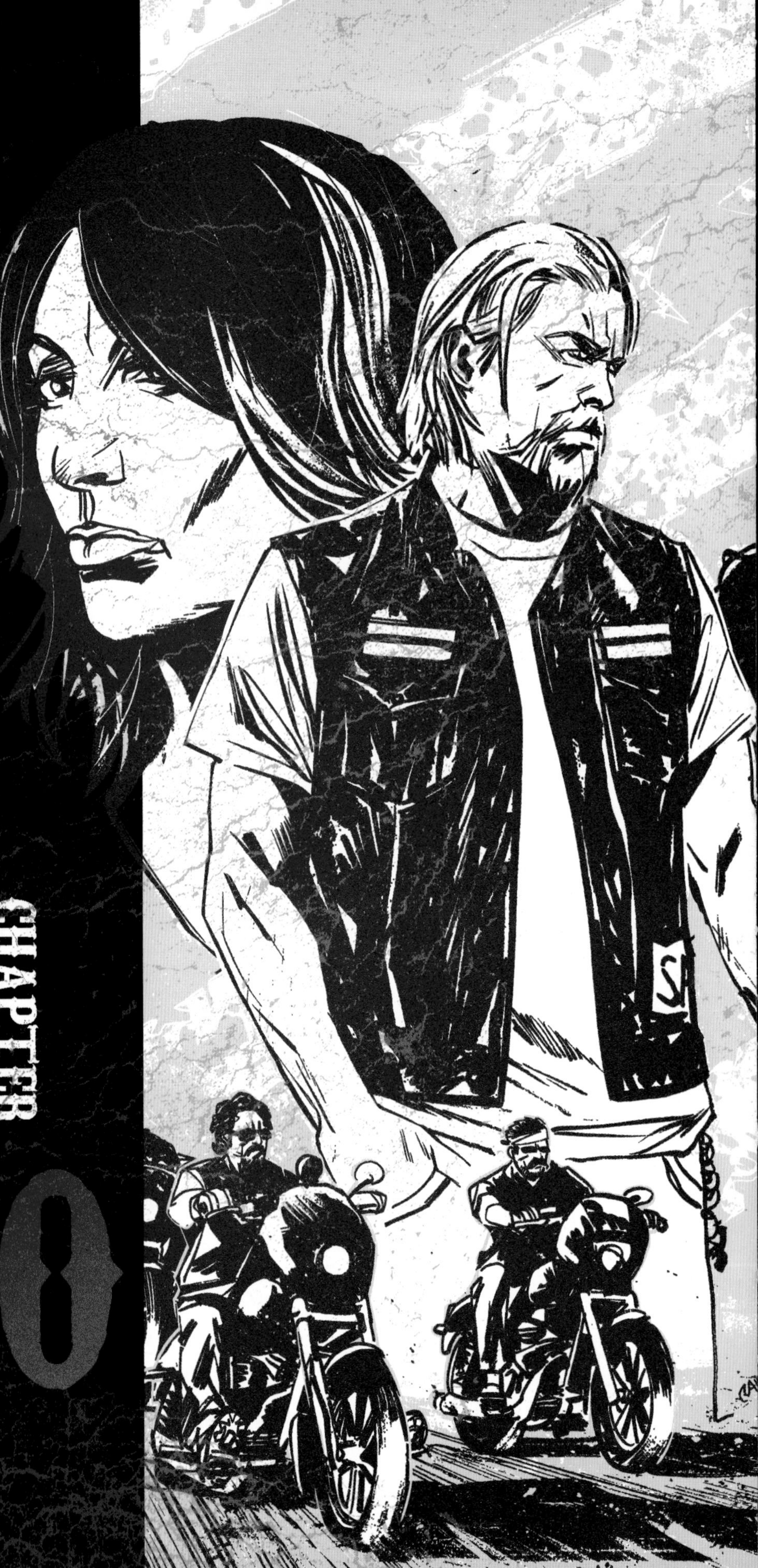

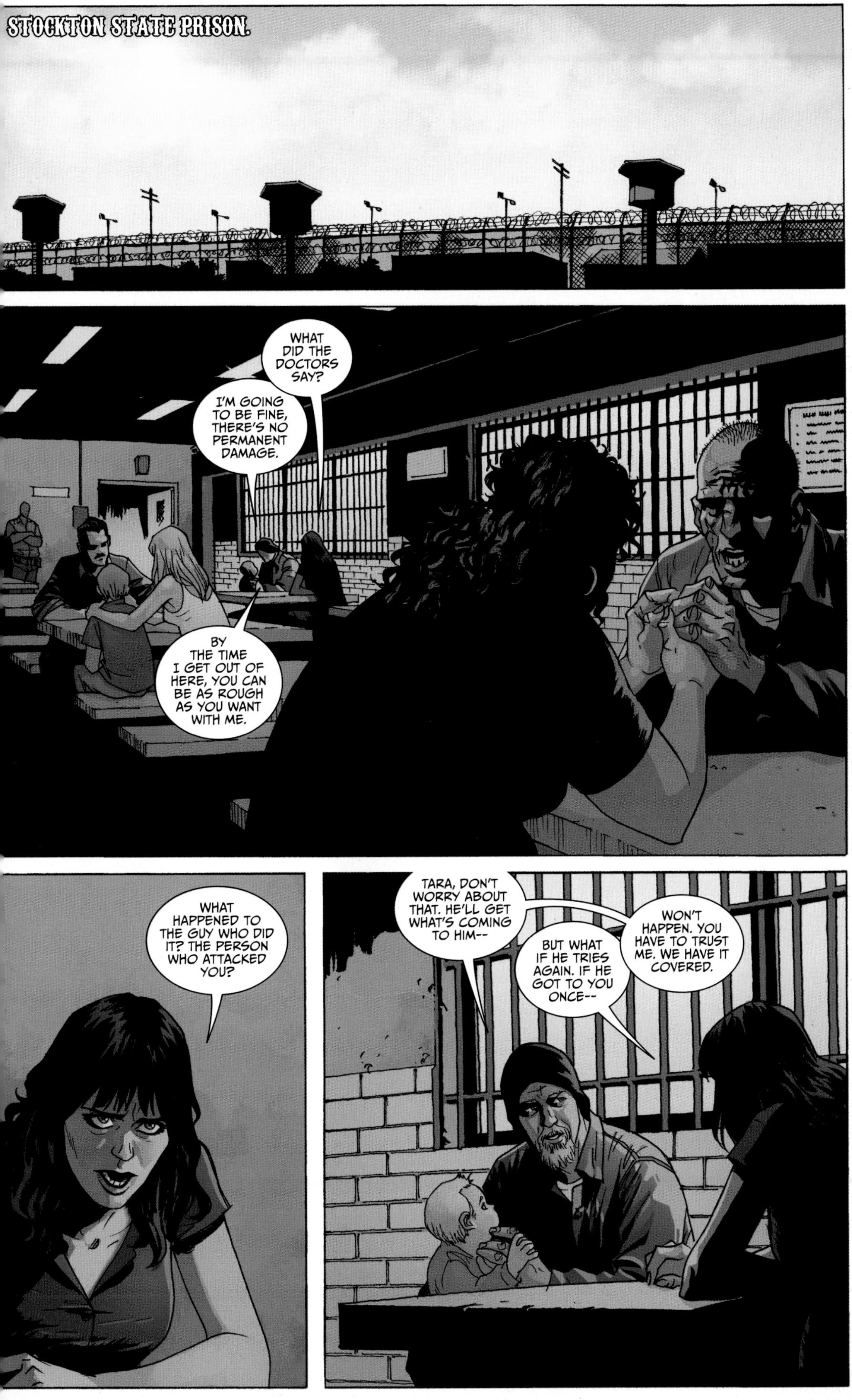
STOCKTON STATE PRISON.
WHAT DID THE DOCTORS SAY?
I'M GOING TO BE FINE, THERE'S NO PERMANENT DAMAGE.
BY THE TIME I GET OUT OF HERE, YOU CAN BE AS ROUGH AS YOU WANT WITH ME.
WHAT HAPPENED TO THE GUY WHO DID IT? THE PERSON WHO ATTACKED YOU?
TARA, DON'T WORRY ABOUT THAT. HE'LL GET WHAT'S COMING TO HIM--
BUT WHAT IF HE TRIES AGAIN. IF HE GOT TO YOU ONCE--
WON'T HAPPEN. YOU HAVE TO TRUST ME. WE HAVE IT COVERED.

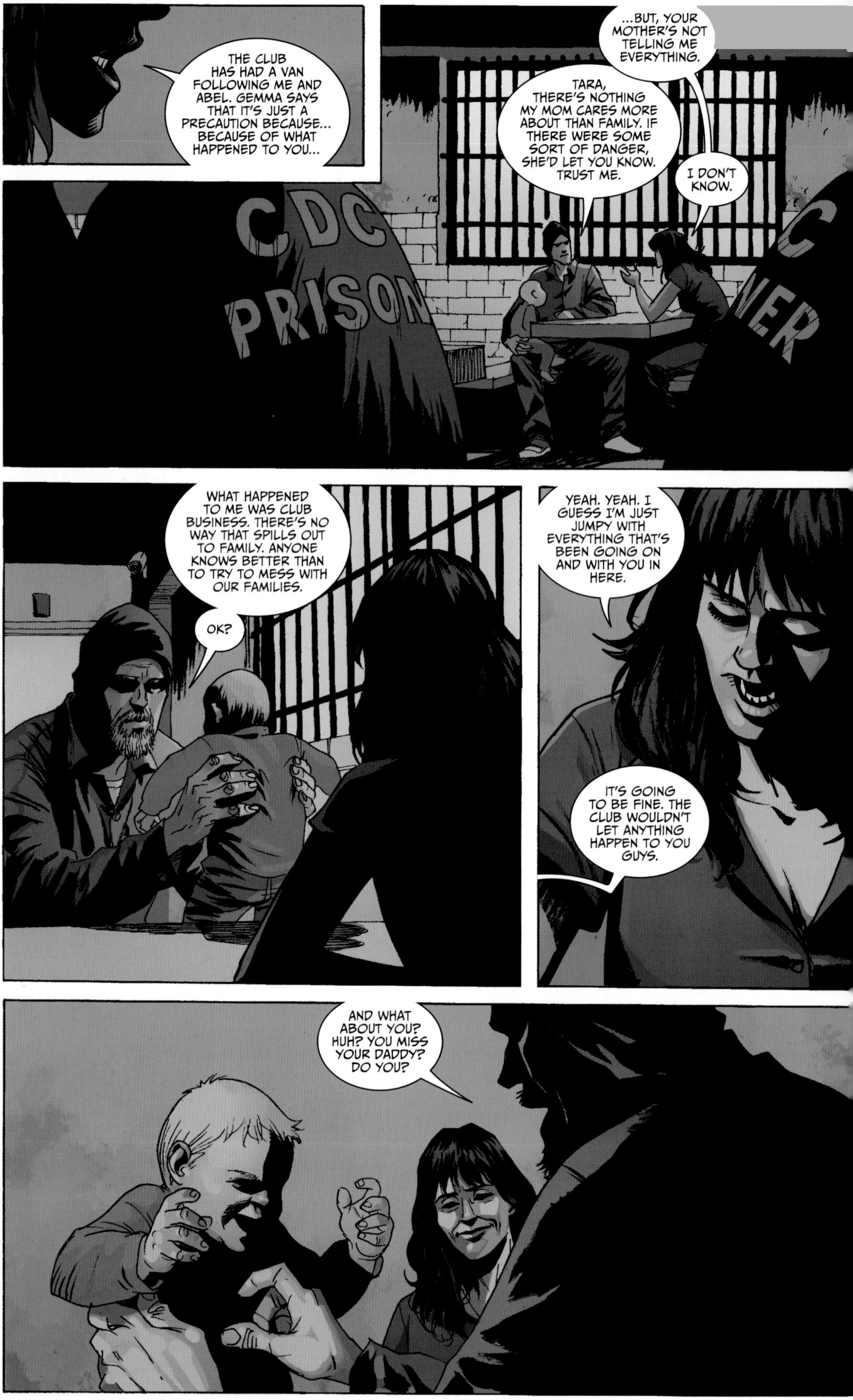
THE CLUB HAS HAD A VAN FOLLOWING ME AND ABEL. GEMMA SAYS THAT IT'S JUST A PRECAUTION BECAUSE... BECAUSE OF WHAT HAPPENED TO YOU...
TARA, THERE'S NOTHING MY MOM CARES MORE ABOUT THAN FAMILY. IF THERE WERE SOME SORT OF DANGER, SHE'D LET YOU KNOW. TRUST ME.
I DON'T KNOW.
...BUT, YOUR MOTHER'S NOT TELLING ME EVERYTHING.
CDC PRISON
WHAT HAPPENED TO ME WAS CLUB BUSINESS. THERE'S NO WAY THAT SPILLS OUT TO FAMILY. ANYONE KNOWS BETTER THAN TO TRY TO MESS WITH OUR FAMILIES.
OK?
YEAH. YEAH. I GUESS I'M JUST JUMPY WITH EVERYTHING THAT'S BEEN GOING ON AND WITH YOU IN HERE.
IT'S GOING TO BE FINE. THE CLUB WOULDN'T LET ANYTHING HAPPEN TO YOU GUYS.
AND WHAT ABOUT YOU? HUH? YOU MISS YOUR DADDY? DO YOU?

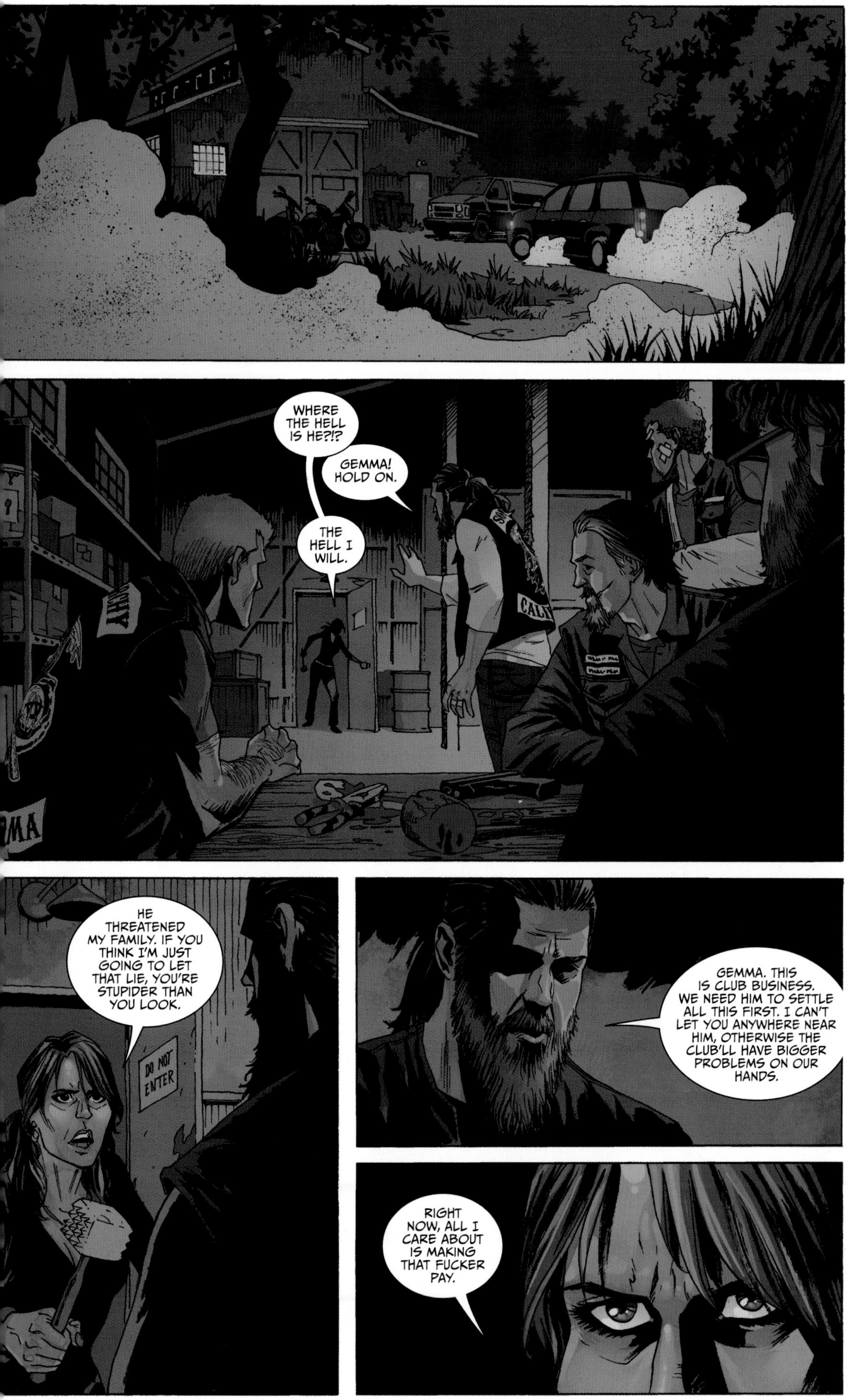
WHERE THE HELL IS HE?!?
GEMMA! HOLD ON.
THE HELL I WILL.
HE THREATENED MY FAMILY. IF YOU THINK I'M JUST GOING TO LET THAT LIE, YOU'RE STUPIDER THAN YOU LOOK.
DO NOT ENTER
GEMMA. THIS IS CLUB BUSINESS. WE NEED HIM TO SETTLE ALL THIS FIRST. I CAN'T LET YOU ANYWHERE NEAR HIM, OTHERWISE THE CLUB'LL HAVE BIGGER PROBLEMS ON OUR HANDS.
RIGHT NOW, ALL I CARE ABOUT IS MAKING THAT FUCKER PAY.

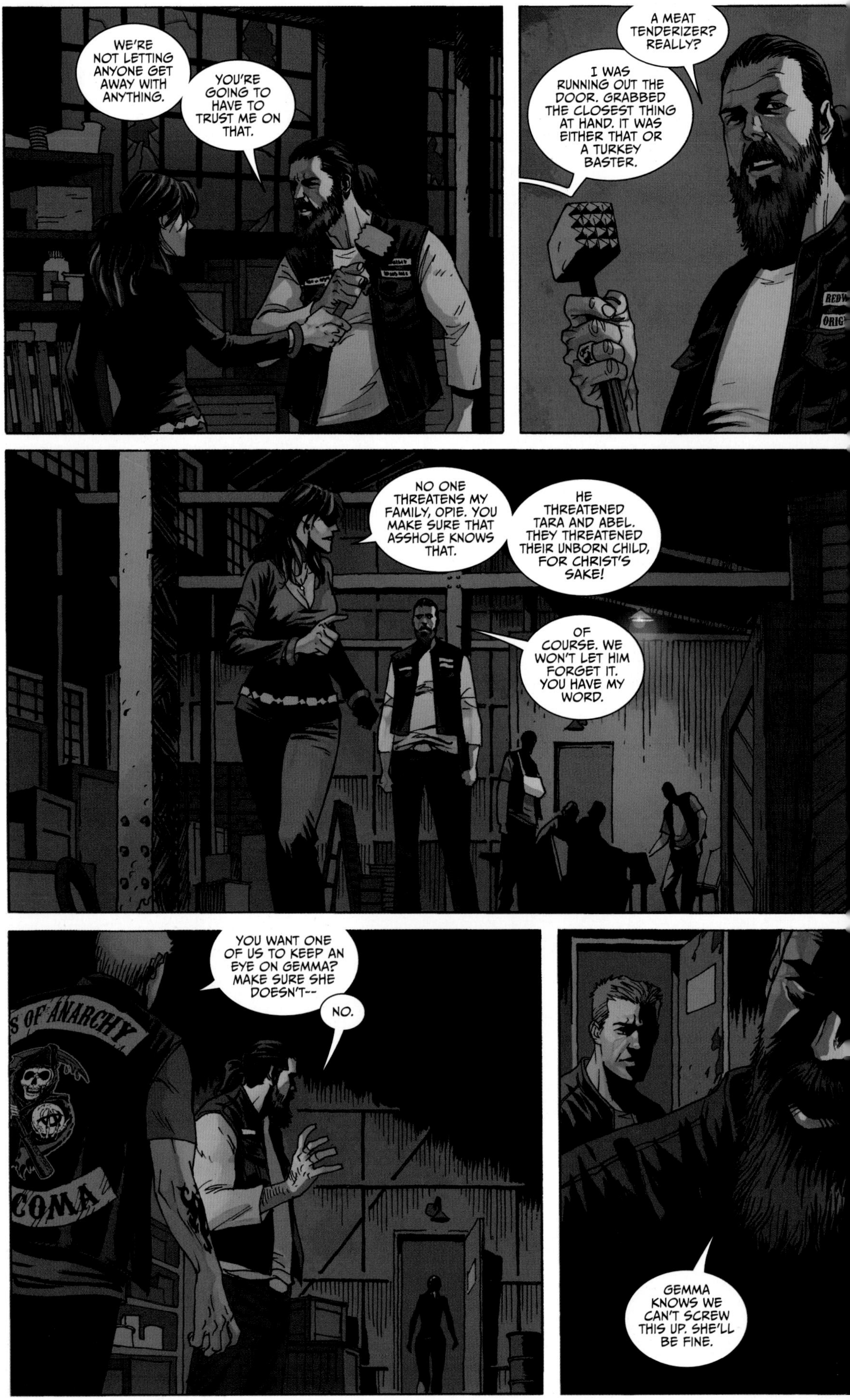
WE'RE NOT LETTING ANYONE GET AWAY WITH ANYTHING.
YOU'RE GOING TO HAVE TO TRUST ME ON THAT.
A MEAT TENDERIZER? REALLY?
I WAS RUNNING OUT THE DOOR. GRABBED THE CLOSEST THING AT HAND. IT WAS EITHER THAT OR A TURKEY BASTER.
NO ONE THREATENS MY FAMILY, OPIE. YOU MAKE SURE THAT ASSHOLE KNOWS THAT.
HE THREATENED TARA AND ABEL. THEY THREATENED THEIR UNBORN CHILD, FOR CHRIST'S SAKE!
OF COURSE. WE WON'T LET HIM FORGET IT. YOU HAVE MY WORD.
YOU WANT ONE OF US TO KEEP AN EYE ON GEMMA? MAKE SURE SHE DOESN'T--
NO.
GEMMA KNOWS WE CAN'T SCREW THIS UP. SHE'LL BE FINE.

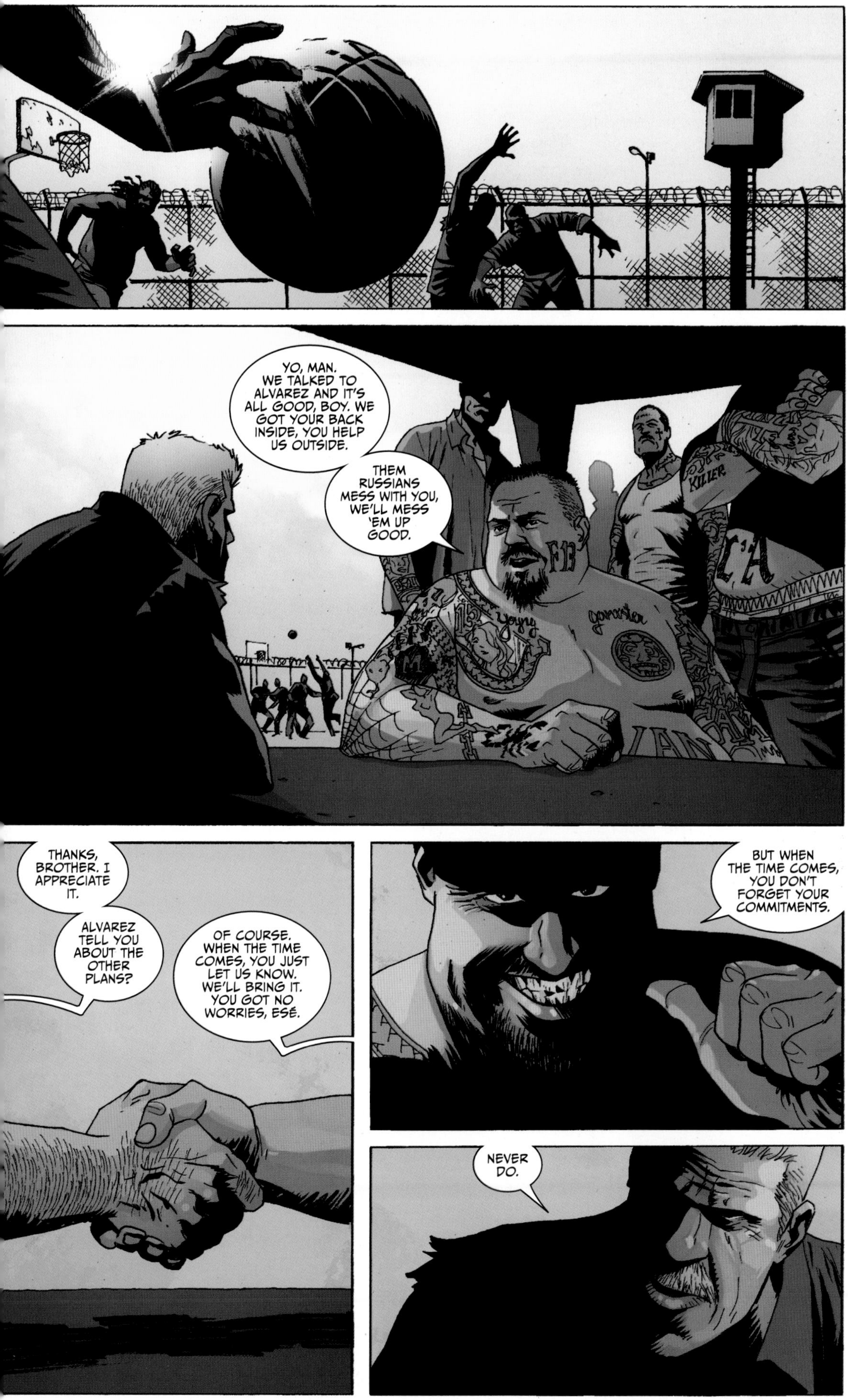

YO, MAN. WE TALKED TO ALVAREZ AND IT'S ALL GOOD, BOY. WE GOT YOUR BACK INSIDE, YOU HELP US OUTSIDE.
THEM RUSSIANS MESS WITH YOU, WE'LL MESS 'EM UP GOOD.
KILLER
THANKS, BROTHER. I APPRECIATE IT.
ALVAREZ TELL YOU ABOUT THE OTHER PLANS?
OF COURSE. WHEN THE TIME COMES, YOU JUST LET US KNOW. WE'LL BRING IT. YOU GOT NO WORRIES, ESÉ.
BUT WHEN THE TIME COMES, YOU DON'T FORGET YOUR COMMITMENTS.
NEVER DO.

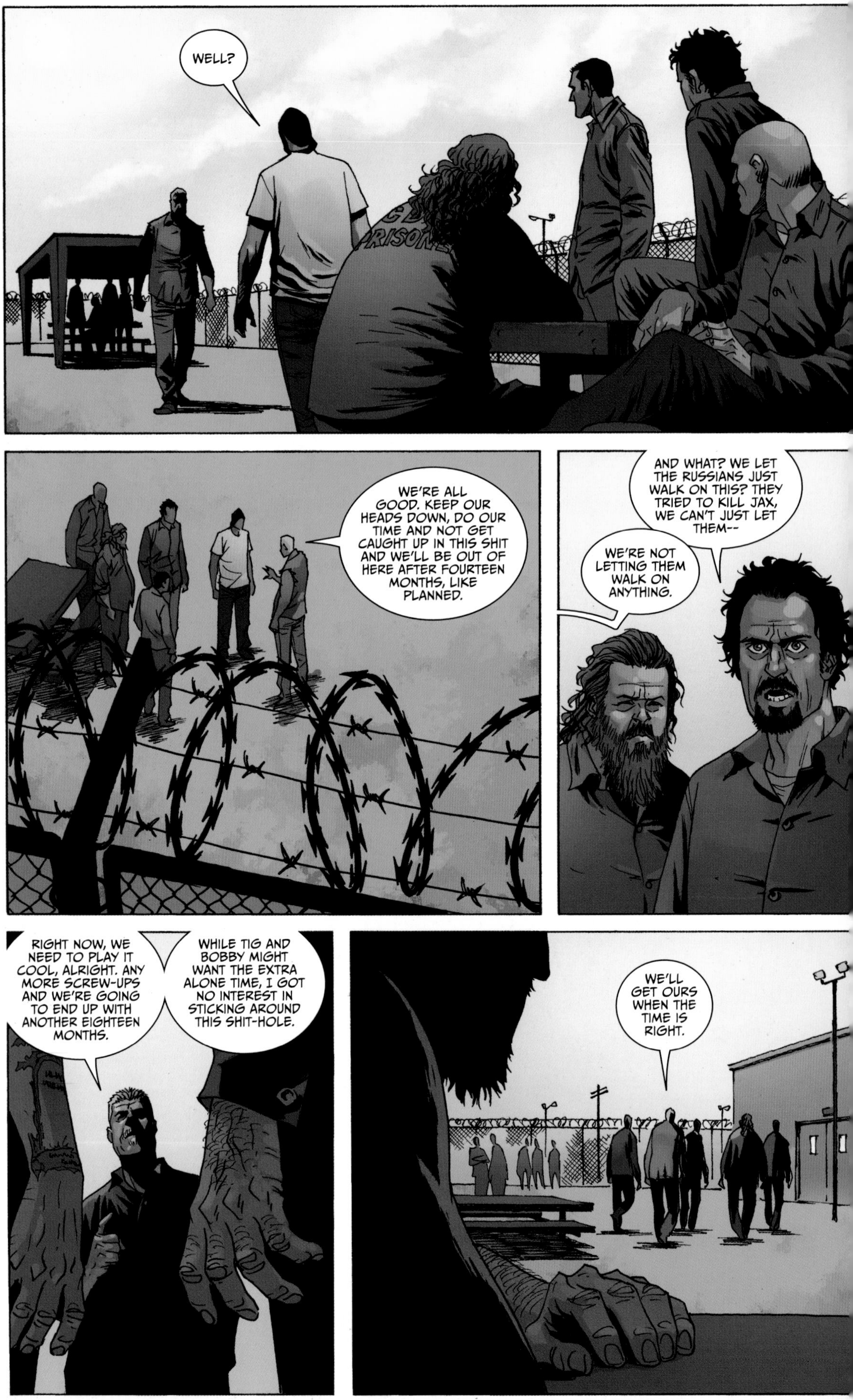
WELL?
WE'RE ALL GOOD. KEEP OUR HEADS DOWN, DO OUR TIME AND NOT GET CAUGHT UP IN THIS SHIT AND WE'LL BE OUT OF HERE AFTER FOURTEEN MONTHS, LIKE PLANNED.
AND WHAT? WE LET THE RUSSIANS JUST WALK ON THIS? THEY TRIED TO KILL JAX, WE CAN'T JUST LET THEM--
WE'RE NOT LETTING THEM WALK ON ANYTHING.
RIGHT NOW, WE NEED TO PLAY IT COOL, ALRIGHT. ANY MORE SCREW-UPS AND WE'RE GOING TO END UP WITH ANOTHER EIGHTEEN MONTHS.
WHILE TIG AND BOBBY MIGHT WANT THE EXTRA ALONE TIME, I GOT NO INTEREST IN STICKING AROUND THIS SHIT-HOLE.
WE'LL GET OURS WHEN THE TIME IS RIGHT.

SUBTLE. LETTING HIM SET THE MEET FOR THE SAME PLACE WE SCREWED HIM OVER LAST TIME.

I DON'T THINK THERE IS A RUSSIAN WORD FOR "SUBTLE."

PLEASE TELL ME THAT MY TWO MILLION DOLLARS IS IN THE VAN.

OTHERWISE, WHY IS IT YOU WANT TO MEET IF NOT TO GIVE ME WHAT IS MINE?

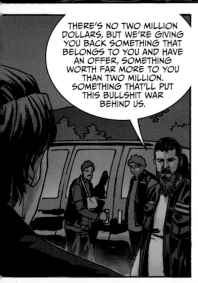

THERE'S NO TWO MILLION DOLLARS, BUT WE'RE GIVING YOU BACK SOMETHING THAT BELONGS TO YOU AND HAVE AN OFFER, SOMETHING WORTH FAR MORE TO YOU THAN TWO MILLION. SOMETHING THAT'LL PUT THIS BULLSHIT WAR BEHIND US.

WHAT THE HELL IS THIS?!?

YOU'VE HAD YOUR MEN STALKING OUR VP'S FAMILY. YOU ATTACKED AND NEARLY KILLED HIM. YOU'RE LUCKY YOU'RE GETTING HIM BACK AT ALL.

FUCK THESE PIECES OF SHIT! PUTLOVA! DO NOT TRUST THEM, THEY ARE FUCKING ANIMALS!

I WILL FIND YOU! I WILL FIND YOU AND I WILL KILL YOU AND I WILL PISS IN YOUR EYES!

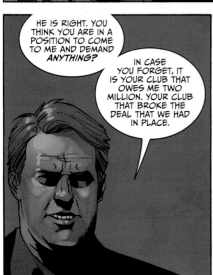

HE IS RIGHT. YOU THINK YOU ARE IN A POSITION TO COME TO ME AND DEMAND *ANYTHING?*

IN CASE YOU FORGET, IT IS YOUR CLUB THAT OWES ME TWO MILLION. YOUR CLUB THAT BROKE THE DEAL THAT WE HAD IN PLACE.

AND NOW YOU BRING BACK ONE OF MY MEN, NEARLY BEAT TO DEATH... THE OTHER DEAD, I ASSUME? AND NOW YOU WANT TO MAKE A NEW DEAL.

YOU THINK ME A FOOL?

YOUR MAN WHO DIED, HE OPENED FIRE ON US. CAN'T FAULT US FOR SHOOTING BACK.

THIS OTHER ONE, HE'S LUCKY HE MADE IT BACK. WE COULD HAVE BURIED HIM, BUT WE DIDN'T.

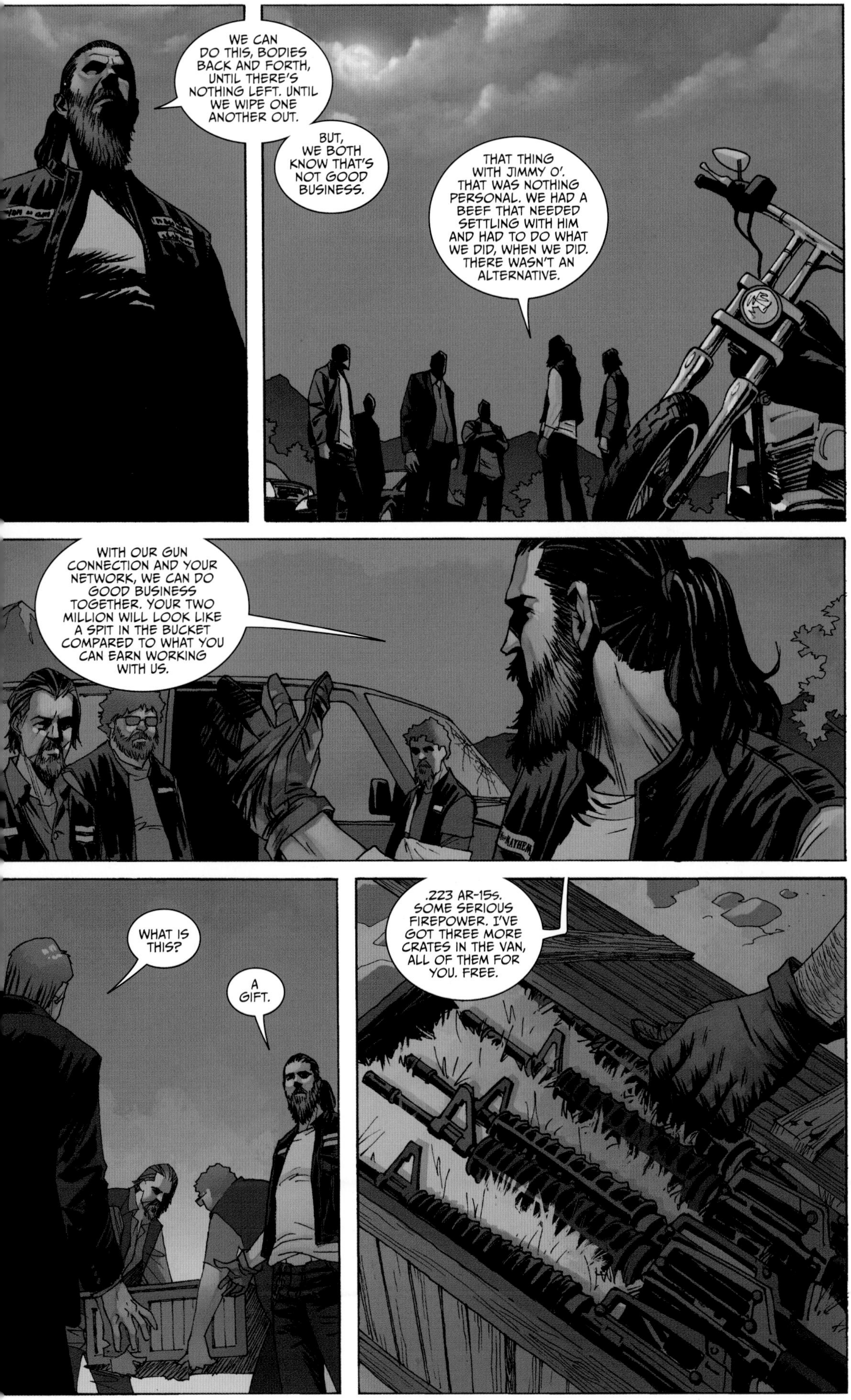
WE CAN DO THIS, BODIES BACK AND FORTH, UNTIL THERE'S NOTHING LEFT. UNTIL WE WIPE ONE ANOTHER OUT.
BUT, WE BOTH KNOW THAT'S NOT GOOD BUSINESS.
THAT THING WITH JIMMY O'. THAT WAS NOTHING PERSONAL. WE HAD A BEEF THAT NEEDED SETTLING WITH HIM AND HAD TO DO WHAT WE DID, WHEN WE DID. THERE WASN'T AN ALTERNATIVE.
WITH OUR GUN CONNECTION AND YOUR NETWORK, WE CAN DO GOOD BUSINESS TOGETHER. YOUR TWO MILLION WILL LOOK LIKE A SPIT IN THE BUCKET COMPARED TO WHAT YOU CAN EARN WORKING WITH US.
WHAT IS THIS?
A GIFT.
.223 AR-15s. SOME SERIOUS FIREPOWER. I'VE GOT THREE MORE CRATES IN THE VAN, ALL OF THEM FOR YOU. FREE.

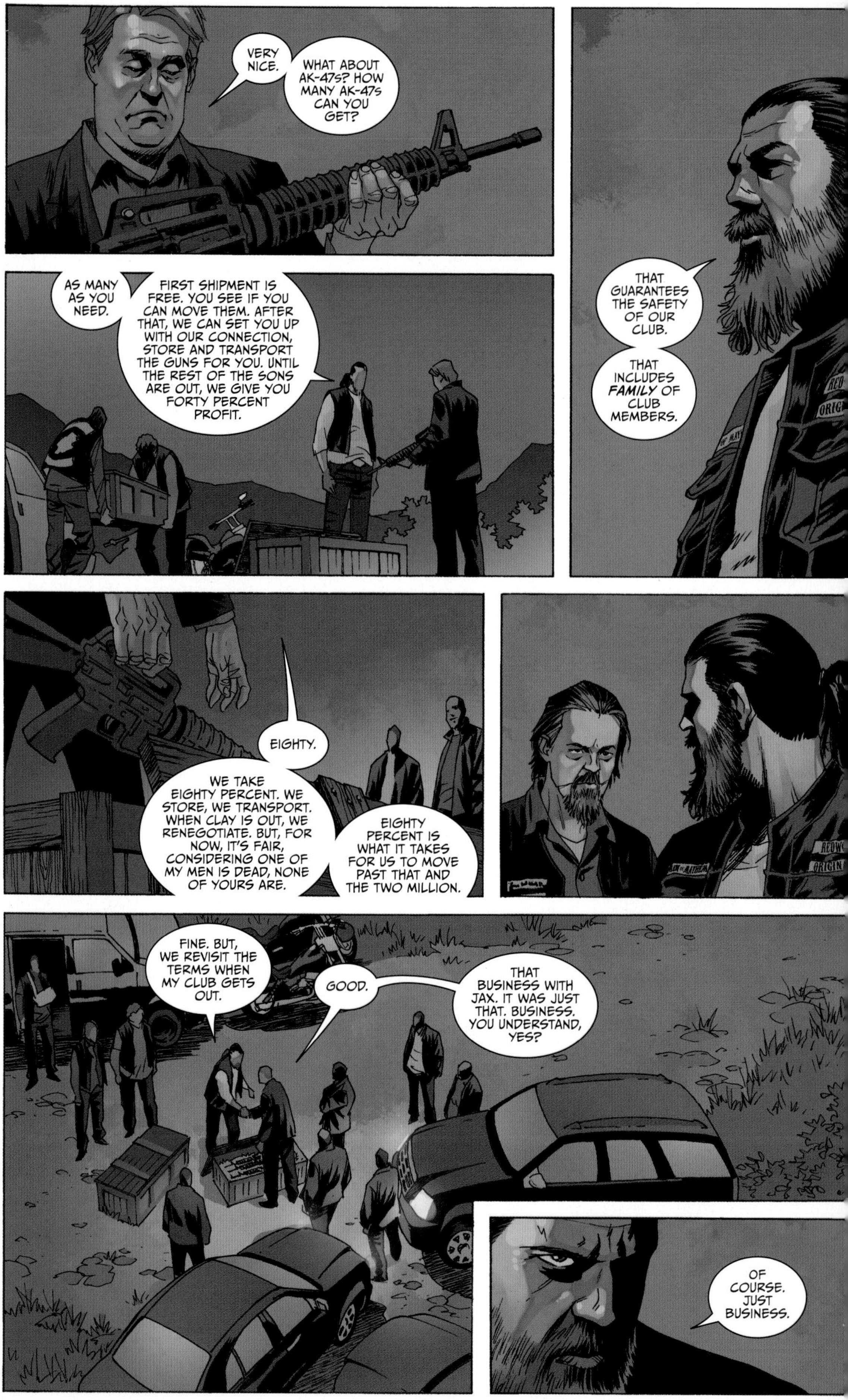
VERY NICE.
WHAT ABOUT AK-47s? HOW MANY AK-47s CAN YOU GET?
AS MANY AS YOU NEED.
FIRST SHIPMENT IS FREE. YOU SEE IF YOU CAN MOVE THEM. AFTER THAT, WE CAN SET YOU UP WITH OUR CONNECTION, STORE AND TRANSPORT THE GUNS FOR YOU. UNTIL THE REST OF THE SONS ARE OUT, WE GIVE YOU FORTY PERCENT PROFIT.
THAT GUARANTEES THE SAFETY OF OUR CLUB.
THAT INCLUDES *FAMILY* OF CLUB MEMBERS.
EIGHTY.
WE TAKE EIGHTY PERCENT. WE STORE, WE TRANSPORT. WHEN CLAY IS OUT, WE RENEGOTIATE. BUT, FOR NOW, IT'S FAIR, CONSIDERING ONE OF MY MEN IS DEAD, NONE OF YOURS ARE.
EIGHTY PERCENT IS WHAT IT TAKES FOR US TO MOVE PAST THAT AND THE TWO MILLION.
FINE. BUT, WE REVISIT THE TERMS WHEN MY CLUB GETS OUT.
GOOD.
THAT BUSINESS WITH JAX. IT WAS JUST THAT. BUSINESS. YOU UNDERSTAND, YES?
OF COURSE. JUST BUSINESS.

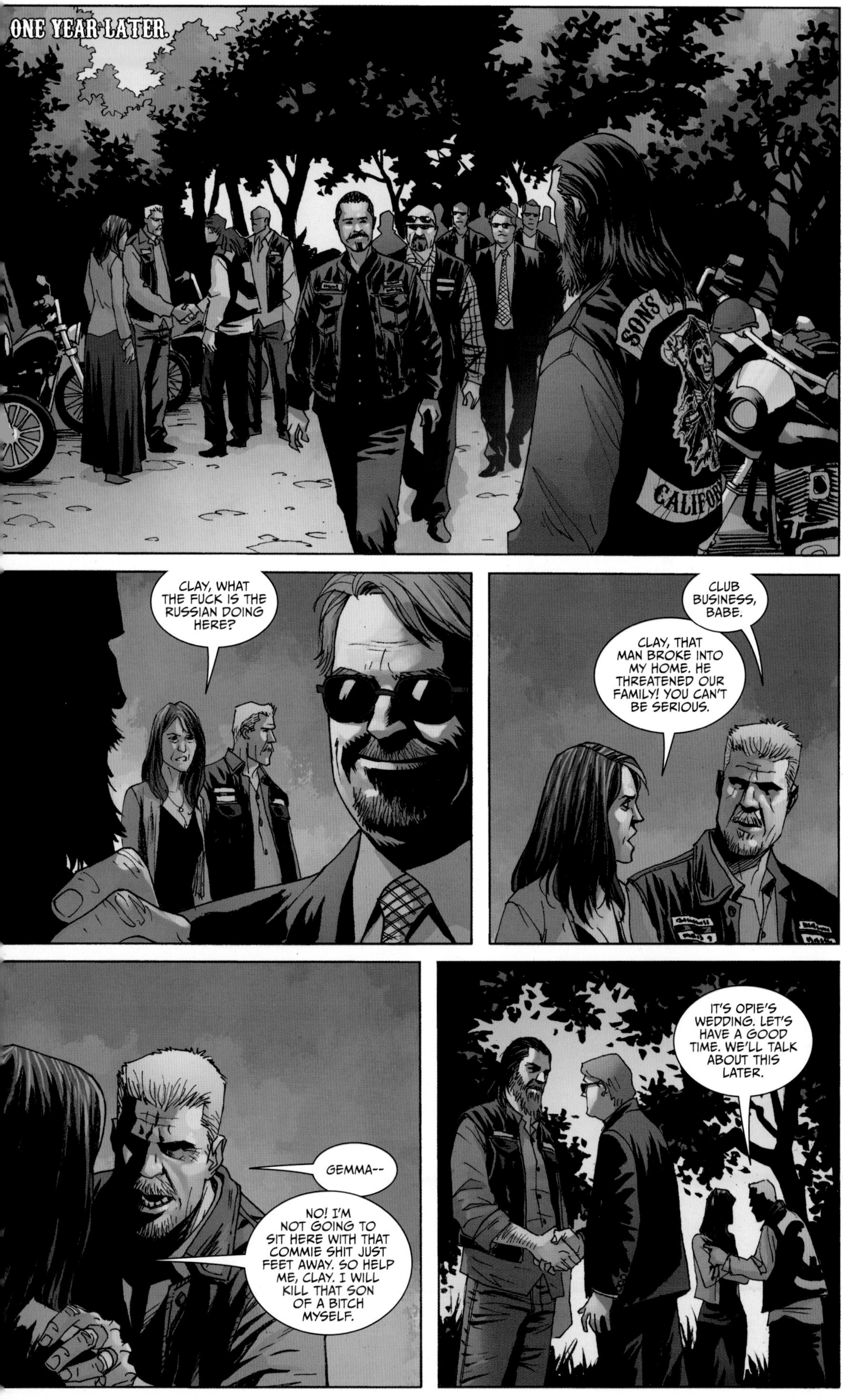
ONE YEAR LATER.
CLAY, WHAT THE FUCK IS THE RUSSIAN DOING HERE?
CLUB BUSINESS, BABE.
CLAY, THAT MAN BROKE INTO MY HOME. HE THREATENED OUR FAMILY! YOU CAN'T BE SERIOUS.
GEMMA--
NO! I'M NOT GOING TO SIT HERE WITH THAT COMMIE SHIT JUST FEET AWAY. SO HELP ME, CLAY. I WILL KILL THAT SON OF A BITCH MYSELF.
IT'S OPIE'S WEDDING. LET'S HAVE A GOOD TIME. WE'LL TALK ABOUT THIS LATER.

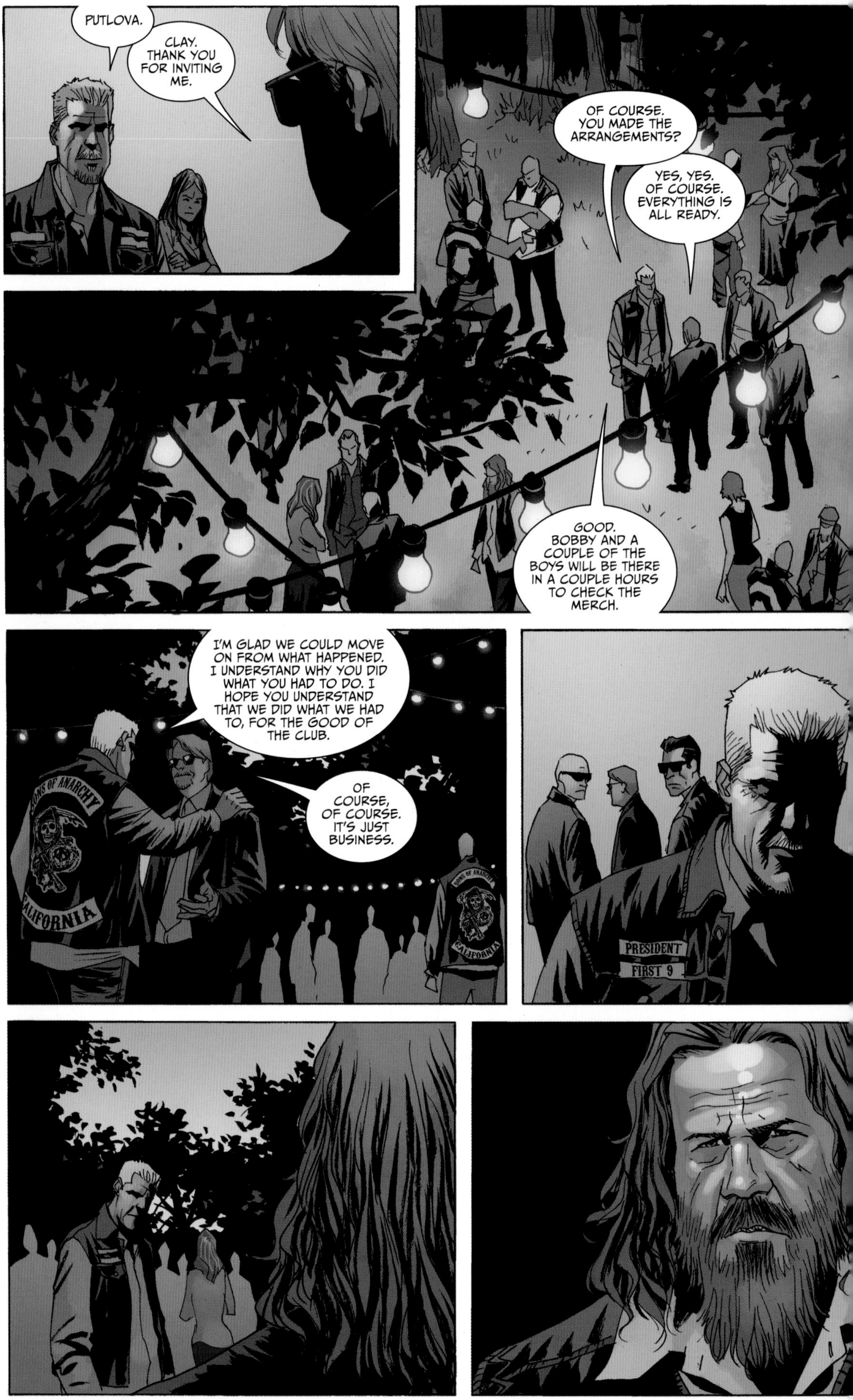
PUTLOVA.
CLAY. THANK YOU FOR INVITING ME.
OF COURSE. YOU MADE THE ARRANGEMENTS?
YES, YES. OF COURSE. EVERYTHING IS ALL READY.
GOOD. BOBBY AND A COUPLE OF THE BOYS WILL BE THERE IN A COUPLE HOURS TO CHECK THE MERCH.
I'M GLAD WE COULD MOVE ON FROM WHAT HAPPENED. I UNDERSTAND WHY YOU DID WHAT YOU HAD TO DO. I HOPE YOU UNDERSTAND THAT WE DID WHAT WE HAD TO, FOR THE GOOD OF THE CLUB.
OF COURSE, OF COURSE. IT'S JUST BUSINESS.
SONS OF ANARCHY
CALIFORNIA
SONS OF ANARCHY
CALIFORNIA
PRESIDENT
FIRST 9

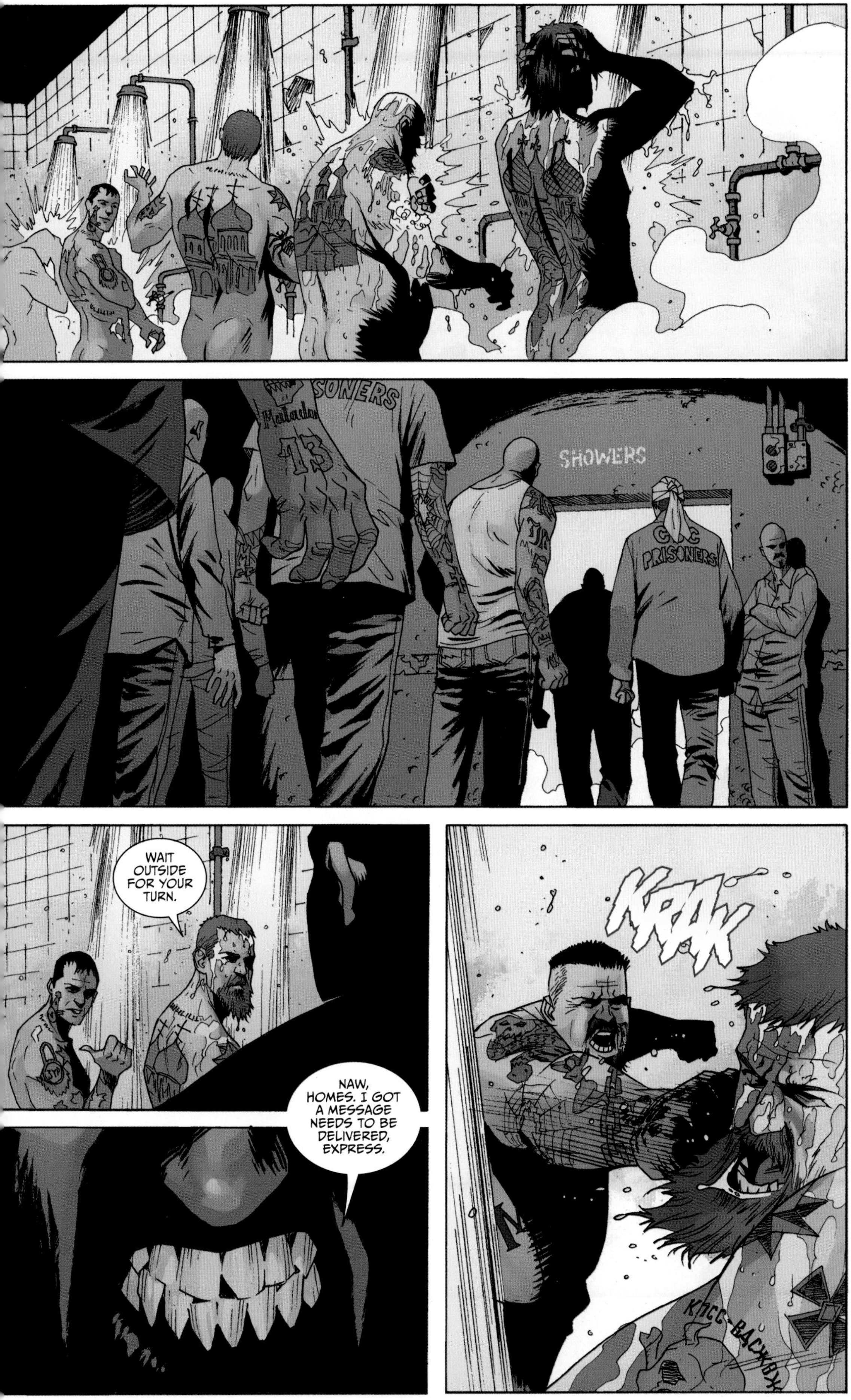

SONERS
SHOWERS
C C PRISONERS
WAIT OUTSIDE FOR YOUR TURN.
NAW, HOMES. I GOT A MESSAGE NEEDS TO BE DELIVERED, EXPRESS.
KRAK

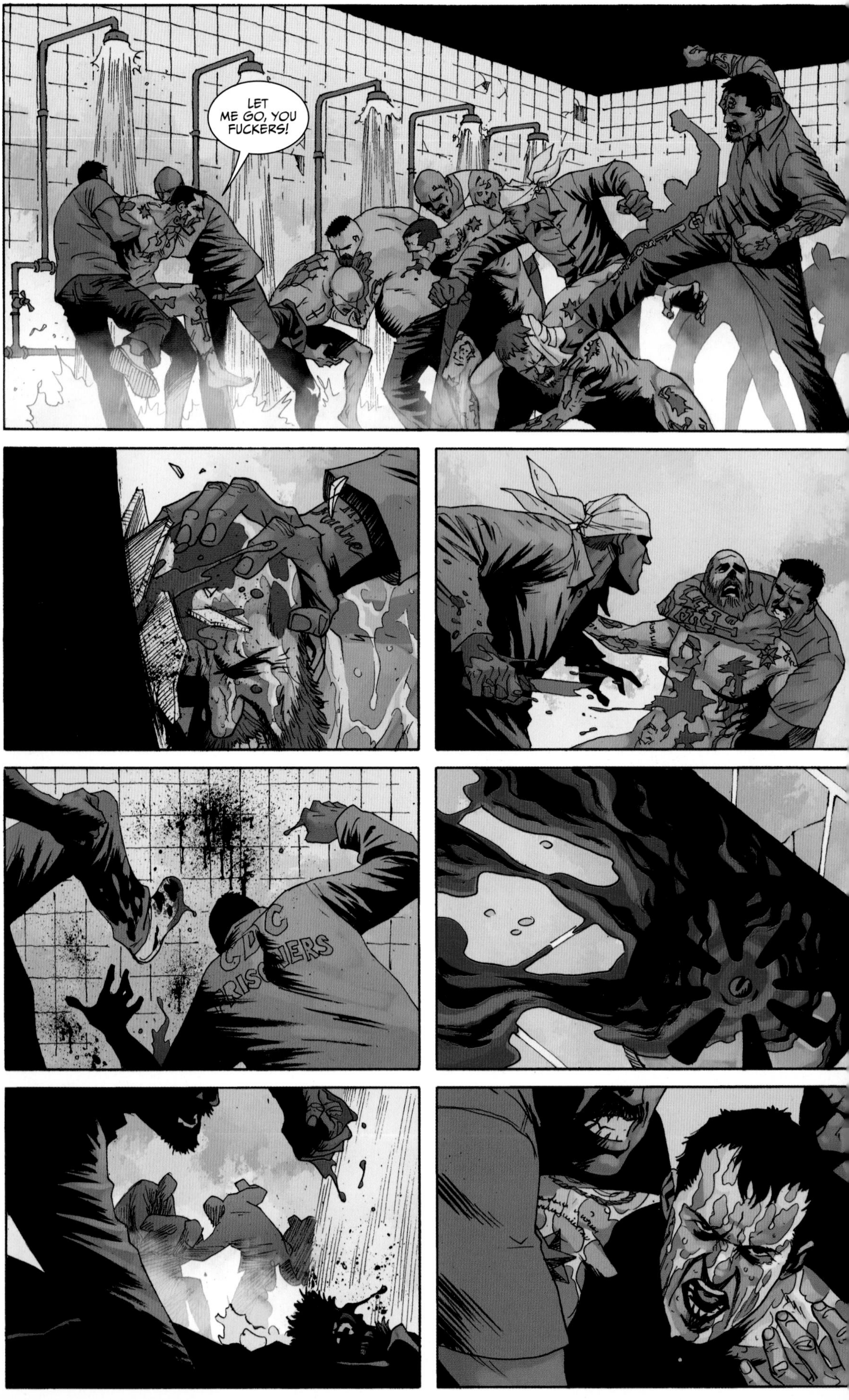
LET ME GO, YOU FUCKERS!

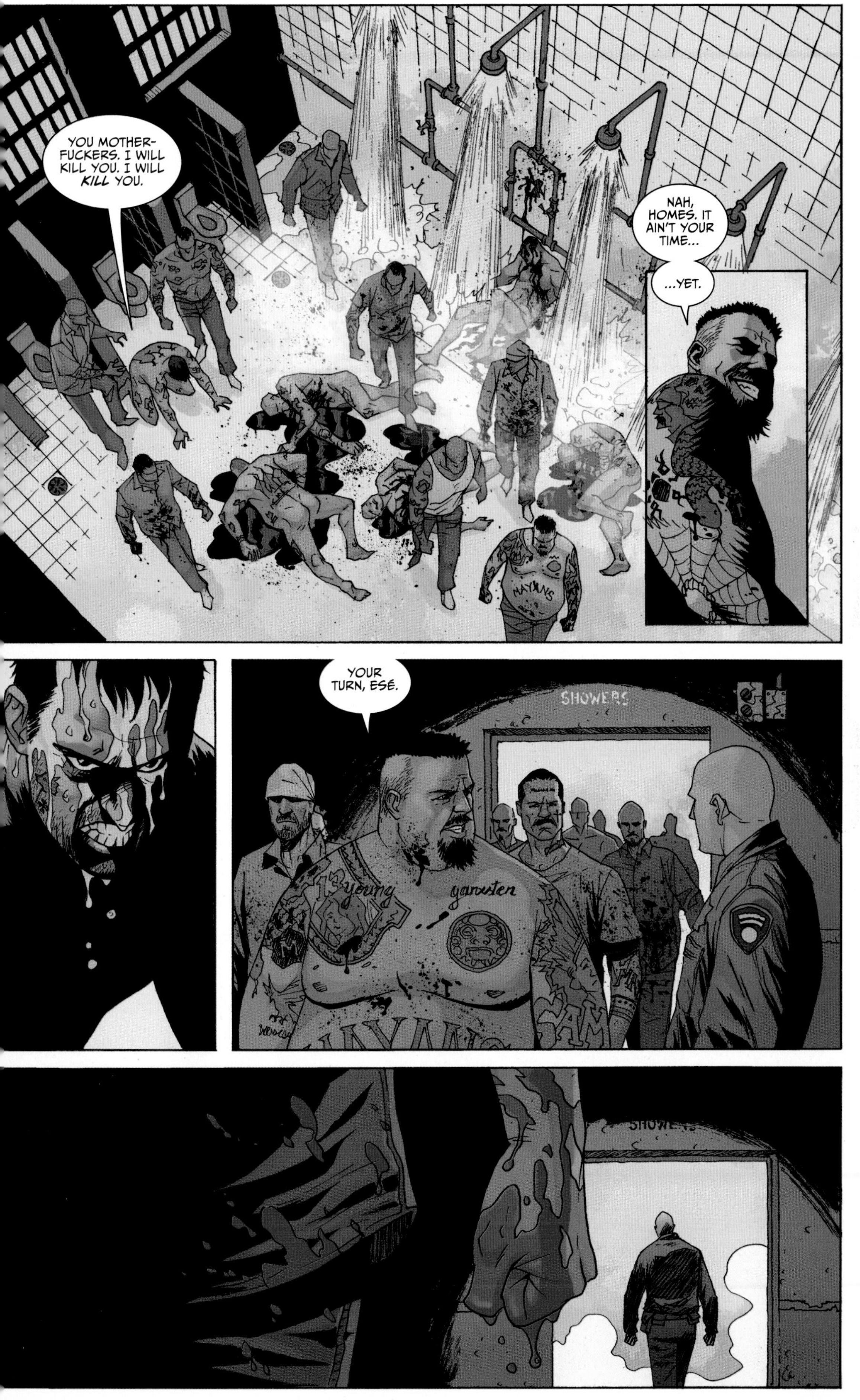

YOU MOTHER-FUCKERS. I WILL KILL YOU. I WILL *KILL* YOU.
NAH, HOMES. IT AIN'T YOUR TIME...
...YET.
YOUR TURN, ESÉ.
SHOWERS

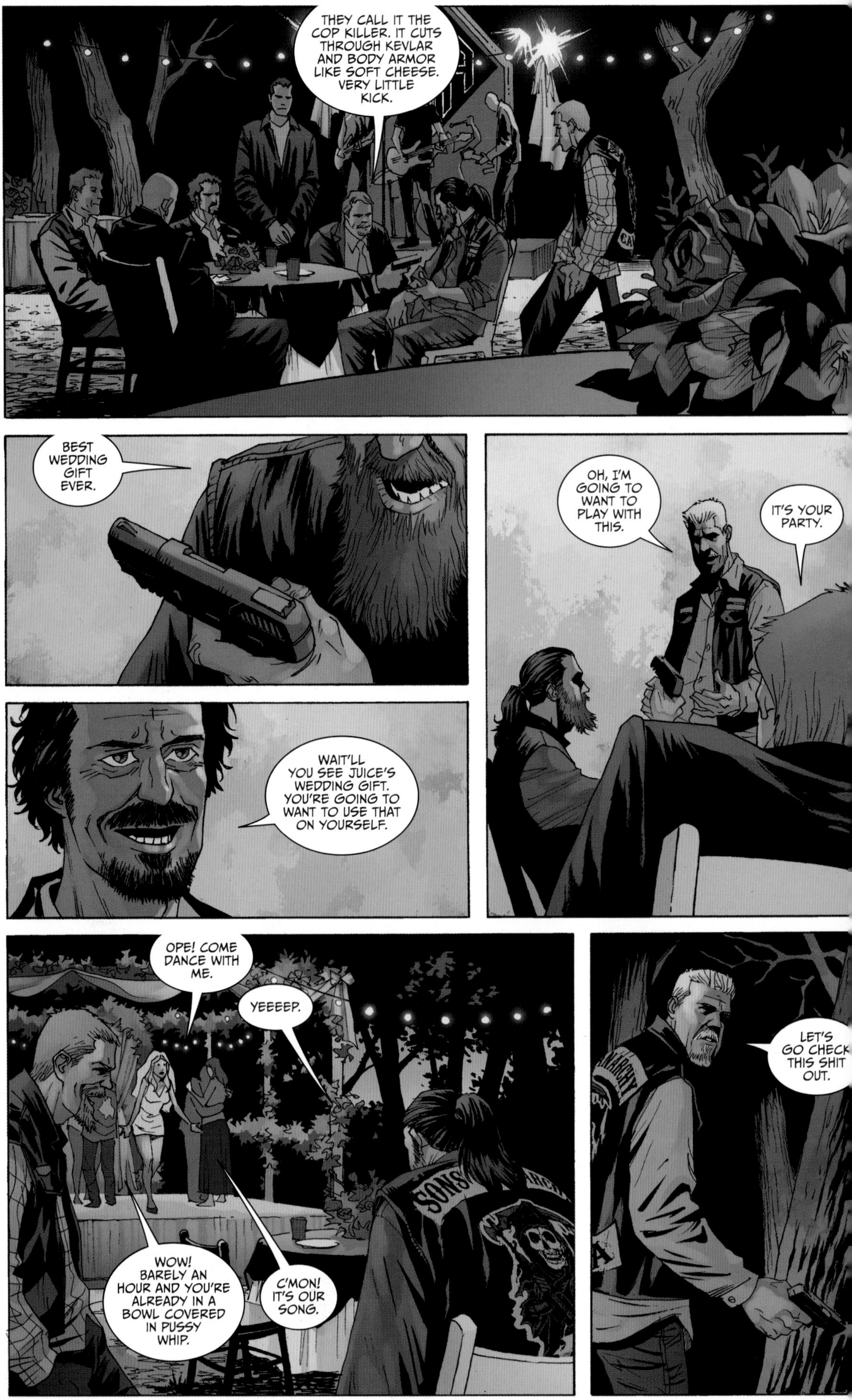

THEY CALL IT THE COP KILLER. IT CUTS THROUGH KEVLAR AND BODY ARMOR LIKE SOFT CHEESE. VERY LITTLE KICK.
BEST WEDDING GIFT EVER.
OH, I'M GOING TO WANT TO PLAY WITH THIS.
IT'S YOUR PARTY.
WAIT'LL YOU SEE JUICE'S WEDDING GIFT. YOU'RE GOING TO WANT TO USE THAT ON YOURSELF.
OPE! COME DANCE WITH ME.
YEEEEP.
WOW! BARELY AN HOUR AND YOU'RE ALREADY IN A BOWL COVERED IN PUSSY WHIP.
C'MON! IT'S OUR SONG.
LET'S GO CHECK THIS SHIT OUT.

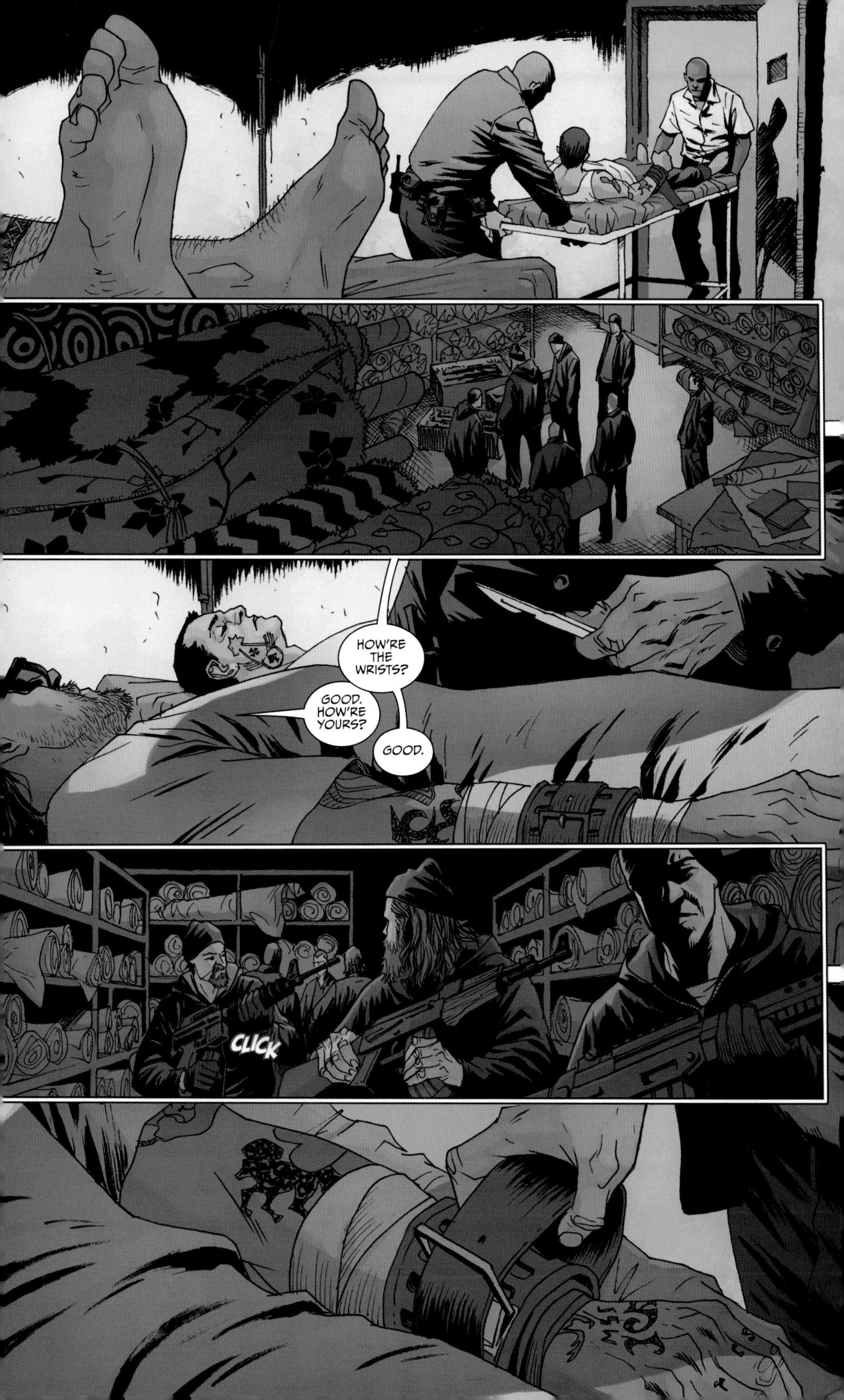
HOW'RE THE WRISTS?
GOOD. HOW'RE YOURS?
GOOD.
CLICK

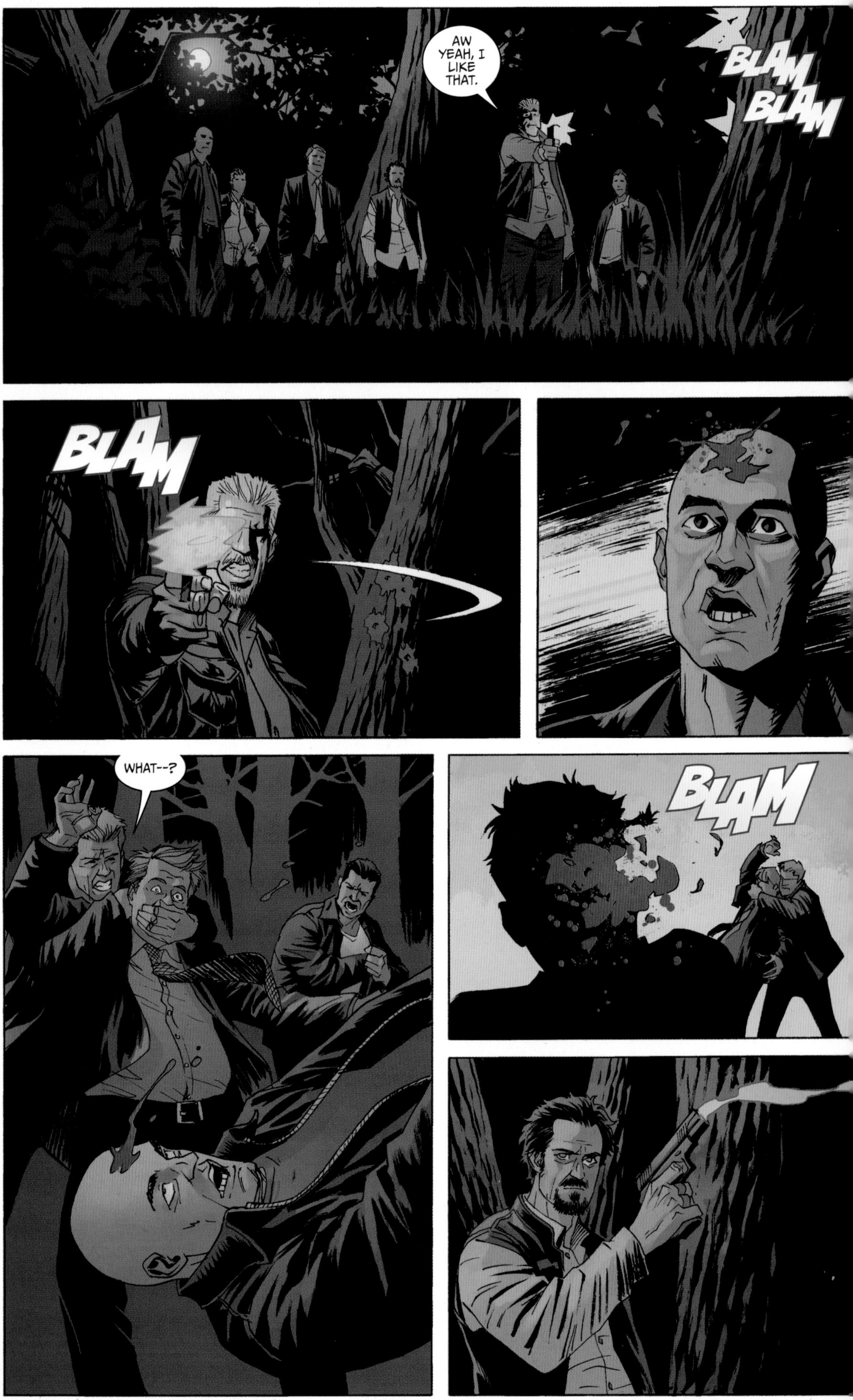
AW YEAH, I LIKE THAT.
BLAM BLAM
BLAM
WHAT--?
BLAM

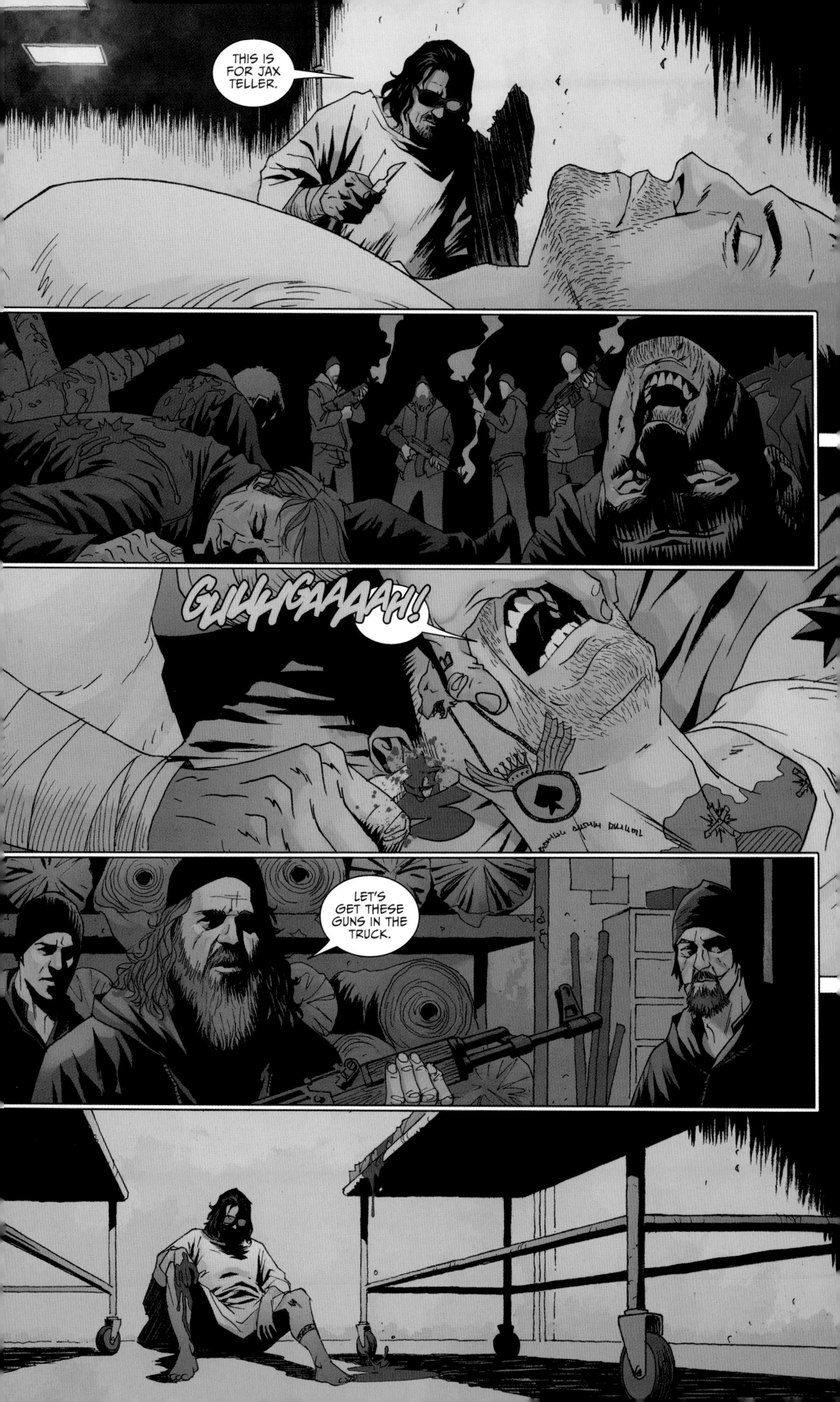
THIS IS FOR JAX TELLER.
GULLLGAAAAAH!
LET'S GET THESE GUNS IN THE TRUCK.

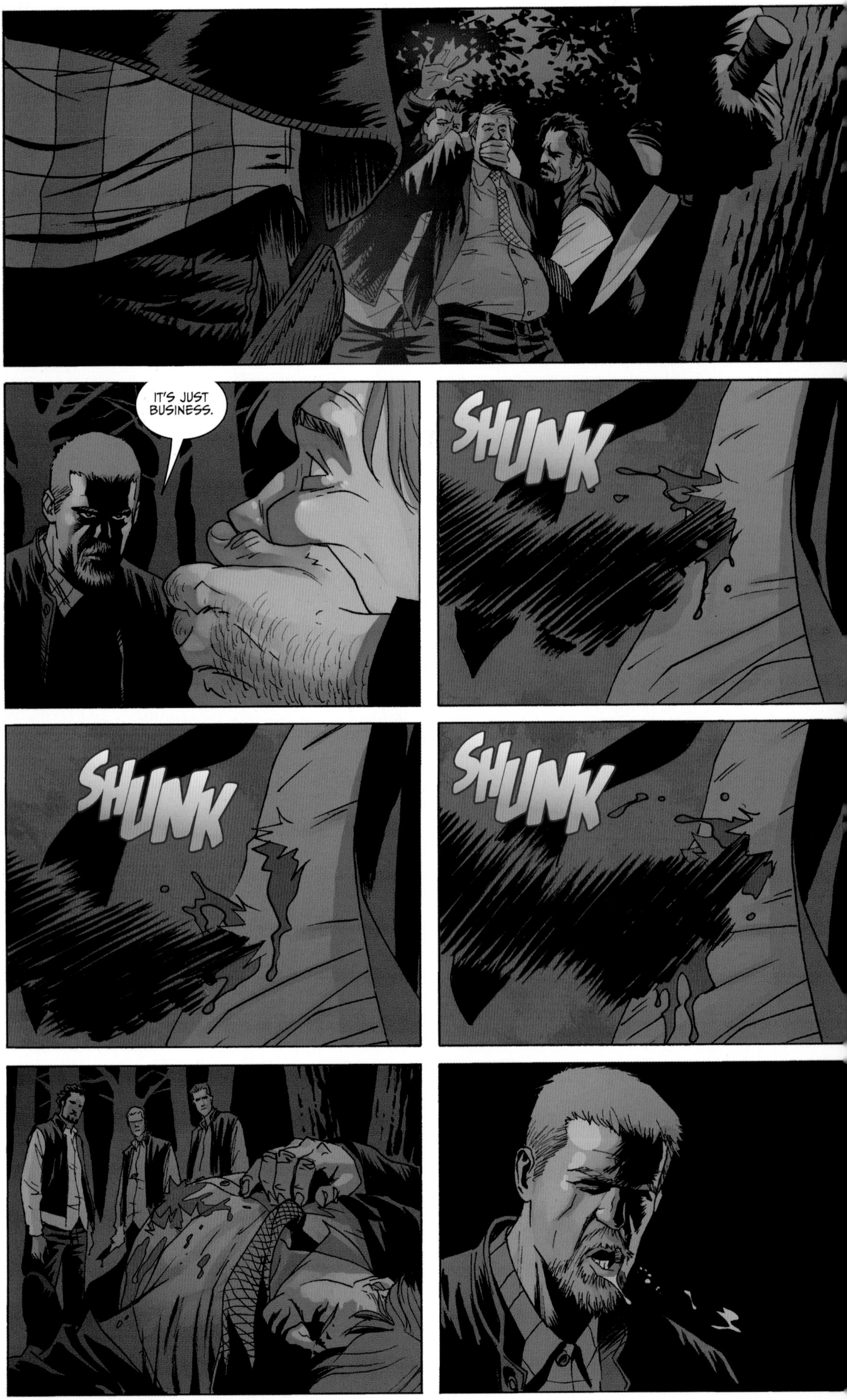
IT'S JUST BUSINESS.
SHUNK
SHUNK
SHUNK

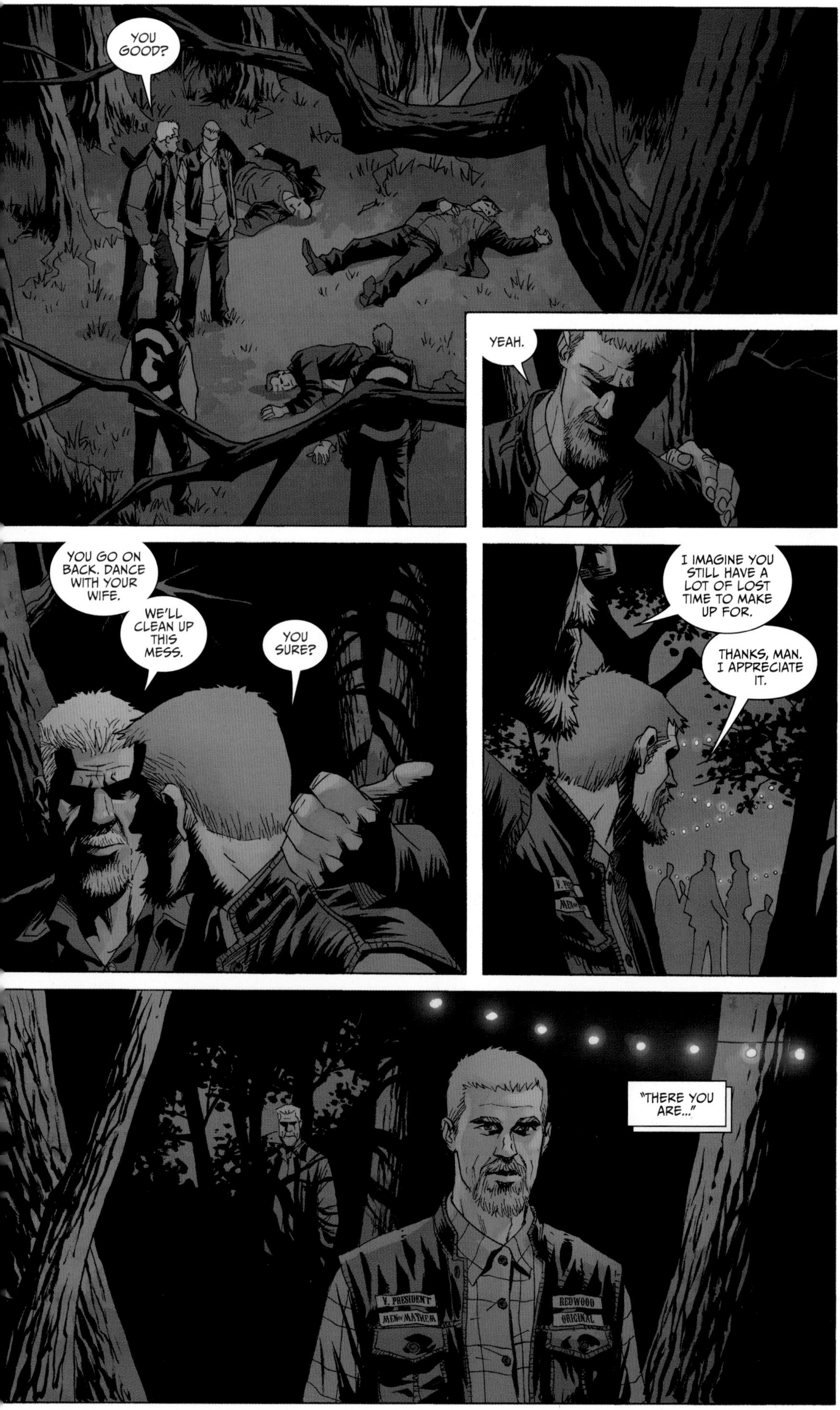
YOU GOOD?
YEAH.
YOU GO ON BACK. DANCE WITH YOUR WIFE.
WE'LL CLEAN UP THIS MESS.
YOU SURE?
I IMAGINE YOU STILL HAVE A LOT OF LOST TIME TO MAKE UP FOR.
THANKS, MAN. I APPRECIATE IT.
"THERE YOU ARE..."
V. PRESIDENT
MEN of MAYHEM
REDWOOD
ORIGINAL

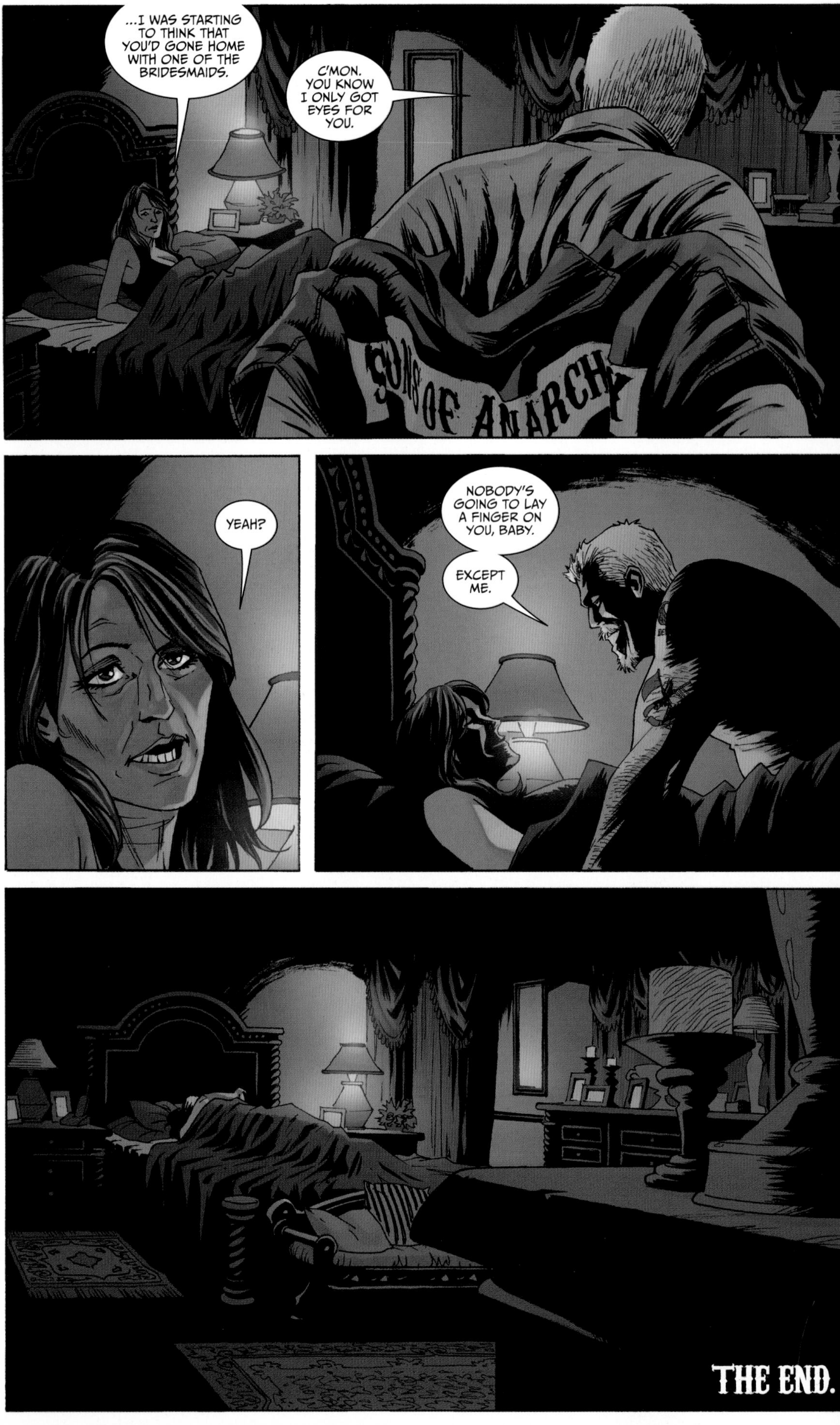
...I WAS STARTING TO THINK THAT YOU'D GONE HOME WITH ONE OF THE BRIDESMAIDS.
C'MON. YOU KNOW I ONLY GOT EYES FOR YOU.
SONS OF ANARCHY
YEAH?
NOBODY'S GOING TO LAY A FINGER ON YOU, BABY.
EXCEPT ME.
THE END.

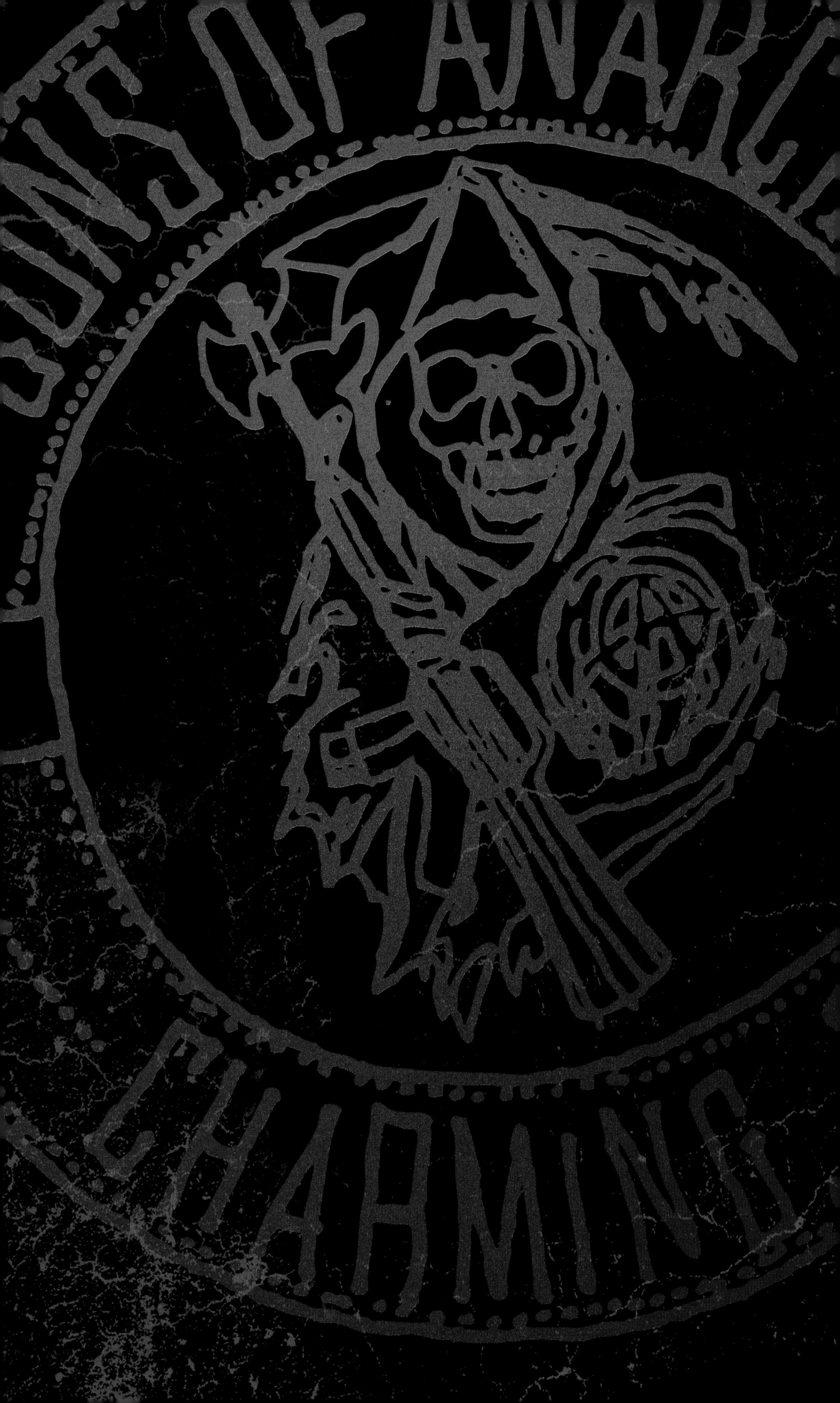
CHARMING

COVER GALLERY

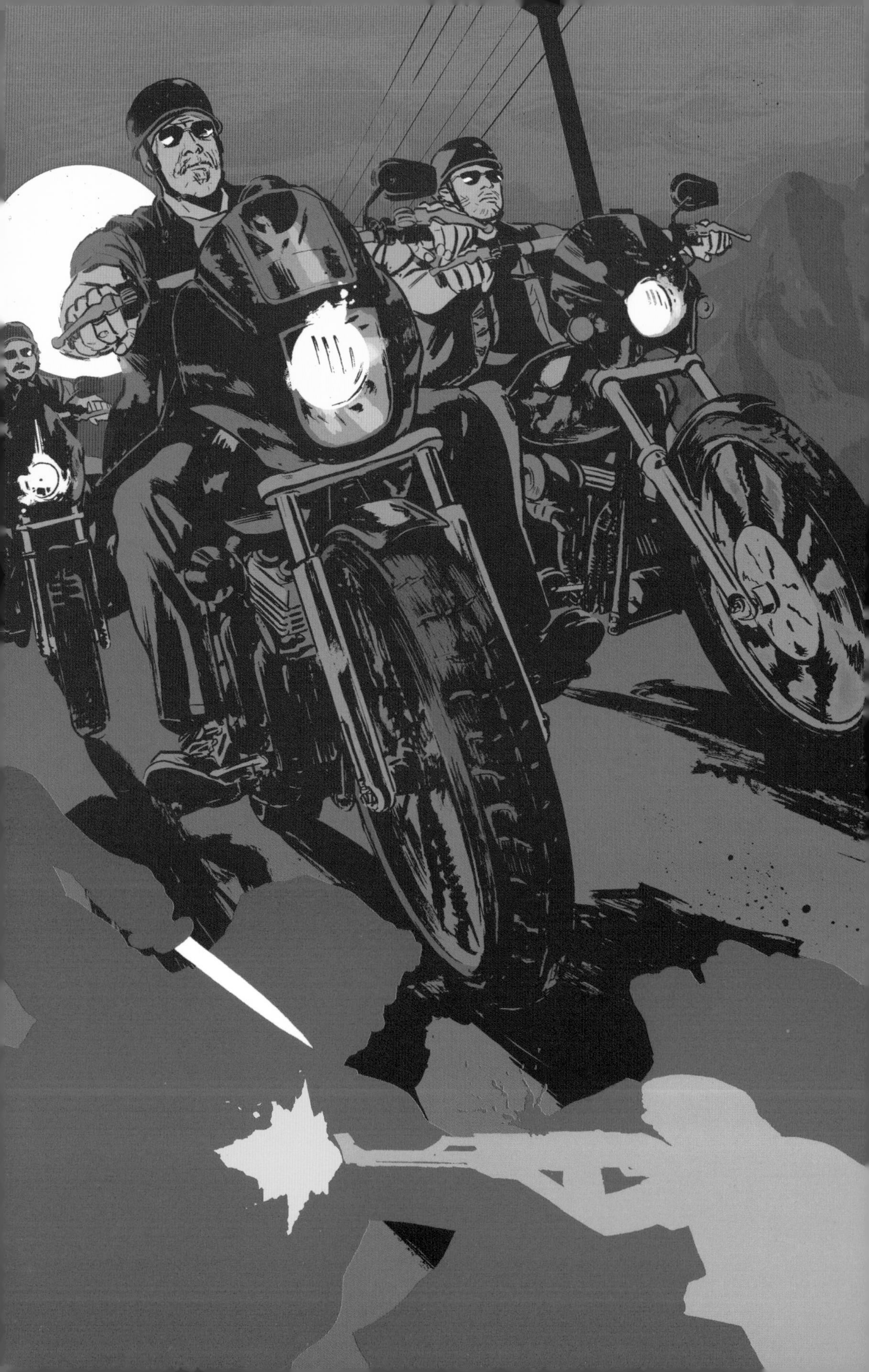

ISSUE SEVEN EMERALD CITY COMICON VARIANT **DARICK ROBERTSON** WITH COLORS BY MATTHEW WILSON

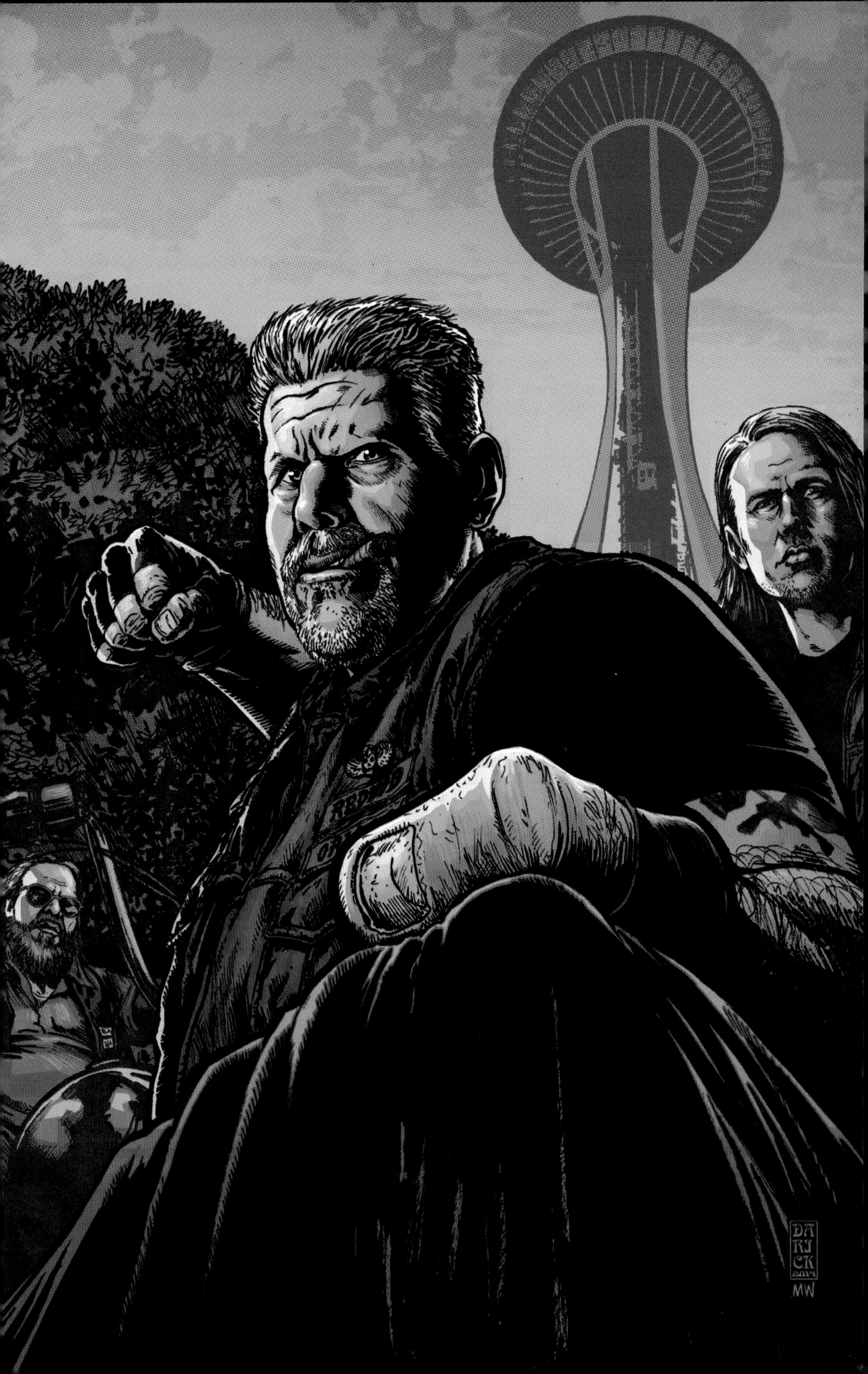

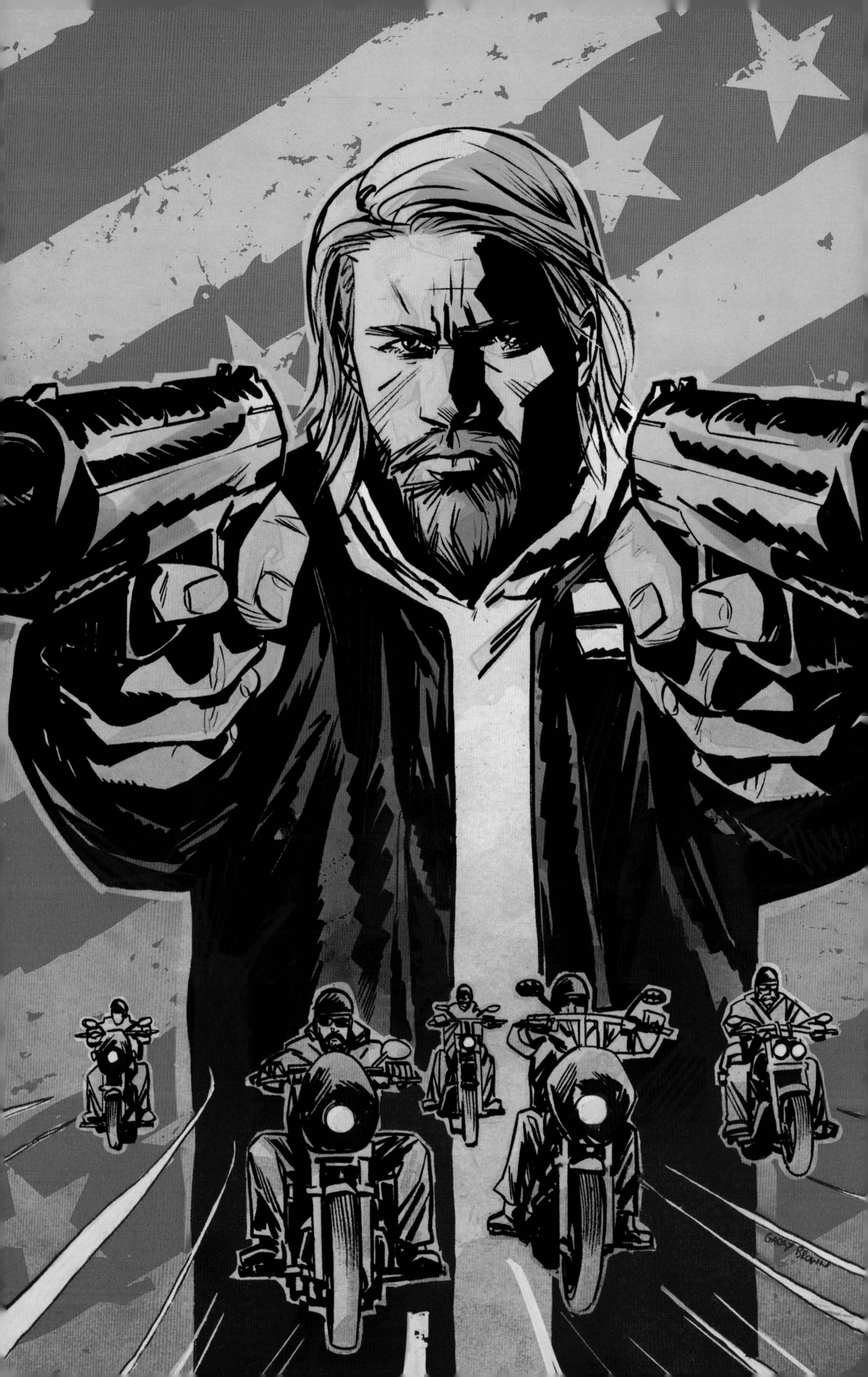

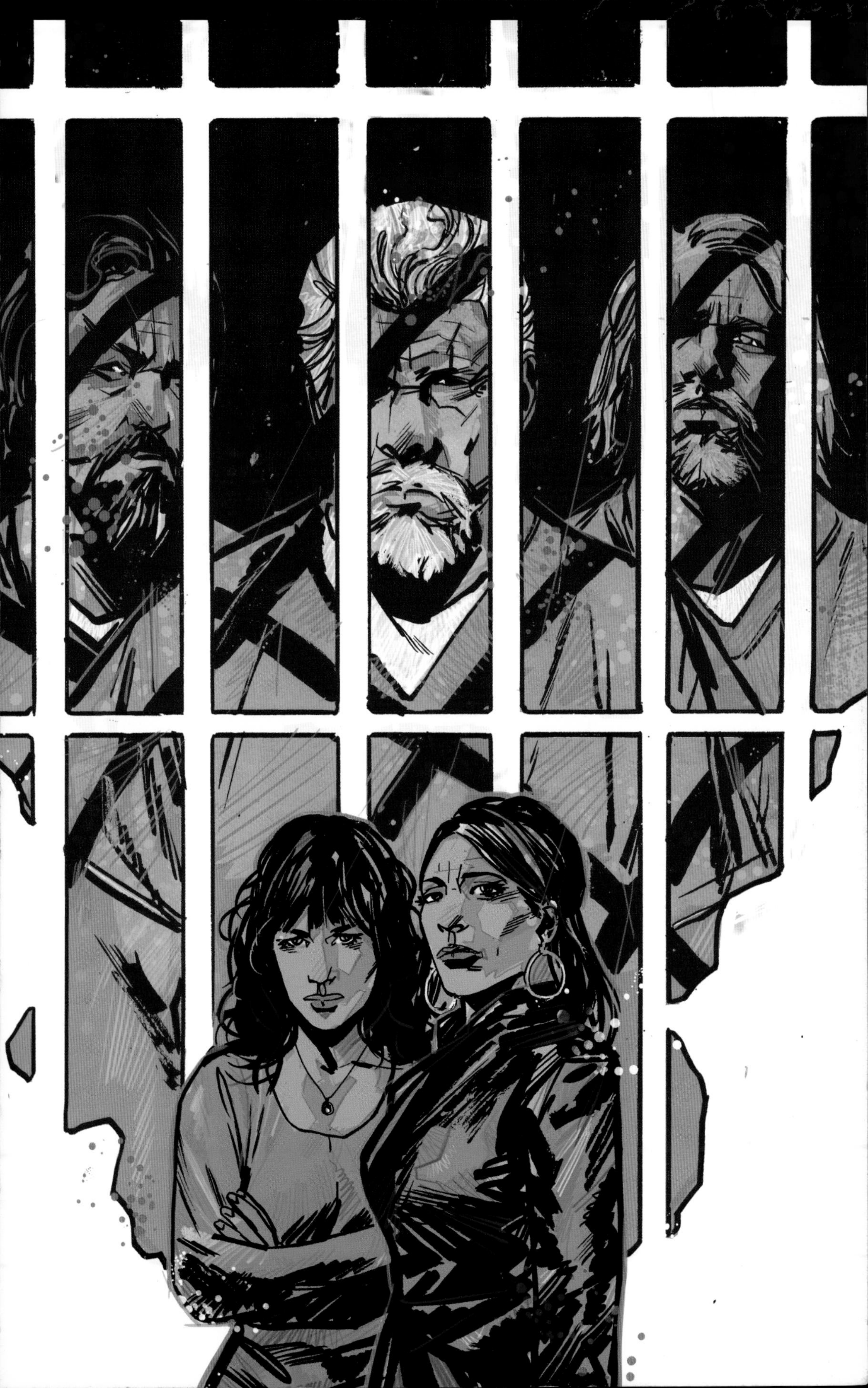

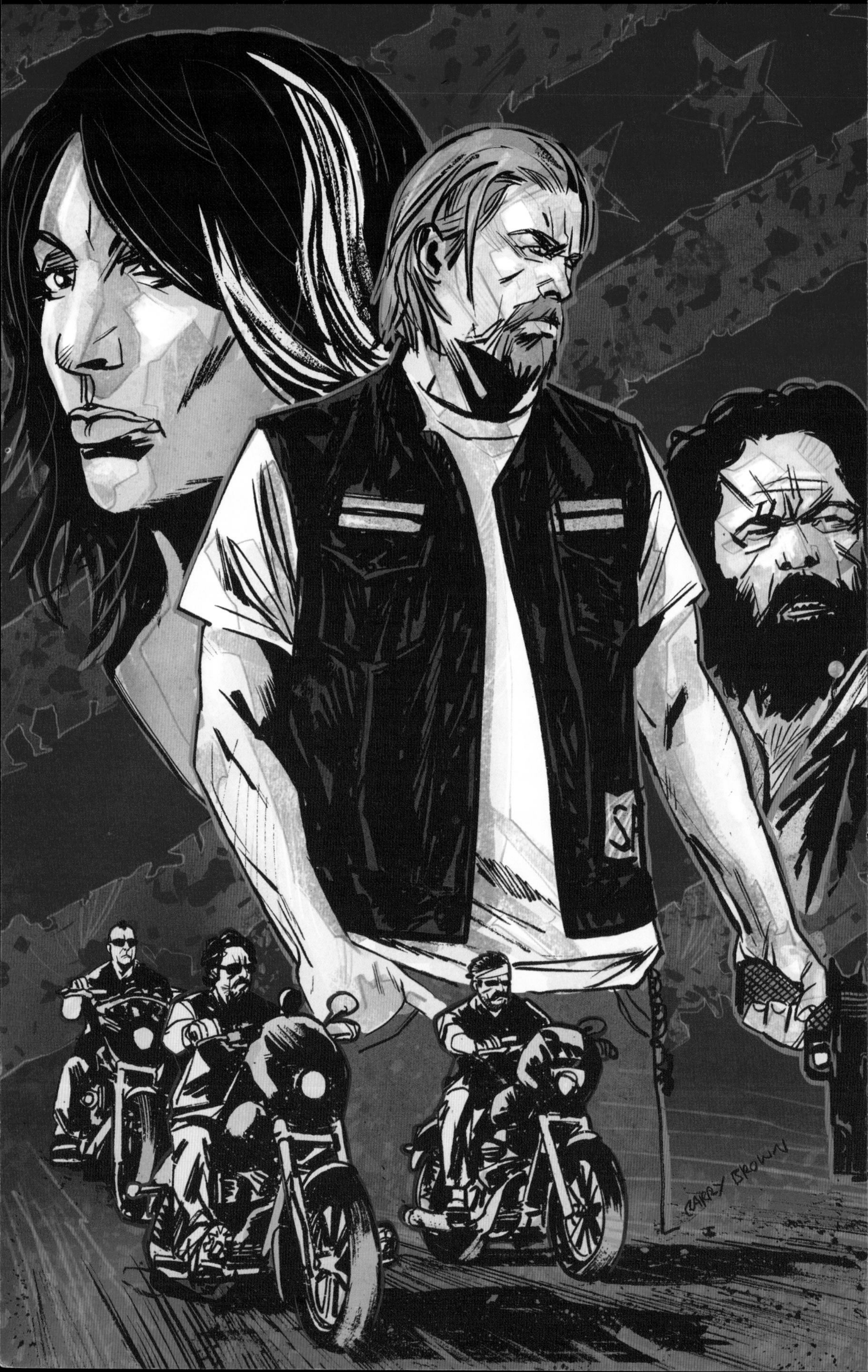
SA
GARRY BROWN

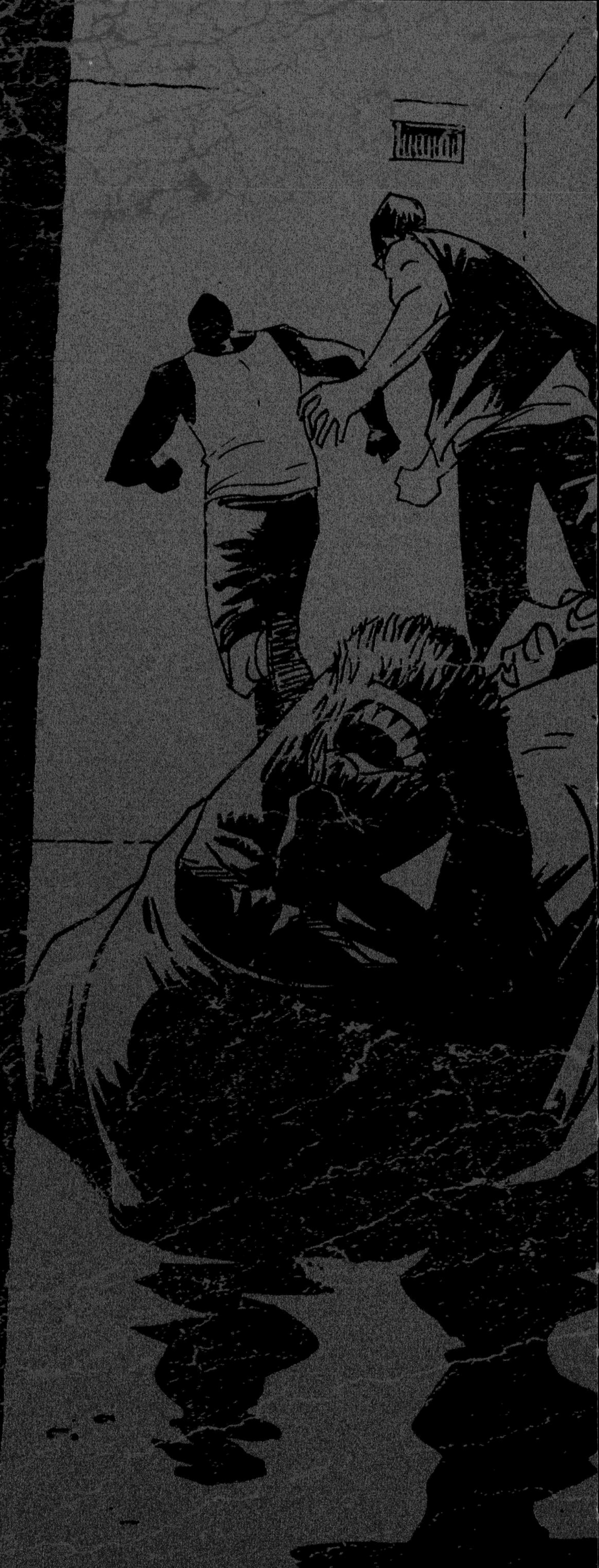

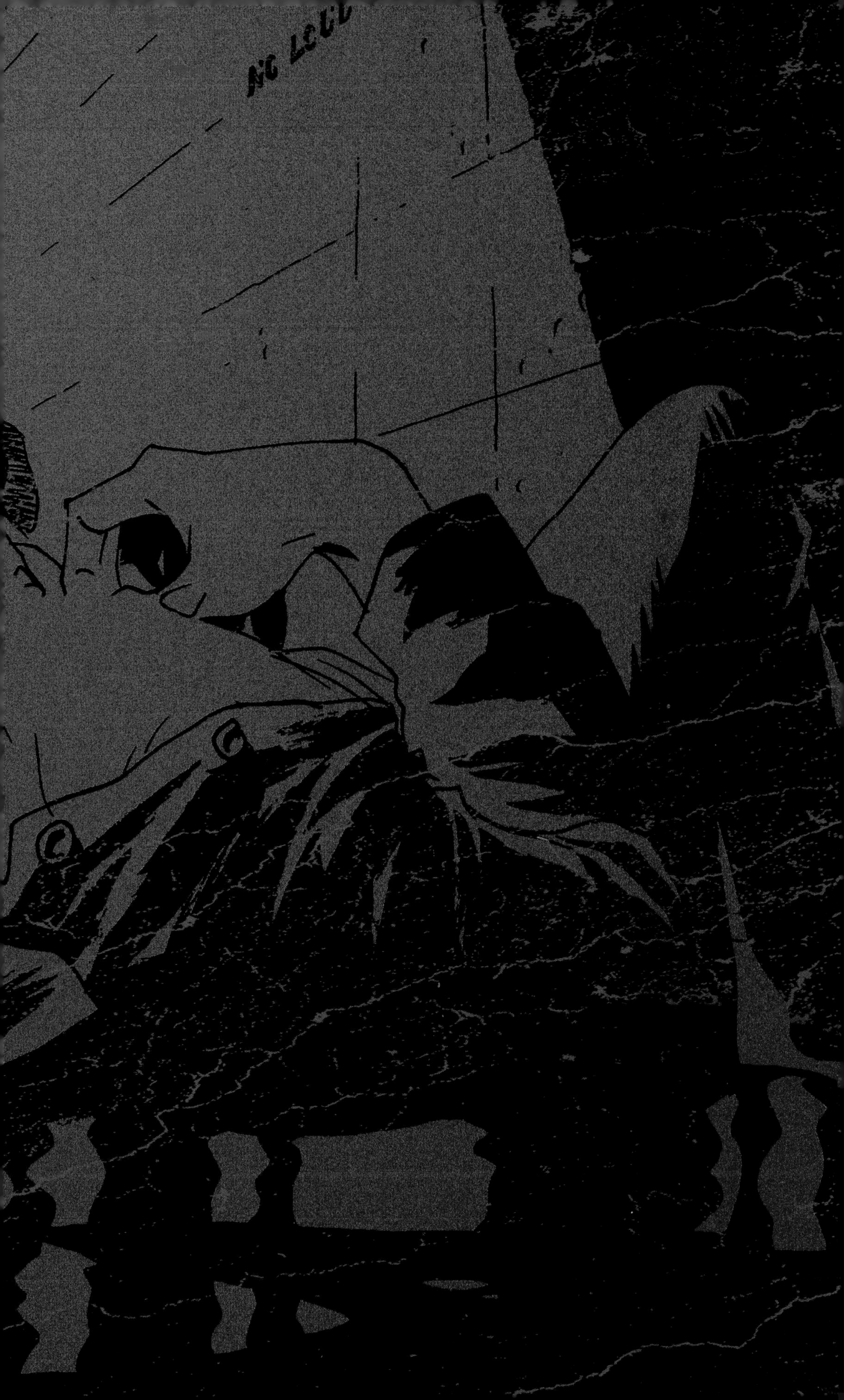

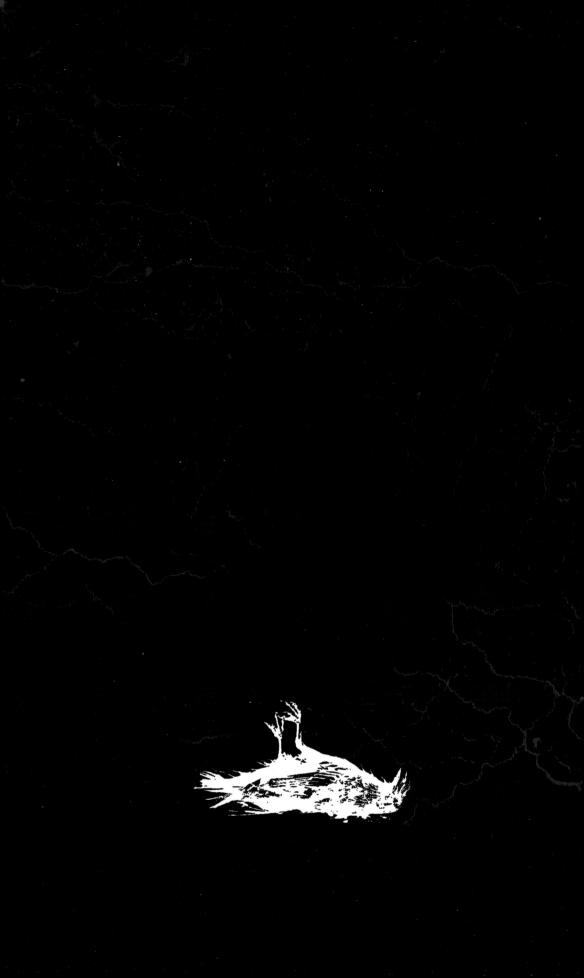